FINANCE KNIGHTS
PUBLICATIONS

ESTATE PLANNING

[ALL-IN-ONE]

Everything to Create Your Estate Plan Without Prior Legal Experience. Organize Wills and Trusts, Protect Your Assets and Heirs, Avoid Probate and Reduce Estate Taxes.

ISBN:
978-1-78793-572-3
978-1-78793-573-0
978-1-78793-574-7

This book is for general educational purposes only. It is not legal, tax, accounting, financial, or investment advice, and does not create an attorney-client or other professional relationship. Always consult a qualified attorney and, where appropriate, a CPA/financial advisor licensed in your state or country before relying on, implementing, or filing anything derived from this book. This publication is intended for general educational purposes only and is not a substitute for personalized legal advice. The information provided should not be used to create legal documents without consulting a licensed attorney in your jurisdiction.

Rules on trusts, last wills, property titling, notarization/witnessing, marital property, probate avoidance, powers of attorney, healthcare directives, taxes, and small-estate procedures vary widely and change over time. You are responsible for verifying current statutes, forms, fees, and filing requirements in your jurisdiction. Examples and sample clauses are illustrative only and may require modification or professional review.

Reviewers and Contributors

Brittany Peck – *Esq.*

"Estate Planning (All-in-One) is a fantastic guide for anyone needing advice on planning their own estate matters. The material is clear, practical, and approachable, and it does a good job guiding readers through complex topics in a thoughtful and accessible way. Its included worksheets do a great job to empower the reader to take action for their own matters."

Louis Grasso – *J.D.*

"This is an exceptional book. Finance Knights Publications breaks down complex estate planning topics into clear, practical guidance. It's organized nicely and is the type of book you should refer back to whenever you review your estate plan. This book is a must-read for individuals curious about estate planning and a good refresher for professionals in the industry."

Michael T. Flannery – *J.D., Distinguished Professor of Law; Associate Dean; Former Special Judge*

"Estate Planning (All-in-One) is a practical guide for anyone who wants to create a comprehensive estate plan designed to meet their specific needs. Covering everything from wills to living trusts and end-of-life directives, this is an invaluable resource for achieving all of your estate planning goals."

Kurt R. Mattson – *J.D., LLM, MLIS, President of Union Legal Research*

"Soup to nuts, this is a great, comprehensive guide to estate planning in plain English. Each chapter offers concise information with a knowledge check. You couldn't ask for a better legal guide for non-attorneys."

Madeline Jackson – *J.M., Legal Administrative Consultant & Estate-Planning Drafting Specialist, Jackson Strategies LLC*

"This is a thorough and reader-friendly guide to estate planning that balances legal accuracy with clear, approachable explanations. The content is well organized and thoughtfully written, making complex concepts accessible to readers with no legal background."

Angie King – *ACP, Senior Trust Administration Paralegal*

"Estate Planning (All-in-One) is a thoughtfully prepared, comprehensive guide to estate planning. I would recommend this book to anyone who is thinking about getting their estate plan in place before you visit a law office or try to do it yourself."

Editing - Design

Shannan Zerance,
Editor, Proofreading & Copyediting

Icreate,
Book Design & Layout Company

Support & Feedback

FINANCE KNIGHTS
PUBLICATIONS

Before we dive in, we want to thank you for choosing to learn about estate planning with us.

This book is packed with everything you need to build a solid understanding of estate planning, and we're holding nothing back because we genuinely want to help you make informed decisions with confidence. Some parts may seem quite technical at times, but we assure you it's all necessary and will prove invaluable as you move forward.

Before moving on, here are a few quick reminders:

1. Access Your Bonus Content

Head over to the section at the end of the book to learn how to download additional resources. These extras were created to help you get even more value out of your reading experience.

2. Share the Start of Your Journey

We'd love to hear your initial impressions and see how you're getting ready to start learning about estate planning. Choose whichever option feels most natural to you:

- Post a photo
  Snap a picture (or more) of your copy and share your initial thoughts.
- Write a few words
  If you'd rather write a few words, we'd love to hear your first impressions and what you hope to learn.

Scan the QR code or click the link (if you're on Kindle):

https://www.amazon.com/review/create-review/?ie=UTF8&channel=glance-detail&asin=B0GS6717MK

Sharing your thoughts **takes less than a minute** and is completely optional.

But if you do decide to share, your photo or a few words might be just the encouragement someone else needs to finally get started.

3. Report Any Issues or Errors

If you find the book unclear or unhelpful, notice any typos, errors, or inconsistencies, or receive a defective copy with torn, missing, or poorly printed pages, please let us know at:

info@financeknightspublications.com

If your feedback helps us identify and fix something that affects the reading experience, we'll make sure you receive a corrected, error-free copy.

TABLE OF CONTENTS

Support & Feedback	**6**
Introduction	**11**
CHAPTER 1 The Estate Planning	**13**
The Main Estate Planning Tools	15
The Probate Process	18
The Pillars of Estate Planning	27
Chapter | 1 | Assessment Test	32
CHAPTER 2 Types of Property	**37**
Inventory	37
Marital Ownership Rules	38
Assets	40
Property Worksheet	51
Chapter | 2 | Assessment Test	53
CHAPTER 3 Last Wills	**57**
Last Wills: The First Building Block	57
Right of Survivorship	60
Executor	62
Guardians and Children's Inheritances	65
Pets	65
Disinheriting a Child	65
After You Sign Your Will	67
What Happens If You Don't Make a Will?	68
Preparing Your Will-Planning Worksheet	68
Chapter | 3 | Assessment Test	70
CHAPTER 4 Living Trusts	**73**
What a Living Trust Actually Is	74
Creating a Living Trust	77
Trustees	79
Beneficiaries	81
Funding the Trust	82
Pour-Over Will	84
Should You Create a Living Trust Yourself?	85

Preparing a Trust-Planning Worksheet	86
Chapter | 4 | Assessment Test	88
CHAPTER 5 How to Pass Property Without a Will or a Trust	**91**
Payable-on-Death (POD) and Transfer-on-Death (TOD) Designations	92
When POD and TOD Accounts Are Not Sufficient	94
Joint Bank Accounts	97
Transfer-on-Death Deeds	98
Small-Estate Affidavits and Simplified Probate	98
Chapter | 5 | Assessment Test	100
CHAPTER 6 Choosing a Guardian for Your Children	**103**
Choosing the Right Guardian	105
Common Problems and Some Solutions	109
After You've Chosen a Guardian	114
Guardian Worksheet	115
Chapter | 6 | Assessment Test	117
CHAPTER 7 Leaving Property to Your Children	**121**
Two Roles to Think About	121
Do Not Name a Minor as a Direct Beneficiary	124
Choosing the Right Structure	125
Custodial Accounts	126
Children's Trusts	129
Naming a Trustee	132
The Property Guardian	138
Life Insurance	139
Chapter | 7 | Assessment Test	146
CHAPTER 8 Estate Planning for Blended Families	**149**
Who Owns What	150
Planning the Estate in Blended Families	155
Planning for Children of Different Ages	160
Chapter | 8 | Assessment Test	162
CHAPTER 9 Taxes in Estate Planning	**165**
Why Estate Taxes Are Rare	165
Income Taxes & Estate Planning	168
Gift Tax and Lifetime Giving	175

The Estate Tax 178
Chapter | 9 | Assessment Test 181
CHAPTER 10 Beneficiaries for Retirement Accounts and Life Insurance 185
Retirement Accounts Aren't Just "Retirement" Anymore 185
The Most Common Plans People Have 187
Beneficiaries and Withdrawal 190
Naming Beneficiaries for Retirement Plans 193
Organize Your Retirement Plans 197
Chapter | 10 | Assessment Test 201
CHAPTER 11 Planning for Incapacity 205
Healthcare Directives 206
Durable Power of Attorney for Finances 213
Chapter | 11 | Assessment Test 221
CHAPTER 12 Living With Your Estate Plan 225
What a Well-Built Estate Plan Usually Includes 226
Chapter | 12 | Assessment Test 232
CHAPTER 13 After a Death 235
What Comes Next 235
Finding the Documents 237
Digital Accounts 239
Notifications 241
Debts, Taxes, and Distributions 242
Chapter | 13 | Assessment Test 246
Conclusion 249
Glossary 251
Bonus Worksheets & Resources 258
About Us 259

INTRODUCTION

Most people don't like thinking about death or what happens after they've passed away. It feels distant, uncomfortable, and easy to push aside with phrases like, "I haven't had time," "I need to understand it better," or "I'll deal with that later." Later becomes later again, until one day, it isn't later anymore.

Last year, Caring.com reported that just 24% of adults have a Last Will. Many Americans die without any estate plan at all, not even a simple Last Will.

When that happens, the people left behind don't just face grief. They often face confusion, paperwork, delays, and stress that could have been avoided with some basic planning.

Modern life demands attention from every direction: maintaining a job, raising children, caring for aging parents, affording housing, and navigating constant news and distractions. Finding time to create an estate plan can feel overwhelming, but it is one of the most valuable steps you can take for yourself and the people you love.

If the words "estate plan" make you tense, you're not alone. Many thoughtful, responsible people feel overwhelmed by the idea. The good news is that you don't need to be a lawyer to learn about the basics or to understand what goes into an effective plan. Much of estate planning comes down to clear thinking, a bit of honesty with yourself, and writing things down.

Ask yourself:

- Who should receive your property and money when you die?
- If you have young children, who would raise them and manage their finances?
- What assets do you actually own, and how are they titled?
- Who would care for your pet?
- Which charities or causes do you want to support?
- What kind of legacy do you want to leave?
- How can you reduce the cost, delay, and burden of probate for your loved ones?

Beginning to answer these questions means thinking about the future of your loved ones in a responsible way, and making certain that what you've built over a lifetime goes into the right hands.

As you do this, it helps to recognize that family life today isn't the same as an old TV sitcom. The classic "nuclear family", a married couple raising their own children, now makes up only a small percentage of U.S. households. Recent census results show that roughly 18% of households contain married parents with children under 18 years of age. Many households are blended, same-sex, single-parent, multi-generational, or centered on chosen family, close friends, and pets who occupy the same emotional space as traditional relatives.

A solid estate plan should reflect that reality. It doesn't assume one "right" kind of family. Instead, it starts where you are: your partner (married or not), your children (biological, adopted, step, or someone you simply treat as your own), your parents or siblings, your closest friends, and the animals and organizations for which you feel responsible. Your documents become a way of saying, "These are my people. This is how I want to take care of them."

In the chapters that follow, these significant questions are translated into concrete steps. You'll learn how to answer them with the appropriate tools, such as Last Wills, trusts, beneficiary designations, healthcare directives, and financial powers of attorney, so that when it matters most, your plan is clear, organized, and ready.

***Note:** If you need to write down information or reminders, you'll find dedicated "Personal Notes" pages at the following pages:*

- *Page **36, 56, 120, 184, 204, 224**.*

CHAPTER 1

THE ESTATE PLANNING

> ***"Plans are worthless, but planning is everything."***
>
> **– Dwight D. Eisenhower,** *five-star U.S. Army general and 34th President of the United States*

Think of an estate plan like a simple set of instructions you'd leave on the kitchen table for someone house-sitting your life. One page covers who's in charge if something goes wrong. Another covers who gets what if you don't come back. Another explains who speaks to the doctors and another points to your retirement accounts and life insurance.

Estate planning, at its core, answers three simple questions:

- **What do you own?**
- **Who should receive it?**
- **How will it get to them?**

More specifically, estate planning entails three simple steps:

- First, you make a list of your assets.
- Second, you choose the people and organizations you want to benefit.
- Third, you decide which tools, wills, trusts, and beneficiary forms, will carry out those choices.

Before you start making a full inventory of every account, policy, and asset you own, you first must decide how you're going to build your plan: will you use a **will**, a **living trust**, or a combination of the two? Once that decision is made, it becomes much easier to list what you own and match it to your loved ones.

Most everyday estate plans are built from the same basic pieces:

- **A will;**
- **A living trust (in some situations);**
- **A durable power of attorney for finances;**
- **An advance healthcare directive (or similar agreement); and**
- **Beneficiary designations** for retirement plans and life insurance.

Each part has a job.

A **will** or a **living trust** is the document in which you state who receives your property and who is responsible for carrying out your wishes. A **durable power of attorney for finances** names someone to step in for you if you can't manage your affairs, handling money and property that isn't already in a trust, paying bills, managing accounts, filing tax returns, and dealing with institutions like banks and government agencies about your benefits, as your document authorizes. An **advance healthcare directive** (or healthcare power of attorney agreement, depending on your state) lets you appoint someone to speak to doctors for you and gives guidance about the kind of care you want.

Retirement plans and life insurance sit outside this framework. They usually pass through according to the **beneficiary forms** on file with each plan or policy, not according to your will. A complete estate plan always includes reviewing these forms and making sure they match your overall intentions.

Why Having Some Plan Is Better Than None

Before comparing wills and trusts, it helps to understand what happens when there is **no** plan at all.

If you die without a will or trust, your state's **intestacy laws** take over. Those rules decide who receives your property. Typically, this starts with a spouse and children, then moves to parents, siblings, and then to more distant relatives. If your estate is above a certain value, it usually goes through a court process called "**probate**," a public and often slow court-supervised process for paying debts and transferring what you owned.

If you have minor children, a judge will appoint guardians after a formal process. The judge will try to make a reasonable choice, but he or she won't know your family history, your values, or the promises you might have made prior to your passing. The judge also won't know that you meant to include your long-term partner, a close friend, or a particular charity.

Intestacy rules might align with your wishes accidentally, but they might not.

And if you:

- Aren't married but live with a partner,
- Have a blended family,
- Are closer to some relatives than others, or
- Want to leave money to friends, charities, or anyone outside your default legal heirs,

relying on those default rules is a gamble. The only way to make your wishes legally clear is to write them down in proper estate planning documents, such as a will or a trust.

The same is true for guardianship. If you want to choose who raises your children if something happens to you, you must say so in writing. A plan doesn't have to be perfect or elaborate. Even a simple will and basic powers of attorney are far better than leaving everything to chance.

The Main Estate Planning Tools

Here's a quick overview of the core documents you'll be using.

Wills

A **will** is the most familiar estate planning document. In a will, you can:

- State who receives your property,
- Name an *executor* (sometimes called a *personal representative*) to handle your estate,
- Nominate *guardians* for minor children, and
- Set up simple trusts for children or other beneficiaries.

If your plan relies on a will as the main tool, your estate will usually go through probate before your beneficiaries can receive their inheritance. In later chapters, we'll look at when a will-centered plan is appropriate, when it might be enough, and how smaller estates sometimes qualify for simplified procedures.

An executor is a **fiduciary**, meaning they have a legal obligation to act with the highest degree of honesty and loyalty toward your beneficiaries, putting the estate's interests above their own.

Trusts

A **trust** is like a legal container you create while you're alive. You transfer certain assets into the trust and usually act as your own trustee during your lifetime, managing and using those assets just as you did before.

Assets properly placed in a trust generally **do not go through probate** when you die. Instead, your chosen successor trustee steps in and follows the instructions you wrote in the trust.

The trust document also spells out what happens to the trust property after your death.

A trust is typically paired with a short "**pour-over" will** that:

- Addresses the distribution of anything you forgot to put in the trust; and
- Names guardians for minor children, if applicable.

In later chapters, we'll look at when it makes sense to add a trust to your plan, especially if you own a home, live in a state with a more involved probate process, or have a blended or nontraditional family.

Durable Power of Attorney for Finances

A **durable power of attorney for finances** lets you name someone to take care of money matters if you can't. This can include paying bills, transacting with banks, signing documents, and handling property that isn't inside your trust. This document is designed to protect you during your lifetime, rather than distribute your estate after death.

Advance Healthcare Directive

An **advance healthcare directive** (also known as healthcare power of attorney or designation of healthcare surrogate, depending on your state) focuses on medical decisions. In it, you:

- Name an individual to speak for you if you can't speak for yourself; and
- Give guidance about the kind of treatment and end-of-life care you want.

This document is a gift to your loved ones because it reduces guessing, guilt, and conflict at a very emotional time.

Retirement Plans and Life Insurance

Retirement accounts and **life insurance policies** are controlled by their **beneficiary forms**. Those forms state who receives the funds at your death. They typically bypass probate and don't follow your will or trust unless you name your estate or your trust as the beneficiary.

As such, part of any good estate plan is reviewing each account or policy and asking:

- Who is currently listed as the beneficiary?
- Is that still what I want?
- Does this designation fit with the rest of my plan?

We'll walk through how to think about those decisions later in the book.

Will, Trust, or Both?

Once you understand the pieces, your initial structural choice is this:

- Will your plan be built mainly around a **will;** or
- Will it rely on a **trust** (with a backup pour-over will) as the primary organizing tool?

Both options are legally efficient. Both can honor your wishes and provide for the people you care about. The differences lie in:

- **How long it takes** to settle your estate;
- **The amount of court involvement**;
- **Up-front cost and effort** to set things up; and
- **Ongoing maintenance** during your lifetime.

For many people, the biggest practical questions are: *Do you want your estate to go through probate? Do you want to direct what happens after you die?*

In some states, probate is slow, formal, and expensive. In those states, using a trust to avoid the full probate process can be a huge gift to your heirs. In other states, especially those that have adopted a set of laws called the **Uniform Probate Code**, probate is relatively quick and streamlined, so a will-based plan may work just fine.

If you're not sure how probate works where you live, you can:

- Consult your state court or legislature website for plain-language explanations;
- Review materials published by your state bar association;
- Read law firm guides; and
- Ask friends or relatives who have been through it about their experiences.

You're looking for a realistic sense of whether probate in your state tends to be routine and manageable, or lengthy and costly.

The following states have adopted the Uniform Probate Code ("UPC") in whole or in substantially similar form:

Alaska	Idaho	Minnesota	New Mexico
Arizona	Maine	Montana	North Dakota
Colorado	Massachusetts	Nebraska	South Carolina
Hawaii	Michigan	New Jersey	South Dakota
			Utah

Here's an example to illustrate how location can change the choice:

> ***Example:*** *Marco and Elena owned a lake home and some savings in a state where court fees and legal costs for probate were known to be high. They decided to create a trust and move the house and investment account into it. Their goal was simple: when one of them died, they wanted the survivor to have quick access to everything without a long court process. Years later, their daughter, Sofia, moved to a state where probate was relatively fast and inexpensive. She chose a different path, a straightforward will because, for her situation and her state's rules, the extra work of managing a trust didn't add enough benefit.*

One size doesn't fit all. A living trust can be wonderful in the right circumstances, and a well-drafted will can be perfectly adequate in others. The next chapters will walk you through both routes so that by the time you decide, you'll understand not just *what* you're choosing, but *why*.

The Probate Process

Most people only hear about probate when someone in their family dies, and they are in the midst of grief and overwhelming sadness. It's often described as something terrible, slow, expensive–a nightmare to be avoided at all costs. Probate can be all those things, but it's a little more nuanced than that.

Probate, by itself, is not "bad." It was created with good intentions: to make certain that when someone dies, their property is gathered; debts and taxes are paid; and whatever is left is passed on in a fair and orderly way. The problem is that, in many places, the system has grown into a slow and sometimes costly process that doesn't always match what families need in real life. Understanding how it works will help you decide how much of it you want your loved ones to face.

What is Probate?

Probate is a court process for settling an individual's estate at death. A judge oversees this process to make sure:

- The will, if there is one, is valid;
- Someone responsible is officially put in charge;
- Creditors and taxes are dealt with properly; and
- The remaining property goes to the right people.

The exact steps differ from state to state, but the basic pattern is similar almost everywhere.

When someone dies, if they have a will, it is usually filed with the local probate court. If they named an **executor** (sometimes called a personal representative), that person asks the court to be formally appointed. Some states, especially UPC states, use the term "personal representative" for both executors and administrators. If there's no will, a close relative or other interested person can ask to be appointed instead; in that case, the court often calls them an "administrator" rather than an executor, but the role is similar: they're the one in charge.

Once the court approves the appointment (or otherwise confirms the person's authority, depending on the procedure), this legal representative steps into the decedent's shoes for a limited purpose: to handle the probate estate. They must notify potential creditors that the person has died, often by publishing a notice in a local newspaper in a format required by state law or the court and by following any state rules about who must also receive direct notice. They then identify and list the property that belongs to the estate and, where required, arrange for formal valuations. They make sure that heirs and beneficiaries are told that a probate case has been opened. Using estate funds, they pay valid debts, taxes, and administration expenses. After those steps are completed, they distribute whatever remains to the people named in the will (or, if there is no will, to the heirs under state law).

In some probates, especially supervised cases, the representative must also prepare and file a final accounting and obtain court approval of the proposed distributions. In other states and in many unsupervised probates, no court approval of the final accounting is required; the representative completes the required steps, makes distributions, and closes the estate using the procedure the state provides.

It's easy to see why a system like this exists. After someone dies, they aren't around to sign documents or confirm what they wanted. Probate serves as a kind of referee. But like many systems, this process can be more complicated and cumbersome than it needs to be, especially for small or simple estates.

Small Estates

The good news is that **not every estate has to go through full probate**. Most states recognize that smaller estates shouldn't be required to jump through the same hoops as large or complicated ones, so they offer shortcuts.

These shortcuts are usually tied to a **"small estate" threshold**. If the deceased person's property, at least the property that would otherwise go through probate, is under a certain dollar amount, the law may allow heirs to collect assets with very little court involvement. In many states, heirs can sign a **small estate affidavit**, a sworn statement saying, essentially, "This person has died, the estate is under the legal dollar amount limit, and I'm entitled to this account or asset as an heir or beneficiary." The affidavit, combined with a death certificate, is given directly to the bank or institution holding the property, and it can release the funds without a full probate action.

Some states use an affidavit system only for money and personal property (like bank accounts, vehicles, or small investments) and require a bit more formality for real estate. Others offer a simplified, "summary" probate for estates under a certain value, which still involves the court but in a much simpler way than a standard, full probate.

Every state sets its own monetary limits, which can change over time. As of the mid-2020s, for example, California allows certain personal property to be transferred without formal probate when the total value subject to that rule is below a specific number that's adjusted every few years for inflation. Other states have their own thresholds and procedures. The basic idea is that small estates can often be settled with minimal paperwork, minimal delay, and minimal cost.

To make that more concrete, imagine this:

> ***Example:*** *When Marco's grandmother died, her only asset in her name alone was a checking account containing about $14,000. Her will left everything to Marco. Because this amount was well under his state's small estate limit and no formal probate had been started, he didn't have to open a court case. Instead, he signed a small estate affidavit, attached a copy of the death certificate, and the bank released the funds to him. That was the entire process.*

Stories like this are common. They're a reminder that "probate" is not automatically years of court visits. For modest estates, the law often provides simple tools to keep things moving smoothly.

If you're an executor or heir facing a possible probate, a good executor's guide or a reputable self-help legal resource can walk you through your state's specific rules and tell you whether a small-estate shortcut is available where you live. For planning purposes, the key takeaway is that the smaller and more organized your probate estate is, the easier things generally are for the people you leave behind.

How Long Does Probate Take?

People often ask, "How long will probate take?" and the only honest answer is, "It depends on a few important things."

First, it depends on your state's probate laws and how busy the local courts are. Some states have modern, streamlined probate systems that move relatively quickly as long as no one is disputing the will. Others require more formal steps and have crowded dockets, which slows everything down.

Second, it depends on how organized the person's finances were. If the decedent kept clear records, paid attention to titles and beneficiaries, and left behind a neat file of accounts and documents, the legal representative can move much more quickly. If, on the other hand, no one knows where anything is, there are mystery accounts, unopened mail, or a house full of unsorted papers, just building a complete picture of the estate can take months.

Third, it depends on family dynamics. If everyone generally agrees on who should be in charge and how things should be divided, probate is mostly paperwork and patience. If there are disputes about the will, suspicions about someone's influence, or hard feelings among siblings or spouses, the process can slow to a crawl. Court hearings, contested motions, and demands for more detailed accountings all cost time and money.

Finally, it depends on where property is located. If you own real estate in more than one state, your personal representative may be required to open a probate proceeding in each state where you own property. That means more court calendars to juggle and more steps to complete.

In practice, even a straightforward probate often takes several months from start to finish. Many estates take a year or more, especially in states with more complex procedures. When there are disputes or complicated assets, the process can easily stretch into multiple years.

For planning purposes, it helps to think of probate as something that almost never resolves quickly, and sometimes takes quite a long time. That doesn't mean it's always awful. It does mean that if you would like your loved ones to have faster, simpler access to what you leave behind, you may want to use tools that reduce how much of your property has to go through that process.

How Much Can Probate Cost?

Just as timelines vary, so do probate expenses. The total cost comprises several components: legal fees, court fees, appraisal costs, publication and notice expenses, and the practical costs of organizing, valuing, and sometimes cleaning out the estate.

In many states, families hire an attorney to help with probate because the rules are technical and the paperwork can be intimidating. Lawyers are typically paid in one of two ways:

- In some states, the law sets a **percentage fee** based on the size of the probate estate. That percentage is usually calculated on the gross value of the estate (what assets are worth before subtracting debts). With a large estate, that can add up to a significant fee, even if it is a small percentage.
- In other states, lawyers charge by the **hour** or sometimes by a **flat fee** for a simple, uncontested case. In those places, the cost is more closely tied to how much work there actually is to do.

On top of attorney's fees, there are court filing fees for opening the case and approving various steps, fees for appraisers to value real estate or other significant property, costs to publish legal notices in a newspaper when required, and ordinary expenses, like paying for document copies, notaries, and sometimes accountants.

To get a feel for how this plays out, imagine three different estates:

***Estate 1**: Maria left behind a home and a small investment account worth a combined **$1 million**. She lived in **California**, where probate attorneys are paid using a statutory percentage of the estate's gross value. The ordinary attorney's fee came to about **$23,000**, and the executor was entitled to the same amount. Even before court costs and appraisals, the estate was already facing close to **$46,000** in fees.*

***Estate 2:** If Maria had lived in **Texas**, the cost would have been very different. Texas allows attorneys to charge **hourly rates or flat fees**, not percentages. For a simple, uncontested estate of the same size, a typical range would be around **$2,500–$7,000** in legal fees, often a fraction of what a percentage-based system would cost.*

Estate 3: *Now imagine a much smaller estate: someone in* ***Illinois*** *dies, leaving only a* ***$12,000*** *bank account and no real estate. Illinois allows the use of a* ***small estate affidavit*** *for estates worth* ***$150,000 or less****, as long as no real property needs to be transferred. The heir completes the affidavit, brings it to the bank, and the funds are released, usually with no lawyer, no probate hearing, and minimal cost beyond notarizing the form.*

None of these numbers are guaranteed. They simply illustrate a larger point: **probate can be relatively modest or surprisingly expensive, depending on the size and complexity of the estate, the state's rules, and whether you've done any advanced planning.** Knowing this helps you decide how important it is for you to reduce probate as part of your estate plan.

What Types of Assets Go Through Probate?

As we said before, when people hear the word *probate*, they often assume it's just a long, expensive court process. At its core, though, probate exists to prevent fraud and to make sure an individual's property goes to its intended recipient at death. The court reviews the will (if there is one), gathers information about what the person owned, and oversees how those assets are distributed.

However, not everything a person owns has to pass through this system. Certain assets already come with built-in instructions about who should receive them. When that happens, the law treats those instructions as a binding contract, and a judge is not needed to step in.

Assets held in a trust, accounts with beneficiary designations, and property that passes to a surviving co-owner with a right of survivorship all fall into this category. In these cases, the owner has already signed valid documents that clearly state who inherits. Because the transfer can happen without a court order, those assets are considered **outside probate**.

For estate planning, it helps to sort everything a person owns into two groups:

- Assets that **go through probate**; and
- Assets that **avoid probate**.

In many law offices, when a new client arrives, the lawyer begins by taking a sheet of paper and drawing a line down the middle. On the left, they write *"Goes Through Probate,"* and on the right, *"Avoids Probate."* Almost everyone looks surprised, not because the idea is complex, but because no one has ever explained things in such a simple way. Once you see your property divided this way, it becomes much easier to understand which tools you actually need.

- The "**Avoids Probate**" side holds everything that already has its own legal pathway to the next owner, for example, an account with a named beneficiary or a house held in joint tenancy with a right of survivorship. Judges do not supervise these transfers, and wills or trusts do not control them. Instead, the beneficiary forms and ownership documents do the work.

- The **"Goes Through Probate"** side includes assets that don't have those automatic instructions. These are the items that typically require a court process and that can be controlled by a will or, in many cases, a trust.

Thinking in terms of these two groups helps clarify what an estate plan actually needs to cover. Beneficiary designations and title documents govern the "Not Probate" side. A will and, where appropriate, a trust will focus on the "Probate" side.

Avoids Probate	Goes Through Probate
Retirement accounts with named beneficiaries	Real estate titled only in the deceased person's name
Life insurance and annuities with beneficiary designations	Investment or brokerage accounts without transfer instructions
Property owned in joint tenancy with a right of survivorship	Bank accounts without pay-on-death instructions
Pay-on-death (POD) accounts	Household items such as furniture, jewelry, artwork, and vehicles**
Transfer-on-death (TOD) investment accounts	Interests in a small business, partnership, or sole proprietorship
Transfer-on-death deeds for real estate (where state law allows)	

*** Solely owned personal property (including vehicles) may require probate, but often can be transferred using small-estate procedures (varies by state).*

Common Assets That Avoid Probate

Many assets can transfer outside probate if they are set up correctly.

Living Trust Property

A living trust is often created specifically to avoid probate. When real estate, bank accounts, or investments are titled in the name of the trust, they no longer need probate when the owner dies. The successor trustee named in the document follows the instructions in the trust and distributes or manages the property without court involvement.

Retirement Accounts

IRAs, 401(k)s, and similar retirement plans require the owner to name one or more beneficiaries. At death, the remaining funds go directly to those beneficiaries, following the rules of the account and current tax law. These assets bypass both the will and the probate process.

Life Insurance

Life insurance policies also rely on beneficiary designations. The insurance company pays the death benefit directly to the listed beneficiaries. These funds are often an important immediate source of money for spouses, partners, or children, and they are typically not delayed by probate.

Annuities

Annuities are contracts with an insurance company or financial institution. The owner contributes money and, in return, receives periodic payments, sometimes for life. Some annuities provide for a death benefit or continued payments to a named beneficiary. When a beneficiary is named, the remaining value can transfer without going through probate.

POD and TOD Accounts

Many banks and investment firms offer:

- **Pay-on-death (POD)** designations for bank accounts; and
- **Transfer-on-death (TOD)** designations for brokerage or similar accounts.

The owner completes a form naming the individual(s) to receive the account when the owner dies. At that point, the financial institution pays or transfers the assets directly to the named person(s). The probate court is not involved in that transfer.

Transfer-on-Death Deeds

In a number of states, the law allows **transfer-on-death deeds** for real estate, and in some states, enhanced life estate deeds (sometimes known as a Lady Bird deed). By signing and properly recording this kind of deed, an owner can name who should receive a property at death, without creating a trust and without going through probate. The rules, terminology, and availability of these deeds vary from state to state, so local law always matters. More than two-thirds of the states permit this type of transfer, including California, Texas, and New York.

Property With a Right of Survivorship

Some forms of co-ownership include a built-in **right of survivorship**. This means that when one owner dies, the surviving owner automatically becomes the full owner of the property. This is common with homes owned by married couples and some other co-owners.

Forms such as:

- Joint tenancy with right of survivorship;
- Community property with right of survivorship; and
- Tenancy by the entirety.

These forms typically allow property to pass automatically to the surviving owner without probate when the first owner dies.

Assets That Go Through Probate

After setting aside the assets that transfer by beneficiary designation, trust ownership, or survivorship, whatever remains is generally treated as the **probate estate**. For many people, this includes:

- Bank accounts without POD instructions;
- Investments without TOD or beneficiary designations;
- Household items such as furniture, appliances, clothing, jewelry, art, or other collections;
- Vehicles and other titled personal property held only in the deceased person's name;
- Real estate owned solely by the deceased person or without any survivorship feature; and
- Ownership interests in a closely-held business, partnership, or sole proprietorship.

> ***Example:*** *Consider Maya, who owns a home and savings accounts jointly with her spouse, Leo, with a right of survivorship. She also inherited a small piece of land in her own name, which she has left to her nephew in her will.*

When Maya dies, her share of the home and the joint savings accounts pass directly to Leo because he is the surviving co-owner. That transfer does not require probate. The land, however, is in Maya's name alone and is meant to go to her nephew. To carry out that gift and update the legal title, the land must pass through probate.

Probate and Estate Tax: Different Questions

Avoiding probate does **not** mean avoiding estate tax and going through probate does **not** automatically trigger tax. They are separate systems.

For federal estate tax purposes, the law looks at the total value of everything a person owned or controlled at death, regardless of whether an asset passes through probate, through a trust, directly by beneficiary designation, or by survivorship.

Only estates above a certain size are subject to the federal estate tax. As of 2026, the federal exemption is **$15 million per person**, with an unlimited deduction for property passing to a U.S. citizen spouse. For a married couple, the combined exemption is $30 million. State estate or inheritance tax rules may differ and can apply at much lower thresholds.

Reasons Many People Prefer to Avoid Probate

In states where probate has not been streamlined, many families choose to plan around it. Common reasons include:

- **Cost and delay.** Court fees, professional assistance, and the time involved can reduce what is ultimately available for heirs and beneficiaries.
- **Lack of added value.** When there is no significant conflict and debts are manageable, families often don't need a judge to supervise every step of distribution.
- **Privacy.** Probate is a public process. Documents such as the will, inventories, and reports to the court usually become part of the public record. A living trust, by contrast, is a private document. Beneficiaries are entitled to information, but there is no automatic public filing in the local courthouse.

There are, however, situations in which probate can be helpful. In complicated estates, or when there is serious disagreement among family members or creditors, having a formal court process and binding court orders can create clarity and finality.

How to Avoid or Minimize Probate

Every state has some version of a **small-estate procedure**. If the value of the probate estate falls below that state's threshold, property can often be transferred with a simplified process, such as an affidavit, rather than a full probate case.

When the probate estate value is larger than the small-estate limit, additional planning is usually needed. Common tools include:

- Establishing a **trust** and transferring assets into it;
- Setting up **POD** and **TOD** designations where available;
- Owning property with **survivorship rights;** and
- Using **transfer-on-death deeds** in states that allow them.

Each step can move an asset from the "Probate" group to the "Avoid Probate" group.

For example:

- A bank account can be turned into a payable-on-death account by naming a beneficiary on the bank's form.
- A property deed can be updated to add a co-owner with a right of survivorship, or to name a transfer-on-death beneficiary, where the law permits it.

These changes can be powerful but may have tax, creditor, or family consequences. Before changing titles or adding co-owners, it is wise to speak with a qualified tax professional or attorney to understand the full impact.

The Limits of Simple Probate-Avoidance Tools

Designations like POD and TOD instructions, joint ownership, and transfer-on-death deeds are very useful, but they do not replace a complete estate plan. By themselves, they generally cannot:

- Manage money or property for minor children or beneficiaries with special needs;
- Provide instructions for managing finances during incapacity;
- Coordinate complex distributions among several beneficiaries;
- Handle forgiveness of loans or gifts made during life; and
- Redirect gifts if a primary beneficiary dies first.

A comprehensive estate plan typically leverages these tools with documents, such as a will, power(s) of attorney, healthcare directive(s), and, when appropriate, a trust.

The Pillars of Estate Planning

For an estate plan to truly be effective, it must do more than simply name a beneficiary on an account or add a survivorship clause to a deed. A complete plan needs to contemplate who receives property, who manages money for children, what happens if someone becomes incapacitated, and whether taxes or court costs can be reduced.

The tools that usually carry this weight are **wills** and **living trusts**. Together, they form the structural core of most estate plans. They can be kept very simple or tailored for complicated family and financial situations, but in one form or another, almost every thoughtful plan relies on at least one of them.

Wills

A will is the traditional starting point. It has two central jobs: (i) it explains **who should receive a person's property** after death; and (ii) it names **who should care for minor children**. Each adult signs a separate will, though spouses or partners often coordinate their documents so they name the same guardians and create a consistent plan.

To put a will in place, a few key decisions must be made. Someone has to be chosen to act as **executor** (sometimes called a personal representative), the person who will gather assets, pay final bills, and carry out the instructions in the will. The will must also spell out **how everything is divided**: who receives the home, savings, investments, and personal items.

If there are minor children, the will usually goes a step further. It names one or more **guardians** to look after them and their property until they reach adulthood (often age 18, depending on state law). This is known as the guardian of their person and the guardian of their property. It also needs to say how money left for those children will be managed until they are old enough to handle it themselves, perhaps through a simple trust or a custodial account overseen by a trusted adult.

For many people, a will can handle the core estate planning tasks. It's generally less expensive to create than a trust and is often easier to understand. But there's an important limitation to keep in mind: a will controls only the assets that are subject to probate. That means that after you die, your estate will likely have to go through a probate proceeding, often with court involvement and required paperwork, before those assets can be transferred to your beneficiaries.

Because a will operates through the probate court, how well it works in practice depends a great deal on the state where the person lives. In some states, probate has been streamlined: the forms are manageable, costs are modest, and the process is relatively quick. In those places, a will may be all that is needed.

In other states, probate is known to be slow, expensive, and procedurally demanding. Non-lawyers may find it confusing, and families can wait months or longer before everything is wrapped up. In that context, people often look for ways to **minimize** the amount of property that must go through probate or avoid the process altogether when possible. This is where the idea of adding a living trust begins to make sense.

The result is that a will on its own may be perfectly adequate in one state and much less attractive in another. The rules have not changed, only how burdensome the local probate process feels.

When a Will Is Enough

Even where probate is not ideal, a will can still be the right choice in many situations. A will may be especially suitable when there is **no real estate, no minor children,** or when the estate is relatively small and simple. It often works well for people whose **main priority is naming guardians for minor children**, particularly young families just getting started. However, a simple will may not accurately provide for the management of finances for a minor, this is a benefit of a trust or a testamentary trust, also known as a trust within a will.

A will also makes sense where the budget is tight and the additional cost and effort of creating a living trust would be a strain. Not everyone needs or wants a more complex structure, and some people do not mind that probate will take some time and money, especially if the estate is modest.

There are also circumstances where having a judge involved can be helpful rather than burdensome, for example, when there are serious creditor issues, and it is useful to have a formal process for sorting out who is owed what. And if most assets will transfer by **beneficiary designations**, joint ownership, or other non-probate methods, a person may reasonably decide that a simple, well-drafted will is enough to tie everything together without creating a trust at all.

For many individuals and couples, a will is an excellent **first layer** of planning. It gets essential decisions on paper. As life changes, when a home is purchased, a business is started, or investments grow, the plan can be revisited and, if appropriate, expanded into a trust-based structure later.

Practical Limits and Financial Reality

There is also the reality of cost. Creating a living trust typically involves more work and higher up-front expense than preparing a basic will. Not everyone is in a position to pay for the "ideal" approach at once. That does not mean they should do nothing.

Putting a **good will** in place is far better than leaving no instructions at all. A person who starts with a will can always create a trust later, when resources and needs align. Estate planning is not a one-time test that must be passed perfectly; it is more like building layers of protection over time.

Living Trusts

A **living trust** (often called *inter vivos*, Latin for "among the living" or a *revocable* trust because it can be revoked or changed) is a legal document designed primarily to keep assets out of probate. Instead of owning certain property directly, an individual transfers ownership of those assets into the name of the trust while they're still alive.

When this is done correctly and consistently, major assets, such as a home, a rental property, or a small business, are no longer counted as belonging to the individual at death. They belong to the trust. The person who created the trust is usually both the initial trustee (manager) and the primary beneficiary during life, so day-to-day control does not change. But when death occurs, the trust, not the probate court, provides the instructions for what happens next.

If a trust is properly **funded**, meaning that titles and beneficiary designations have been updated, so the trust owns or controls the intended assets, the individual may die with only a few minor items in their own name: perhaps a checking account, a car, and ordinary personal belongings. To the probate system, this looks like a **small estate**, which often qualifies for simplified procedures or even avoids probate entirely.

In that scenario, the person named as **successor trustee** can step in, follow the instructions in the trust, and distribute or manage the assets without going through a traditional probate case. The process is usually faster, private, and less expensive than a full court-supervised administration.

Even when a living trust is in place, a simple **"pour-over" will** is still needed. This kind of will has a narrower role: it names guardians for minor children and directs that any assets accidentally left outside the trust should be gathered and transferred into the trust after death. The trust then governs how everything is ultimately handled.

Why a Living Trust Can Be Useful

A living trust offers benefits that extend beyond probate avoidance. One is **privacy**. In many states, a will must be filed with the probate court, and this court file is open to the public. A trust, by contrast, generally is not filed in court. Beneficiaries and certain institutions that need proof of authority will see it, but it does not automatically become part of a public record.

Another key advantage is **planning for incapacity**. If the person who created the trust becomes unable to manage their financial affairs, then the successor trustee can step in and manage the trust assets for that person's benefit while they are still alive. This can make it much easier to pay bills, maintain property, and make financial decisions without the delay and expense of a separate court proceeding to appoint a guardian or conservator.

Trusts can also be written with a great deal of **flexibility**. They can be used to manage money for children or adults who are not ready to handle large sums on their own, to protect a child with special needs without disrupting public benefits, to handle unusual or closely held assets, or to balance competing interests in blended families, for example, providing income for a current spouse while preserving the underlying property for children from an earlier relationship.

When planning reaches this level of complexity, it is technically possible to create similar structures through a will that takes effect at death. In practice, however, people who need sophisticated, long-term arrangements often find that a living trust provides a clearer and more flexible framework, especially when probate would otherwise be lengthy or costly.

Who Is Likely to Benefit From a Trust

A trust is not mandatory for everyone, but it is often a strong choice in certain circumstances. It can be particularly helpful when someone owns **real estate**, especially in more than one state, or when the total value of assets that would otherwise go through probate is clearly above the local small-estate threshold. It also becomes more attractive as an estate grows larger and the possibility of taxes or complex administration increases.

A trust may be especially well-suited to people in **second marriages**, families with children from different relationships, or situations involving **complicated assets**, such as a privately held company or investment properties that will need active management after a death. It can also be the right tool where a beneficiary has special needs and requires careful, long-term financial protection rather than an outright inheritance.

In short, the more moving parts an estate has, multiple beneficiaries, significant assets, business interests, or delicate family dynamics—the more likely it is that a living trust will be worth the extra effort to set up.

Wills and Living Trusts, Side by Side

When wills and living trusts are compared directly, each has clear strengths. A will is generally easier and less expensive to create. It works well for smaller or simpler estates and is often the best starting point for young adults and families whose main goal is naming guardians. The trade-off is that a will usually requires probate, with the delays, costs, and publicity that it can involve.

	Living Trust	Will
Privacy	Usually stays private; it is not filed with the court. The trustee handles transfers outside public view, though beneficiaries are entitled to see the document.	Typically filed with the probate court after death and becomes part of the public record, with a judge overseeing the process.
Cost to create	Generally more expensive and time-consuming to set up, especially if a lawyer is involved.	Often less expensive and easier to prepare; many people can create a basic will without a lawyer.
Effort to set up	Requires retitling key assets into the trust's name, which means updating deeds and account paperwork. It is manageable, but it takes organization and follow-through.	No retitling of property is required during life; assets stay in the person's name until handled through probate.
What it can do	Allows you to direct who receives property and to appoint someone to manage trust assets if you become unable to do so yourself.	Allows you to decide who inherits your property and to name guardians for minor children.
After a death	Assets in the trust are usually distributed without a full probate case, so the process is often faster and less costly.	Estates that rely mainly on a will usually need probate, which tends to take longer and involve more court and professional fees.

A living trust, by contrast, usually costs more to establish and requires additional work to fund properly. But in return, it can reduce or eliminate the need for probate, keep details more private, and provide a structure for managing assets both during life and after death.

For many people, the right answer is not "either/or" but **"both, working together"**: a living trust to hold and manage major assets and a will to catch anything left outside the trust and to name guardians for children.

Chapter | 1 | Assessment Test

Welcome to the Chapter Assessment test. You'll find a short quiz at the end of every chapter to help you gauge your understanding of the key concepts covered. It's recommended that you achieve at least 60% before moving on to the next chapter. If you don't reach this target, take some time to review the chapter before trying again. Good luck!

1. At its core, estate planning answers which three fundamental questions?

a. How much tax you will owe, who will manage your assets, and where documents are stored

b. What you own, who should receive it, and how it will get to them

c. Which court will handle your estate, how long probate takes, and who pays the fees

d. Whether you need a lawyer, a trust, or insurance

2. Why is it recommended to decide between a will and a living trust *before* completing a full asset inventory?

a. Because beneficiary designations depend on the inventory order

b. Because inventory worksheets are legally binding

c. Because the choice of structure helps determine how assets will be listed and transferred

d. Because trusts eliminate the need to identify assets

3. Which of the following is NOT typically part of a basic estate plan?

a. A durable power of attorney for finances

b. An advance healthcare directive

c. A beneficiary designation for retirement accounts

d. A prenuptial agreement

4. What generally happens if a person dies without a will or trust?

a. Their assets automatically pass to whoever paid the funeral expenses

b. A judge distributes property based on what seems fair

c. State intestacy laws determine who inherits

d. All assets are transferred to the state

5. **Why are beneficiary designations for retirement accounts and life insurance so important?**

   a. They usually control distribution regardless of what the will or trust says

   b. They reduce estate taxes automatically

   c. They replace the need for any other estate planning documents

   d. They require court approval before taking effect

6. **Which statement best describes probate?**

   a. A private administrative process handled entirely by family members

   b. A court-supervised process for settling a deceased person's estate

   c. A tax audit triggered by large inheritances

   d. A mandatory process for all estates, regardless of size

7. **What is one major reason many people try to reduce how much of their estate goes through probate?**

   a. Probate prevents heirs from receiving property

   b. Probate eliminates beneficiary designations

   c. Probate can involve delay, cost, and public court records

   d. Probate increases estate tax liability

8. **Which of the following assets most commonly avoids probate when properly set up?**

   a. Household furniture owned solely by the deceased

   b. A bank account without a pay-on-death designation

   c. Real estate titled only in the deceased person's name

   d. A retirement account with a named beneficiary

9. **How does a living trust help with incapacity planning?**

   a. It automatically authorizes medical decisions

   b. It allows a successor trustee to manage trust assets without court involvement

   c. It eliminates the need for powers of attorney

   d. It transfers assets to beneficiaries immediately

10. According to the chapter, which statement best reflects the relationship between probate and estate tax?

a. Avoiding probate also avoids estate tax

b. Only probate assets are subject to estate tax

c. Probate and estate tax are separate systems with different rules

d. Estate tax applies only if probate is required

Answers

1. **B** – Estate planning focuses on what you own, who should receive it, and how the transfer will occur.
2. **C** – Choosing the structure first makes it easier to organize assets and match them to the right planning tools.
3. **D** – A prenuptial agreement can affect estate planning but is not a core estate planning document.
4. **C** – Without a plan, state intestacy laws control how property is distributed.
5. **A** – Beneficiary forms usually govern these assets and often override a will or trust.
6. **B** – Probate is a court-supervised process for settling an estate after death.
7. **C** – Many people seek to avoid probate due to its cost, delays, and lack of privacy.
8. **D** – Retirement accounts with named beneficiaries typically pass outside probate.
9. **B** – A successor trustee can step in to manage trust assets during incapacity without a court order.
10. **C** – Estate tax looks at total assets, regardless of whether they pass through probate.

Personal Notes

CHAPTER 2

TYPES OF PROPERTY

> *"The things you own end up owning you."*
>
> ***– Chuck Palahniuk,***
> *American novelist and essayist*

Inventory

Before any estate plan can take shape, it helps to know what, exactly, is in your estate. Even if you don't think of yourself as someone with "an estate," every adult has one: a collection of accounts, property, insurance, personal items, and financial interests that add up to the picture of what will eventually pass to others. Most people don't own sprawling ranches or complicated businesses, but everyone still benefits from taking stock of what they have, how each asset is titled, what it's roughly worth, and where the important documents can be found.

The idea of listing everything can feel tedious, but it doesn't have to be overwhelming. The inventory can be done in small pieces, one category today, another next week, until the picture is complete. Most people already have nearly all the information they need scattered across bank statements, email accounts, old folders, or insurance documents; it simply hasn't been gathered in one place before.

Creating an inventory often gives people their **first clear snapshot** of what they truly own. Seeing everything laid out can be reassuring, surprising, or even motivating. If the picture shows that resources are thinner than hoped, it may be a good moment to consider steps like purchasing additional life insurance or contributing more consistently to savings.

The value of this process becomes especially clear after a death. Without some organizing up front, it can take heirs months or even years to identify accounts, locate property, or interpret scattered paperwork. Worse, assets sometimes go undiscovered entirely. Families occasionally find out about forgotten investments only because a stray dividend check arrives in the mail or a state's unclaimed property office reaches out years later. A simple inventory dramatically reduces the chance that something will slip through the cracks.

Once the initial list is created, maintaining it becomes easy. A quick review once a year, often at the same time tax documents are gathered, is usually enough to keep everything up to date.

When estimating the value of assets, rough numbers are fine. Financial figures change all the time, and an estate inventory is not the same as a formal financial plan. The purpose is simply to understand whether taxes might someday be an issue (most families never reach the federal estate tax threshold) and get a sense of what will eventually pass to heirs and beneficiaries.

Knowing **what types of assets** you own is just as important as knowing their value. Wills and trusts control only certain property. Other assets, such as retirement accounts, life insurance, transfer-on-death accounts, or real estate held with survivorship rights, may pass outside your will or trust entirely. Think of your estate like a large pie: your will or trust directs a significant slice of it, but the crust and a few pieces may take a different route because of the way they are titled. Later chapters explain these mechanisms in detail, but the first step is simply being aware of what category each asset falls into.

A complete and organized inventory makes sure your estate plan actually addresses everything you own. That is the foundation for the rest of this book, and it begins with a little homework.

Marital Ownership Rules

Ownership rules vary significantly across the United States, especially for married couples. In some states, ownership is determined by whose name appears on a deed or account. In others, ownership is determined by where the money came from; wages earned during the marriage may automatically belong to both spouses. These systems can feel counterintuitive at first, but knowing which one applies is essential.

If, after reviewing this chapter, you and your spouse are unsure how your property is categorized, it is wise to consult a local family-law attorney. They are the experts in determining what belongs to whom within a marriage.

Community-Property States

In nine states, mostly in the western United States, property acquired during the marriage is generally treated as **community property**. This means each spouse owns one-half of the property, no matter whose name appears on the paperwork. Each spouse is free to decide what happens to their half, but they cannot control their partner's share.

This system can create misunderstandings when people assume something is "theirs alone" because their name is on the account, only to discover later that only half of it truly belongs to them. The source of the funds matters most: if an asset was purchased with income earned during the marriage, both spouses own half.

States That Allow an Optional Community-Property System

A small number of states allow married couples to opt into community-property treatment, usually through a written agreement or a specially designed trust. Unless a couple takes that formal step, their assets remain classified under common-law rules.

Type	States
Full community-property states	Arizona, California, Idaho, Louisiana*, Nevada, New Mexico, Texas, Washington, Wisconsin*
States that allow an optional community-property system	Alaska, Florida, Kentucky, South Dakota, Tennessee

** Louisiana's community-property system is rooted in civil law rather than the common-law tradition followed by the other eight states, but the practical result is similar. * Wisconsin uses the term "marital property" under the Uniform Marital Property Act, but the effect closely mirrors community-property rules.*

Common-Law States

In the remaining states and in Washington, D.C., ownership generally follows the name on the title or account. A home titled in one spouse's name belongs to that spouse alone. To prevent unfair results for surviving spouses, these states typically give the survivor the right to claim an **elective share** of the deceased spouse's estate. Exercising that right can require a formal legal filing, and sometimes court involvement, which careful planning can often avoid.

> ***Note:*** *Elective share rules vary widely by state, including deadlines, what property is counted, and how the share is calculated.*

Common-Law Property States

Alabama	Indiana	Montana	South Carolina
Alaska*	Iowa	Nebraska	South Dakota*
Arkansas	Kansas	New Hampshire	Tennessee*
Colorado	Kentucky*	New Jersey	Utah
Connecticut	Maine	New York	Vermont
Delaware	Maryland	North Carolina	Virginia

Florida*	Massachusetts	North Dakota	Washington, D.C.
Georgia	Michigan	Ohio	West Virginia
Hawaii	Minnesota	Oklahoma	Wyoming
Illinois	Mississippi	Oregon	

* ***Alaska, Florida, Kentucky, South Dakota, and Tennessee*** *are common-law states that* ***allow an optional community-property agreement or trust****.*

Changing the Default Rules

The rules of either system can be altered by written agreement. When the agreement is signed before marriage, it is called a **prenuptial agreement**; when signed afterward, it is called a **postnuptial agreement**. These agreements can be essential tools when couples want to adjust ownership rights, protect children from previous relationships, or simply bring clarity to shared property. Although the conversations behind them can be difficult, avoiding them can lead to expensive disputes later, particularly during divorce or after a death.

> ***Example:*** *Imagine a couple living in a community-property state. They have been married for many years and live in a house that one spouse inherited. Under typical community-property rules, inherited assets are treated as that spouse's separate property. If that spouse dies first, the surviving partner may* ***not*** *automatically inherit the entire house; state law may require that some or all of it pass to the deceased spouse's children, including children from a previous relationship. This can be a real shock for a surviving spouse who has always thought of the house as fully "theirs."*

In this example, an attorney could help them correct this by changing the legal character of the home from separate property to community property, usually through a postnuptial agreement and a new deed. With both steps completed, each spouse owns half, and the surviving spouse keeps the entire home if the other dies first.

Assets

Now that you have a clearer sense of how different kinds of property move from one owner to another, it is time to take the next practical step: understanding what you actually own.

Many people discover during this stage that their financial life is more scattered than they expected. A bank statement tucked in one drawer, an insurance policy in another, investment paperwork hiding inside last year's tax folder. There's nothing unusual about that; most of us have the pieces, just not in one place.

Creating an inventory brings everything together. Now we'll break your property into manageable categories, so you can work through them one at a time.

Cash and Everyday Accounts

A good place to start is with the most familiar assets: your cash. For this inventory, "cash" simply means money sitting in:

- Checking accounts;
- Savings accounts; and
- Certificates of deposit (CDs).

Begin by listing each account. For every one, note:

- The name of the bank or credit union;
- The type of account and its account number;
- Whose names are on it (just you, you and a partner, or you and someone else); and
- An approximate balance and the date recorded.

It doesn't matter if the numbers fluctuate. What you want is a realistic snapshot; it does not need to be perfect.

Alongside this, it's very helpful to record how someone could access the account if they needed to handle things for you. In today's world, that often means writing down where login details are stored, how two-factor authentication works, or whether there's a password manager in use. You don't have to put all the raw passwords in your book if that feels unsafe; you can simply indicate, for example, "Online banking login details are in the blue notebook in the study drawer," or "All financial passwords are stored in my password manager, with access details in my letter of instructions."

A simple table in your workbook might look like this (with your own details, of course):

Cash Asset	Where Is It?	Who Owns It?	Approx. Value	How to Access It
Checking account ending 4421	Riverbank, Main Street branch	Alex and Jordan, joint owners	~$5,200	Online banking; credentials note in desk file
Savings account ending 8930	Oak Hill Credit Union	Alex only	~$1,750	Passbook in home safe
2-year CD ending 1174	NorthCity Bank	Jordan only	~$15,000	Statement in "Investments" binder

Once you have completed this section, you already have a clearer picture than most people ever do. The next step is to look at money that is technically meant for someone else: accounts and plans set aside for children.

Accounts for Children and Education Savings

Many families open accounts in a child's name without thinking of them as part of "the estate." Grandparents might have started an investment account "for the grandchildren." Parents may have opened a small savings account when a child was born. Even if you do not think of that money as yours, your inventory should still include it. If something happens to you, others will need to know what financial support is already waiting for your children.

Custodial Accounts

Bank and investment accounts created "for the benefit of" a child are often custodial accounts. Legally, the child is considered the owner, but the money is managed by an adult custodian until the law says the child is old enough to take control, often at 18 or 21, depending on the state.

You can usually identify a custodial account by how it is titled, not by its tone. The account name typically includes language such as "as custodian for" or references a state's UTMA or UGMA statute.

Account statements might say "for benefit of" or use abbreviations like **UTMA** or **UGMA**, referring to the Uniform Transfers to Minors Act or the Uniform Gifts to Minors Act. Until the child reaches the required age, only the custodian can make decisions about investing or spending that money, and everything must be used for the child's benefit.

In your inventory, it helps to record:

- Which child the account is for;
- Who is acting as custodian;
- Where the statements are kept; and
- An approximate value.

This way, if others have to step in, they know what's already available for that child.

College Savings Plans

In addition to custodial accounts, many families now use **tax-advantaged education savings plans**. These can form a significant part of what eventually supports a child or grandchild. As such, they belong on your list as well.

The most common are **529 plans**. Every state offers at least one. You don't have to live in a state to use its plan, but some states offer tax breaks to residents who use the home-state version. The funds in a 529 plan grow tax-free as long as withdrawals are used for qualified education expenses, which now often include both college costs and some K-12 tuition.

There are also **Coverdell Education Savings Accounts**, which allow smaller annual contributions but can be used for a wide range of education expenses.

Here, your inventory might include a simple entry such as:

Education Asset	Where Is It?	For Whom?	Who Controls It?	Approx. Value
BrightFuture 529 Plan	Sunrise State 529 program; statements in "College" folder	Emma	Alex (account owner)	~$9,200
Coverdell Education Account	Managed by Harbor Investments; online access	Liam	Jordan (account owner)	~$3,400

Once you include these children's assets, the picture becomes more realistic: you see not only what will pass to adults, but also what is already earmarked for the next generation.

Safe Deposit Boxes

Some people prefer to keep their most important items in a safe deposit box at a bank or credit union. If you use one, it should be listed in your inventory along with its location, the name of the financial institution, and where the key can be found.

What often surprises families is that, in some states, accessing a safe deposit box after the owner dies can take time. The bank may require court documents, and it may be several weeks before the executor or trustee can gain access. If your original will, trust, or other vital information is locked in the box, the delay can complicate everything.

For that reason, your inventory should note:

- The bank and branch;
- The box number;
- Who is listed as an authorized user; and
- Where the key is stored

That way no one is left wondering whether a hidden box exists or how to reach it.

> ***Note:*** *If you decide to store your original estate planning documents in a safe deposit box, be sure to keep a copy of your estate plan where the person who will handle your affairs,* ***your successor trustee or your executor/ personal representative****, can easily obtain it if you become incapacitated or after your death. Access rules for safe deposit boxes vary by state and by the bank, and family members or fiduciaries may not be able to retrieve originals immediately without proper authority.*

Real Estate

For many people, the most valuable part of their estate is real estate: a primary home, perhaps a holiday property, or a small rental. Understanding these assets is not just a matter of knowing addresses and values. It is equally important to understand **how each property is owned** because the form of ownership controls what happens to it after a death.

If you recently bought your property, you may remember signing a thick stack of paperwork at closing. Somewhere in that pile is the key document: the **grant deed** (or warranty deed or similar), which transfers legal ownership to you. That deed usually states exactly how you hold title to the property.

Many people do not know where that deed ended up, and that's completely normal. If you can't find it, don't panic. Once a deed has been recorded at the county land records office, it becomes a public record and can be copied.

If your deed is missing from your files, the process to get another copy is simple. The office you need may be called the county recorder, land registry, land records office, or county clerk, depending on where you live. A quick phone call or website visit will tell you the cost of requesting a copy, usually just a modest fee.

You can then send a short letter or follow the online instructions, giving your name, the property address, and any other requested details, and the county will mail you an official copy. Title companies can obtain deeds as well, but they often charge more than the county.

Once your deed arrives, look closely at the words that describe how you own the property. Those few phrases matter a great deal.

Deeds usually include language such as:

- "Alex Rivera, a married man as his sole and separate property;"
- "Alex and Jordan Rivera, husband and wife, as joint tenants;"
- "Alex and Jordan Rivera, husband and wife, as community property;"
- "Alex and Jordan Rivera, husband and wife, as community property with right of survivorship;"
- "Alex and Jordan Rivera, as tenants by the entirety;" or
- "Alex Rivera, Jordan Rivera, and Mia Park, as tenants in common."

Each of these phrases tells a different story about who owns what and what happens next when one of the owners dies.

Separate Property

If the deed names only one person, the property is usually that person's separate property. In general, they are free to leave it to anyone they wish in a will or trust.

In community-property states, however, the analysis can be more complicated. If joint marital funds were used to pay down the mortgage or make improvements, the spouse may have a legal interest, even though their name does not appear on the deed. For this reason, couples in those states are often encouraged to review title carefully and, if necessary, consult a local attorney to confirm who owns what.

Joint Tenancy

Joint tenancy is a very common way for couples, relatives, or even friends to own property together. In joint tenancy, each owner has an equal share, and the defining feature is the **right of survivorship**. When one owner dies, the other joint tenants automatically inherit that share. The property does not pass through the deceased owner's will or trust; the transfer happens by law.

This can be a very effective way to avoid probate for that property, but it also means an owner cannot leave their share to anyone else in their will. The surviving joint tenant or tenants will own the whole property, no matter what the will says.

Community Property

In community-property states, married couples and, in some places, registered domestic partners can hold real estate as community property. Each spouse owns an undivided half. Unlike joint tenancy, there is no automatic survivorship built in. Each spouse can leave their half through a will or trust. After a death, an additional step is needed to transfer or confirm ownership of the deceased spouse's share.

Community Property with Right of Survivorship

Some states allow a version of community property that includes a survivorship feature. In those states, couples can hold property, so that it is both community property during their lifetimes and automatically passes to the surviving spouse at the first death. This blend offers some tax and planning advantages while avoiding probate for that asset.

Tenancy by the Entirety

Tenancy by the entirety is available to married couples (and in some states, registered partners). It resembles joint tenancy with survivorship, but often includes stronger protection against certain individual creditors. If one spouse is sued, for example, a creditor may be more limited in what can be taken from property held this way. When one spouse dies, the other becomes the full owner automatically.

Tenancy in Common

Where ownership is shared but survivorship is not mentioned, the default is usually tenancy in common. Co-owners may each hold different percentages, one might own 70%, another 30%. Each owner's share can be left to anyone in a will or trust, and at death, the share does not automatically move to the other co-owner. It passes according to the deceased owner's estate plan.

Your real estate inventory might note for each property:

- The address;
- How title is held (exact wording from the deed);
- Approximate market value and mortgage balance; and
- Any online access information for the loan account.

Seeing this information in one place helps you understand not just what you own, but how each piece will actually move when the time comes.

Retirement and Investments Accounts

As you move from cash and real estate into the next category of your inventory, the picture becomes a little more layered. Many people find this part eye-opening, because investments tend to accumulate slowly over time: an IRA opened years ago, a 401(k) from an old job, a mutual fund bought during a good market year. To bring order to all of this, start by gathering every investment statement you can.

Once you have them, divide them into two piles. One includes everything that qualifies as a retirement account: IRAs, Roth IRAs, 401(k)s, 403(b)s, pensions, and annuities. The other pile holds everything else: brokerage accounts, individual stocks, mutual funds purchased directly from investment companies, or shares you may own from programs offered by large corporations.

This simple split matters because retirement accounts must adhere to very different rules. Each one typically has a named beneficiary on file with the plan administrator or financial institution. When you die, those assets do not pass through your will or trust; they go directly to the person listed on that beneficiary form. If you ever want to change who inherits a retirement account, you won't find the solution in your estate plan, you'll need to update the company's records with a beneficiary-change form. That's why keeping these accounts in a distinct pile makes everything easier as you move forward in the planning process.

The second pile contains your non-retirement investments, and these behave more like the other financial assets in your estate. How they pass will depend on how the account is titled. If the investment is held jointly with someone else, often as joint tenants, the surviving owner will simply inherit the entire account, without probate or court involvement. On the other hand, if the account is in your name alone, you're free to direct it through your will or trust. Some companies also allow you to add a payable-on-death or transfer-on-death designation, which allows you to name a beneficiary directly, much like with retirement accounts.

As you look through each account statement, check the names printed at the top. The owner listed there is the legal owner. If two names appear, both people are considered owners. If only one appears, the account belongs to that person alone, unless you live in a community-property state, where the analysis may be more nuanced. You may also see small abbreviations near the names: **FBO** ("for the benefit of"), **JTWROS** (joint tenants with right of survivorship), **CPWROS** (community property with right of survivorship), or **TE** (tenancy by the entirety). These codes tell the story of how the asset will move when the time comes.

Businesses

For small business owners, the company is often one of the largest, and most personal, assets they'll ever own. It represents years of late nights, big risks, and steady determination. But that same business can be one of the hardest things for loved ones to manage if the owner dies unexpectedly.

A business can easily stall during probate. Court delays, paperwork requirements, and the need for judicial approval can leave employees unsure who's in charge and customers unsure whether the business is still operating. Even a strong company can lose value quickly if no one has the legal authority to keep it going.

That's why your inventory should go beyond listing the business as a single asset. Take a moment to think about **what you actually own**:

- Do you operate as a sole proprietor?
- Do you share ownership through a partnership or LLC?
- Do you hold stock in a corporation, whether fully or partially?
- Is there a governing document that spells out what happens to your share if you die?

Understanding the structure is the first step toward making sure your estate plan protects the business you worked so hard to build.

Sole Proprietorships

If your business is simply "you," not a separate legal entity, this part is straightforward.

A sole proprietorship can be listed just like any other personal asset. Be sure your inventory includes:

- The business name;
- The equipment or tools used in the business;
- Inventory or accounts receivable (if applicable); and
- The business bank account.

One item many people overlook is the **goodwill** connected to the business—the reputation, client relationships, and name recognition you've built. Treat it as part of the business and include it in your inventory so it's clear that it, too, can be transferred along with everything else.

Partnerships

If you co-own a business with others, the rules are a bit more complex. Most partnership interests can be transferred as part of your estate, but partnership agreements often include rules about what must happen when one partner dies. Some give the surviving partners the right to buy the deceased partner's share; others require certain approvals before ownership can be transferred.

These rules don't stop you from planning ahead, they just determine what your heirs ultimately receive. When adding a partnership to your inventory, note:

- The name of the partnership;
- The percentage you own;
- Where the partnership agreement is kept; and
- Whether the agreement restricts transfers at death.

If anything in the agreement is unclear, or problematic, this is a good moment to clarify it with the other partners or a business attorney. Sometimes a simple amendment can solve an issue that would otherwise cause trouble later.

Corporations You Own Entirely

If you're the sole shareholder of a corporation, your shares generally can be transferred without much difficulty.

Include in your inventory:

- The corporate name;
- The number of shares you own;
- Where the corporate records are kept; and
- Whether there are bylaws or resolutions related to transfers.

Even with a single-owner corporation, good paperwork matters. Keeping your records clear ensures that whoever steps in after your death, whether it's a family member, executor, or trustee, can act quickly and confidently.

Closely Held Corporations and LLCs

Many people share ownership with one or several partners, either in a closely held corporation or in a limited liability company (LLC). These entities often have internal rules about how ownership can be transferred and who is allowed to hold voting rights.

When you add these businesses to your inventory, look for:

- The operating agreement (for LLCs) or bylaws (for corporations);
- Any restrictions on transfers; and

- Buy-sell provisions that may give other owners the right to purchase your interest at a set price or formula.

These rules don't prevent estate planning, they just shape it. If co-owners have a contractual right to buy your share after you die, your estate plan simply ensures that the purchase price goes to your heirs rather than requiring them to fight for it in court.

Special Case: Subchapter S Corporations

If your business is an S corporation, your estate planning needs become more delicate.

S corporation shares can only be held by certain types of owners, and **only specific trusts** are allowed.

If your estate includes S corporation stock, make a note in your inventory, so you can raise the issue with your lawyer later. A few lines of the wrong trust language can unintentionally terminate S-corp status, which can be costly to fix.

Life Insurance

Investments and retirement accounts often shape the long-term picture of your estate, but life insurance plays a different and equally important role--providing immediate financial support to those you leave behind. For many families, especially those with young children, the payout from a policy can be the single largest source of liquid funds after a death.

Your inventory should list all the policies you own and the ones offered through your workplace. Start by checking what coverage your employer provides. Many workplaces offer group life insurance, sometimes equal to a year or more of your salary, and some allow employees to buy additional coverage at reasonable rates.

These group policies can change insurers over time, but they always have a certificate number, which is usually enough to trace the policy. Some employers also provide accidental-death policies, which offer an additional payout if the death is the result of an accident.

Next, turn to any life insurance you purchased on your own. The details you need, policy number, benefit amount, and beneficiaries, are usually listed on the policy itself or on your premium statements. If you can't find the physical document but know the company's name, a phone call or online account should help you recover everything you need.

Life insurance is also a place where outdated beneficiary designations tend to hide. People often forget to update beneficiaries after major life events like marriage, divorce, or the birth of a child. If you discover inconsistencies while building your inventory, don't worry; they can be corrected.

Annuities

Annuities sit somewhere between an investment and an insurance product. They begin with a contract: you deposit funds, and the company promises to pay the money back over time, often with interest. Some annuities offer payments only during your lifetime, while others continue to a surviving spouse or designated beneficiary. Because the rules vary widely, it's important to confirm whether any annuity you own includes survivor benefits. A quick call or online inquiry with the issuing company can usually answer that.

Add any annuity contracts to your inventory, with the contract number, issuing company, and payout terms, if they're available.

Government Benefits

Before you leave this section, make note of any government benefits for which you or your spouse may qualify. These can include:

- **Veterans' benefits**, such as VA disability compensation, survivor benefits, pensions, burial benefits, or healthcare benefits through the VA;
- **Social Security benefits**, including retirement benefits, spousal benefits, survivor benefits, and disability benefits;
- **Social Security Disability Insurance (SSDI)** or **Supplemental Security Income (SSI);**
- **Military survivor benefits**, such as Survivor Benefit Plan payments for eligible spouses;
- **Federal or state disability programs** related to a work injury or long-term disability;
- **Public employee benefits**, including pensions or survivor benefits for government workers;
- **Healthcare-related benefits**, such as Medicare, Medicaid, or state-specific assistance programs; and
- **Educational or housing benefits** available to surviving spouses or dependents, particularly for veterans.

These don't always take the form of lump-sum payments, but knowing they exist helps your loved ones claim what they're entitled to.

Royalties, Copyrights, and Patents

Intellectual property often lives on, well past the person who created it. A song, a book, a design, or a patent can keep generating income for many years. These assets are often forgotten during estate planning simply because they don't sit in a traditional account.

If you own intellectual property, add each item to your inventory along with:

- Where the registration documents are stored;
- Any licensing agreements;

- The agency or publisher that pays royalties; and
- The account where payments are deposited.

These rights can usually be transferred very easily, often with a short assignment document. Making sure they're accounted for protects both your creative legacy and the income it may continue to generate.

Pensions

If you've worked for a government agency, a school, a union, or an employer that still offers traditional defined-benefit pensions, make sure to include those here. Pensions come with their own set of rules, and not all of them continue paying benefits after the recipient dies. Some provide generous survivor benefits; others end immediately. Knowing which type you have helps your family understand what support they may or may not receive.

Locate your most recent pension statement, visit the plan's website, or call the administrator to learn whether survivor benefits are available and what they look like. Your inventory should include contact information for the plan, your employee ID or account number, and any relevant notes about eligibility.

Digital Assets

Your estate includes more than physical property. It includes your "digital life" such as your cryptocurrency, monetized social media accounts, domain names, and loyalty points. These require specific planning because they exist without a physical paper trail.

Automobiles & Other Personal Property

Compared with houses, pensions, and investment accounts, everyday personal property tends to shift more quickly over time. Cars are traded in, furniture is replaced, and belongings come and go. For that reason, your inventory only needs to capture items that are either valuable or meaningful. For example, a car with a loan attached, jewelry with sentimental value, or a collection of artwork are worth noting. Everyday household items, however, don't need to be cataloged piece by piece.

Property Worksheet

Now that you've walked through the different kinds of assets you may own and how they really work, this is the moment to turn all that understanding into something practical. The next step is your **Property Worksheet**. This is where you pull everything together: what you own, roughly what each item is worth, and how it's titled. You don't need exact figures to the cent; good estimates are enough. What matters is that you see, on one page, the outline of your estate and the building blocks of your future plan.

Think of the worksheet as a map of your financial life. When each asset is clearly listed and described, it becomes much easier for you to plan, and one day, it will be easier for the people you appoint to locate, manage, and transfer those assets without confusion. The clearer you are now, the smoother things will be for them later.

To make this as easy as possible, below you'll find a QR code that lets you download a printable Property Worksheet. You can print it and fill it out by hand, or reprint pages as your circumstances change. Take your time with it, work through it in small pieces if you need to, and remember: completing this worksheet is not just paperwork, it's the foundation of a thoughtful, well-informed estate plan.

Scan the QR code to download the printable worksheet, or if you are on digital, click on this link:

https://drive.google.com/file/d/1hyCPx2AejNGz60ov3mfkV1NrwgzSxvoR/view?usp=drive_link

What Comes Next

By the time you finish this part of your inventory, you've done more than list your belongings, you've taken the first real step toward understanding how your estate fits together. It's a careful kind of detective work, and it can be surprisingly emotionally exhausting. Remind yourself that it is okay for you to take a break. Set your papers aside. Let the information settle.

What comes next in your planning will be more personal. Now that you know what you own, you can start shaping a plan that reflects the people you care about and the future you want for them. Everything you've organized up to this point becomes the foundation for smart, thoughtful decisions.

And you've already done the hardest part. Good work.

Chapter | 2 | Assessment Test

1. Why is creating an estate inventory important even for people who don't consider themselves "wealthy"?

- **a.** Because inventories are required by law
- **b.** Because every adult owns assets that will eventually pass to others
- **c.** Because it automatically reduces estate taxes
- **d.** Because banks will not release funds without one

2. What is the primary purpose of estimating asset values in an estate inventory?

- **a.** To calculate exact tax liability
- **b.** To prepare court-required appraisals
- **c.** To understand the overall picture and whether planning issues may arise
- **d.** To lock in values for future probate

3. Why is it important to identify how each asset is titled or owned?

- **a.** Because titles determine interest rates and fees
- **b.** Because titling determines whether an asset is subject to probate and, therefore, whether it passes under a will or outside probate
- **c.** Because assets without titles cannot be inherited
- **d.** Because courts require uniform ownership formats

4. In a community-property state, which statement is generally true about property acquired during marriage?

- **a.** It belongs entirely to the spouse whose name is on the account
- **b.** It belongs to whichever spouse earned the income
- **c.** Each spouse generally owns one-half, regardless of title
- **d.** It automatically passes to children at death

5. What is the main feature that distinguishes joint tenancy from tenancy in common?

- **a.** Joint tenancy allows unequal ownership shares
- **b.** Joint tenancy includes a right of survivorship
- **c.** Tenancy in common avoids probate
- **d.** Tenancy in common is limited to married couples

6. Why should custodial accounts for children be included in an estate inventory?

- **a.** Because the money legally belongs to the parents
- **b.** Because courts require them to be listed
- **c.** Because the accounts are frozen at death
- **d.** Because others will need to know what resources already exist for the child

7. Which asset is most likely to pass outside a will or trust due to a beneficiary designation?

- **a.** Household furniture
- **b.** A sole proprietorship
- **c.** A retirement account
- **d.** A personal checking account without POD instructions

8. Why can owning real estate in more than one state complicate estate administration?

- **a.** Property values must be recalculated annually
- **b.** Multiple probate proceedings may be required
- **c.** Federal law overrides state property rules
- **d.** Beneficiaries must live in the same state

9. What is one reason business interests require special attention in an estate inventory?

- **a.** Businesses are always taxed at higher rates
- **b.** Business assets cannot pass through trusts
- **c.** Probate delays can disrupt operations and reduce value
- **d.** Courts automatically dissolve businesses at death

10. What is the main purpose of completing the Property Worksheet at the end of the chapter?

- **a.** To create a legally binding estate plan
- **b.** To replace the need for a will or trust
- **c.** To provide exact financial statements for heirs
- **d.** To see, in one place, what you own and how it is titled

Answers

1. **B** – Every adult owns assets that will eventually pass to others, making an inventory useful for everyone.
2. **C** – Rough estimates help reveal the overall picture and whether planning issues may arise.
3. **B** – Ownership and title determine whether an asset is governed by a will, trust, or other mechanism.
4. **C** – In community-property states, each spouse generally owns one-half of property acquired during marriage.
5. **B** – Joint tenancy includes a right of survivorship, meaning the surviving owner automatically inherits the share.
6. **D** – Including custodial accounts helps others understand what resources already exist for the child.
7. **C** – Retirement accounts typically pass according to beneficiary designations.
8. **B** – Real estate in multiple states can require separate probate proceedings.
9. **C** – Probate delays can stall business operations and quickly reduce value.
10. **D** – The worksheet provides a clear, single-page overview of assets and ownership.

Personal Notes

CHAPTER 3

Last Wills

> ***Where there is a will, there is a way.***
>
> **— George Herbert,**
> *Welsh poet, orator, and Anglican priest*

Now that you've taken the time to understand what you own, how it's titled, and where it fits within your estate, the next step is deciding how those assets should be passed on. For many people, this decision leads to one central tool: a Last Will, sometimes simply called a *will*.

A Last Will may not be the flashiest document in your estate plan, but it's one of the most important. It spells out who receives your property that is not titled in a trust or that does not have a beneficiary designation, who is in charge of settling your affairs, and, if you're a parent, who will step in to care for your children, also known as guardianship provisions. Even in an era of trusts, beneficiary designations, and digital accounts, a will is at the core of nearly every thoughtful estate plan, as it disposes of property titled in your individual name.

Last Wills: The First Building Block

Before drafting any will, whether you use a lawyer, software, or the worksheet included with this book, there are four critical questions that every person must answer:

1. What do you own, and how do you want to give it away?

Everything begins with the property worksheet you created in Chapter 2. That list isn't just a record; it's the blueprint for your will. Your next task is to use that information to complete the **Will Worksheet**, which helps you match each asset (or group of assets) with the people or organizations you want to benefit.

Be sure to think about your estate as a whole, including the assets your will does *not* control, such as assets titled in a trust or with named beneficiary designations. Coordinating everything, including probate and non-probate property, is what makes an estate plan work smoothly.

2. Who should settle your estate?

Every will needs an **executor,** also called a personal representative. This is the person who will file your will at the courthouse, gather your assets, pay any outstanding debts, and distribute your assets according to your instructions. Some people choose a spouse or adult child; others prefer a trusted friend or professional. What matters most is the individual's reliability and the ability to stay organized during a stressful time.

3. Who should care for your children?

If you have minor children, this is often the hardest part of the entire will. Naming guardians requires considering values, personalities, and practical realities. Chapter 6 thoroughly walks through that decision, and it's worth reading before you complete the guardian section of the Will Worksheet.

4. How should money for my children be handled?

Many parents want their children to inherit, but not all at once, and not at a young age. Chapter 7 explains the different ways to set up custodial accounts or trusts so that a child's inheritance is protected and managed until they're mature enough to handle it. A will can put these arrangements in place with just a few clear instructions.

Depending on your life circumstances, it may help to skim ahead. Estate planning is interconnected; each choice affects the rest, so it's normal to move back and forth as you build your plan.

A well-drafted will is more powerful than many people expect. It can:

- Leave your property to the people or charities you choose,
- Spell out what should happen if a beneficiary dies before you,
- Name an executor and a backup,
- Choose guardians for your children,
- Set up a trust or custodial structure for young beneficiaries, and
- Provide for the care of a pet.

If, after reading Chapter 1, you expect that a **living trust** may fit your situation better, that's perfectly fine. In fact, most of the decisions you make when filling out the Will Worksheet apply directly to trusts as well. You still need to know what you own, who you want to benefit, and who should carry out your wishes. The only difference is the tool you use.

Making Your Will Legal

The good news is that making a will legally valid is straightforward in nearly every state. The law is designed to honor your wishes without requiring complicated procedures. In most places:

- You must be an adult of sound mind,
- Your will should be typed or printed (handwritten wills are legal in many states but can cause problems),
- You must sign and date it in front of two witnesses who don't inherit under the document, and
- The witnesses must sign as well.

Most professionals also recommend attaching a **self-proving affidavit**. This short statement, signed by the witnesses, sometimes in front of a notary, confirms that you signed the will voluntarily and understood what you were doing. It makes probate far easier later because no one has to track down witnesses years or decades afterward. Some states require notarization; others don't.

If you choose to create your will through reputable online software, it will guide you through the correct process for your state so you won't have to memorize these details. What matters most is clarity: what you own, who receives it, and how everything should be managed.

A Will Is Just One Piece of the Puzzle

Even though a will is foundational, it doesn't cover everything. Many of your most valuable assets may never pass through your will at all. Real estate with survivorship rights, retirement accounts, life insurance policies, beneficiary-designated financial accounts, and assets held in a trust all bypass your will entirely.

This surprises many people. But the logic is simple: a will governs only assets that go through probate. Anything that passes by **contract**, like beneficiary designations or by **survivorship,** isn't controlled by the will.

The key is coordination. Think of your estate as running on two parallel tracks:

- **Track 1**: Probate assets directed by your will.
- **Track 2**: Non-probate assets directed by beneficiary forms, joint ownership, or a trust.

If the tracks aren't aligned, the results can be messy. Beneficiary designations and joint ownership with right of survivorship often operate like contracts that a bank, brokerage, or insurance company will honor quickly, usually without court involvement. Because these transfers typically happen outside probate, a judge generally can't use your will to change who receives them. But if no valid beneficiary designation is on file, if all named beneficiaries can't take the asset, or if the joint ownership arrangement has been broken or isn't effective at death, the asset may end up in the probate estate and then be distributed under the will (or under state intestacy law if there is no will).

A few real-world examples simplify the point:

Example 1*: You leave everything to your partner in your will, but your old retirement account still lists your sister as beneficiary. The retirement company will pay your sister, no matter what the will says.*

Example 2: *You leave equal shares of your estate to your three children, yet your life insurance names only the oldest child because you opened the policy years ago and never updated it.*

Example 3: *You leave your entire estate to a charity, but your home is jointly owned with your brother, who automatically becomes the full owner at your death.*

Right of Survivorship

When you own property together with someone else, the way you own the property can completely override the instructions in your will for disposing of that asset. In some cases, your share doesn't pass under your will at all; it goes automatically to the other owner the moment you die.

This happens when the property is held with a **right of survivorship**. The most common example is joint tenancy. If the deed to a home states that two people own it "as joint tenants with right of survivorship," when one of them dies, the survivor automatically owns the entire property. So the first person's will doesn't control who receives that asset at the first death.

However, the survivor's estate plan will matter later: when the surviving joint tenant eventually dies, the home will be distributed according to the survivor's will or trust (unless the survivor changes the title again, such as by placing the property into a trust or creating a new survivorship arrangement).

Several forms of ownership can include this automatic inheritance feature. Joint tenancy is the one most people use, but some states also allow married couples to hold property as **community property with right of survivorship**, and others allow **tenancy by the entirety** for spouses. All of these forms share the same core idea: when one owner dies, the surviving owner takes full title without probate and without regard to what the will says. Chapter 2 explains these ownership forms in more detail, but here the key takeaway is simple: if property is owned with a right of survivorship, your will does not control where it goes.

This is why understanding **how** you own property is just as important as knowing **what** you own. If the title doesn't match your intentions, your estate plan can fail, even if the will itself is perfectly drafted.

When Joint Ownership Doesn't Match Your Wishes

Consider this example:

Leah owns a house with her long-term partner, Daniel. Years ago, when they bought it, the deed was set up as "joint tenants with right of survivorship," which felt natural at the time, they were building a life together. Leah also has an adult son, Marco, from a prior relationship. In her will, Leah leaves everything to Marco.

When Leah dies, Daniel automatically becomes the full owner of the house because of the right of survivorship. Marco inherits Leah's savings, investments, and personal belongings, but **no share of the property**, even though Leah imagined that "her half" would eventually become his. She had pictured Daniel living there for a time, then buying Marco out or the property being sold and Daniel and Marco sharing the proceeds. Because the title was never changed, that plan never had a chance to work.

If Leah had wanted Marco to inherit her half of the house instead of letting it pass outright to Daniel, she would have needed to retitle the asset to eliminate the automatic survivorship clause before she died. In many states, a joint tenant can do that without the other owner's consent. Two common approaches are:

- Changing the owner's interest from joint tenancy to **tenancy in common**, or
- Transferring her share into a **trust**, which then leaves the property as she directs.

In either case, Daniel would still own his half, but Leah's half could pass to Marco through her will or trust instead of going to Daniel automatically.

Of course, that kind of arrangement raises a practical issue. Daniel and Marco could end up co-owning the same house, with one living there and the other owning a partial interest. That can create tension or pressure to sell. One way to ease that is to have Leah's share pass into a trust for Daniel's lifetime. The trust could allow him to stay in the home or even require the trustee to let him live there, while ensuring that Marco ultimately receives the value of Leah's half when Daniel moves out or dies, or when the property is sold.

The point isn't that there is only one "right" answer, but that **title must match your intentions**. Without changing the form of ownership, the law will follow the deed, not the will.

Survivorship Rules Aren't Limited to Houses

Homes are often held in joint tenancy, but they're not the only assets where survivorship can exist. Bank accounts, brokerage accounts, and even vehicles can be titled in a way that gives the surviving owner everything automatically.

This can work well in some situations. Unmarried partners sometimes use joint tenancy to make sure the survivor can keep using shared funds without delay. Older parents might add an adult child to an account to make bill-paying easier, not realizing they've created a survivorship arrangement that gives that one child the entire account at death.

The important thing to remember is that you **cannot override** the right of survivorship with your will. If two siblings own a rental condo as joint tenants, and one sibling's will leaves "everything to my spouse," the surviving sibling, not the spouse, will own 100% of the condo when that sibling dies. The income and the property follow the survivorship deed, not the will. If you want your share to go to someone other than the co-owner, the property must be titled as tenants in common, not joint tenants.

Another Example: Joint Ownership and Unintended Consequences

Imagine two sisters, Nina and Carla, inherit a lakeside cabin together when their father dies. The deed lists them as joint tenants with right of survivorship. Over the years, they rent out the cabin during the summer and use it with their families in the off-season. Nina is married to Alex, and in her will she leaves her entire estate to him.

Nina assumes Alex will one day receive "her half" of the cabin. But when she dies, the law doesn't consider her will, it refers to the deed. Because the cabin is owned in joint tenancy, Carla automatically becomes the sole owner. Alex receives Nina's other assets, but the cabin and its rental income belong entirely to Carla.

If Nina had wanted Alex to inherit her interest in the property, she could have taken steps while she was alive to change the title. In many states, she could have unilaterally converted her interest from joint tenancy to tenancy in common or moved it into a trust for Alex's benefit. Carla would still own her share as before, but Nina's share could have been left to Alex under her will or trust.

Again, the principle is simple: joint tenancy and other forms of survivorship ownership are powerful, but they only work in your favor if you've chosen them intentionally and understand how they interact with the rest of your plan.

Executor

Once you have a sense of what your will should say, who inherits, how children are protected, and what happens to your property, the next question is a practical one: **who will actually carry all of this out?** That individual is your **executor**.

In simple terms, your executor is the person who steps into your shoes after you die. They gather your property, work out what you owned and what you owed, pay any remaining bills and taxes, and then pass what is left to the **beneficiaries** you've named in your will according to your wishes. To do that, they must follow your instructions and your state's **probate** rules. In many families, the executor also ends up helping coordinate things like **life insurance** payouts and **retirement account** benefits, even though those assets pass by **beneficiary designation** rather than through the will. It's often easier for everyone if one trusted person keeps an eye on the whole picture.

If your **estate plan** is built mainly around a will, your executor will likely need to open a probate case with the local court, or hire a lawyer to do it using estate funds. If you also have a **living trust** and most of your larger assets are already in that **trust**, there may be little or no probate for those assets. In that case, the heavier responsibilities fall on your **successor trustee**. Often, the same person fills both roles, which keeps things simple. Still, even when a **trust** handles the big items, someone must close remaining accounts, cancel subscriptions and cards, deal with points and rewards, clear out your home, and file your final **tax return**. That "someone" is usually the executor.

With that picture in mind, the choice becomes: who is the right person to trust with this job?

What Makes Someone a Good Executor?

A common misconception is that an **executor** needs to be a financial expert, a lawyer, or a tax professional. They don't. People with those skills can be hired, when and if needed, and the **estate** can pay for the help. What matters most is character and temperament.

A good executor is someone who is reasonably organized, honest, and willing to follow through. They should be comfortable keeping track of deadlines, dealing with paperwork, and asking questions when they don't understand something. They don't have to know everything; they just need to know when to pick up the phone and get advice.

It also helps enormously if your executor can communicate well with your **beneficiaries**. Settling an **estate** happens at an emotional time, and small misunderstandings can turn into big conflicts when people are grieving. Someone who can explain decisions calmly, listen to concerns, and keep people informed will make the process feel much easier and fairer for everyone.

Practical considerations matter too. An executor who lives near you will usually find the job easier than someone far away. There will be papers to sign, property to inspect, and sometimes in-person **court** appearances. Most states allow out-of-state executors, but **probate courts** often impose extra safeguards, such as requiring a **bond** (an insurance guarantee to protect the **beneficiaries**) before appointing them. If you have more than one suitable candidate, choosing someone close by often saves time and prevents hassles.

Who People Commonly Choose as Executor

Many married people choose their **spouse** as executor. A spouse is usually familiar with the family finances and is often the person who will receive much of the **estate**. When the relationship is stable and the surviving spouse is capable of handling details, this is a natural and practical choice.

But naming a spouse isn't required. If your spouse would be overwhelmed by paperwork, has health issues, or if there are complicated family dynamics that could make the job emotionally heavy, you might prefer to name someone else. In those situations, a trusted sibling, adult child, or a close friend may be a better fit.

For single or divorced people, the executor is often an adult child, sibling, or a long-time friend who knows them well. Many people worry they are "burdening" someone by naming them; but in practice, people are often honored to be chosen and happy to help, especially when they know professional help can be hired and paid from the estate.

Parents of adult children sometimes feel torn about whether to name one child or several. Naming one child can raise questions of fairness; naming all of them as **co-executors** can create practical problems, because co-executors usually have to sign documents together and agree on decisions. If your children naturally cooperate and communicate well, sharing the role can work fine. If they live far apart or have a history of tension, asking all of them to run the **estate** together may make things more difficult. Here, your knowledge of your own family is more important than any general rule.

In some situations, especially when an **estate** is large, contains unusual assets, involves ongoing **trusts** or businesses, or is likely to spark conflict, a **professional executor** can be a wise choice. This might be a bank's **trust department** or an individual professional **fiduciary** who makes a living acting as **executor**, **trustee**, or financial guardian. A professional brings experience, neutrality, and systems built for exactly this kind of work. They charge fees, often a percentage of the **estate** that passes through **probate** or an hourly rate, and many have minimum estate sizes they will accept. But in a complicated estate, a skilled neutral person can prevent mistakes and reduce stress for the family.

First Choices, Alternates, and Honest Conversations

As we said before, legally, the person creating the will (called the **testator**) "nominates" an executor. If a probate case is opened, the court then formally appoints that person and gives them official documents (often called **letters testamentary)** that prove their authority.

But if your executor cannot or does not want to serve, the court will move to whomever you've named as an **alternate**.

This is why it's important not only to choose a primary executor, but also to list at least one backup, and ideally two. Life changes. Someone you choose today may be ill, overwhelmed, or no longer a good fit many years from now. Naming alternates gives the court a clear path if your first choice cannot act and eliminates delay and expense.

Whatever choices you make, one step ties it all together: **talk to the people you are naming**. It is much better to ask, *"Would you be comfortable doing this for me one day?"* than to surprise someone with the responsibility after your death. A person who is hesitant can decline now when you still have time to adjust your plan. A person who is willing can ask where you keep important records, whether you have a list of accounts, and who your main advisers are. These early conversations can feel awkward at first, but they are often a relief on both sides. You get the comfort of knowing someone is willing and prepared; they get the chance to understand what you are asking and why you chose them.

Those conversations are an act of care, for you, for your **executor**, and for the people who, one day, will rely on both of you. With the right person in place, your **will** becomes more than a document; it becomes a plan that can actually work.

Guardians and Children's Inheritances

Once you've chosen an executor, the next question is more personal: *Who will take care of your children if you're not there to do it yourself?* And just as importantly, *who will manage any money left for them until they're ready to handle it?*

These decisions can feel heavy, which is why Chapters 6 and 7 explore them in depth. Still, it helps to have a clear picture of what you'll eventually need to write into your will, so this section gives you a simple, high-level road map before you dive deeper.

If you have minor children, you will need to do two things: name a **guardian** to care for them and put a structure in place to manage the money they inherit. Some parents use a custodial account; others prefer a trust that lasts until the child reaches an age at which they feel the child will be responsible. There isn't one "right" answer, just the system that best reflects the values and stability you want for your family.

Pets

Not everyone has children, but nearly everyone has someone, or *something*, that depends on them. For many people, that's a pet. Pets can't inherit property directly, but you can make a plan for their care.

Some people simply leave money to a trusted friend and ask that the friend look after the animal. This approach relies on trust rather than legal force. For example, Noah might leave $3,000 to his neighbor, Ava, with a note asking her to care for his greyhound, Max. Ava legally receives the money outright, but the intention is clear, and for many owners, that's enough.

Others prefer something more formal, such as a **pet trust**, which every state now allows. A pet trust works just like any other trust: you name the pet or pets, appoint someone to care for them, set aside a specific amount for their needs, and describe how you want them treated. You also name someone who can go to court if those instructions aren't followed. If money is left over after the pet passes away, you choose where it goes.

You can also arrange for a "forever sanctuary," a rescue or care organization that accepts pets and promises lifetime care. For example, Dina might leave funds to a bird rescue that agrees to care for her parrot, Mango, for as long as he lives. It's a thoughtful way to support both your pet and an organization you trust.

Disinheriting a Child

Disinheriting a child or close relative is one of the few moments in estate planning where clarity is absolutely essential. If you simply omit someone's name, the law may treat them as an **omitted heir**: someone who can claim a share of your estate because they were mistakenly left out. Courts often assume an omission was accidental unless you clearly say otherwise.

A clear sentence is enough to avoid misunderstandings. For example, a parent who has chosen not to provide for a child might write, *"I am intentionally making no provision for my son, Marcus."*

Compare that with the problems caused by silence: imagine a parent who wrote a will years before their youngest child, Lena, was born and never updated it. Even if the parent intended to divide everything among their older children, Lena would still be entitled under law to a full share.

Being straightforward is both kinder to the family and safer for your plan.

Make Your Will

At this point, you've spent time thinking through your assets, your beneficiaries, and the people you want to put in charge. Now comes the practical question many readers ask: *Do I really need a lawyer to write my will?*

The reassuring answer is that most people can certainly create a simple, valid will on their own. Wills follow a familiar structure, almost like recipes with standard ingredients, and the law intentionally keeps the requirements straightforward. As long as the essential information is included and the document is properly signed and witnessed, your will becomes a legally binding expression of your final wishes.

In addition, some states will provide an example or template for a valid will in that state. For example, Minnesota includes a template in its chapter of probate statutes.

For most people, the easiest path is to use a **DIY will-making tool**, which walks you through the questions you need to answer and inserts the correct legal language automatically. These tools take away the mystery and let you focus on the decisions that matter most.

But do-it-yourself doesn't fit every situation. If your family is blended, if you're intentionally leaving someone out, or if you own complex assets, such as a business, property abroad, or real estate shared with family, working with an attorney can be the safer choice. Lawyers are also invaluable when you expect conflict or when someone in your family might challenge your mental capacity later. The more unusual the situation, the more important it is to have professional support.

Even so, doing your homework makes the process faster and less expensive. Completing the Will Worksheet and reading the chapters that relate to your circumstances help you walk into a lawyer's office clear-headed and prepared. Clients who arrive organized generally end up with cleaner documents, fewer hours billed, and a plan that feels genuinely tailored to their lives.

Choosing a DIY Tool

If you decide to prepare a simple will on your own, you won't be starting from a blank page. There are now several reputable online services that guide you through the process step by step, asking you questions in plain language and then generating documents designed to follow your state's rules.

Some well-known examples include **Trust&Will.com**, which offers will packages that typically include a Last Will, an advance healthcare directive, and a financial power of attorney, all built through an online questionnaire and tailored by state law.

Platforms like **FreeWill** focus on making basic estate planning documents (such as wills and advance healthcare directives) widely accessible, often at low or no direct cost to the user. They clearly state that they are self-help tools, not law firms, and are designed for straightforward situations.

Services such as **LegalZoom** and **Rocket Lawyer** also offer online will packages and often bundle in powers of attorney and healthcare directives, sometimes with access to a network of licensed attorneys for an additional fee.

All of these tools work in more or less the same way: you answer guided questions about your family, your assets, and your preferences, the software builds a document that fits your state's requirements, and you then print and sign it with the proper witnesses. For someone with a relatively simple situation, no complicated business interests, no cross-border assets, and no expected family disputes, this can be an efficient and affordable way to put a basic plan in place.

That said, even the best software has limits. None of these services truly "replace" a lawyer in complex cases. If you're in a second marriage, if you want to treat children differently, if you own a closely held business or real estate in more than one country, or if you suspect a relative might challenge your will, a human attorney is usually a much better investment than trying to push a complex life through a standard online template.

A good rule of thumb is this: the more unusual your family or assets look compared to the "standard" nuclear family with a home and a few accounts, the more you should lean toward professional advice. And even if you do choose to work with a lawyer, using a worksheet or an online tool first, just to organize your thoughts, can make your time together far more productive.

After You Sign Your Will

Once you've signed your will in front of two witnesses, preferably with a **self-proving affidavit** attached, the final task is storing it safely.

Keep the original somewhere protected but accessible, such as a fire-resistant home safe or a cloud digital vault. Lawyers rarely store originals, and a photocopy may not be enough for probate in some states.

Just as important, make sure your executor knows where the will is kept. You don't need to show it to anyone now, and you certainly don't need to hand out copies, but the person responsible for settling your estate must be able to find it easily later. If you want to leave a personal letter explaining your choices or sharing guidance, keep it in the same place with instructions to open it only after your death.

What Happens If You Don't Make a Will?

Many people assume their property will "automatically go where it should." Unfortunately, the law doesn't work that way. If you die without a will, your assets pass according to **intestate succession**, a state-created framework that distributes property based strictly on family relationships.

Typically, your spouse receives the largest share, followed by your children. If you have neither, the estate passes to parents, siblings, and more distant relatives in a fixed order. What intestacy does *not* do is honor personal relationships: unmarried partners, close friends, charities, and anyone outside your bloodline or legal marriage receive nothing.

Real families are much more complicated than the state's one-size-fits-all rulebook. Frequently, a long-term partner of the deceased will inherit none of their home or savings simply because no will was ever made. Another high-profile example is the musician Prince: despite his wealth and his generosity during his lifetime, his lack of a will meant that charities he cared about received nothing.

These rules also matter deeply if you have minor children. Without a will naming a **guardian**, a judge will choose someone to raise them and someone else to manage their inheritance. Judges work hard to make good decisions, but they don't know your family dynamics, your values, or the promises you've made. Only a will gives them your voice.

And finally, without a will or trust, children receive their entire inheritance the moment they become legal adults, 18 or 21, depending on the state. For many parents, that's far too young. The only way to delay or structure a child's inheritance is to put those instructions in writing.

Preparing Your Will-Planning Worksheet

Once you've thought through guardians, caretakers, and the people you want to include in your plan, you'll be ready to start filling in the Will Worksheet. This worksheet doesn't ask you to list every asset you own; that's the job of your inventory. Instead, it focuses on the decisions that make a will work.

You'll write out basic information about your family and yourself, who should receive specific items or gifts, and then choose who receives everything else, what's known as the **residuary estate**. If you're leaving money to young children, you'll decide how long their trust should last and whether you want them to receive part of their inheritance earlier for milestones such as education, housing, or starting a business.

You'll also confirm your executor and alternate choices, as well as your nominations for guardians and trustees for any minor children. These choices repeat across your estate plan, so it's normal to see the same two or three names appear several times. Most of us have a small circle of trusted people, and that's exactly what an estate plan relies on.

When your thoughts are clear, download the Will Worksheet using the QR code or link provided below.

https://drive.google.com/file/d/13R19dOTGEn-zKKEaUilCfPGbZ9pRXQ_I/view?usp=sharing

Whenever you're ready, we can move on to the next section.

Note: Why a Worksheet and Not a Will Form?

You may wonder why this book offers a worksheet instead of a fill-in-the-blank will form. The reason is straightforward: a single form can't realistically account for the many differences in state law, family situations, and personal priorities without becoming confusing or misleading.

Rather than trying to turn estate planning into a mechanical exercise, this worksheet is designed to help you ***think through*** *how you want your will to work, who should inherit, in what order, and under what conditions, and who should carry out those wishes. This tool focuses on intent and structure, not legal drafting.*

Shared with an estate planning attorney, the worksheet can reduce the time spent gathering background information and allow the conversation to move more quickly toward drafting a will that accurately reflects your wishes and complies with your state's law.

Chapter | 3 | Assessment Test

1. Why does the chapter describe a will as "the first building block" of an estate plan?

- **a.** Because it automatically avoids probate
- **b.** Because it replaces the need for trusts and beneficiary designations
- **c.** Because it coordinates key decisions about property, executors, and guardians
- **d.** Because it controls all assets you own

2. Which of the following decisions must be addressed in every will?

- **a.** How estate taxes will be minimized
- **b.** Who will act as executor
- **c.** Which court will supervise probate
- **d.** How retirement accounts are invested

3. What is the main role of an executor?

- **a.** To rewrite the will if circumstances change
- **b.** To supervise beneficiaries' spending
- **c.** To manage trust assets during incapacity
- **d.** To gather assets, pay debts, and distribute property according to the will

4. Why is a self-proving affidavit commonly recommended when signing a will?

- **a.** It allows the will to bypass probate
- **b.** It replaces the need for witnesses
- **c.** It makes probate easier by avoiding the need to locate witnesses later
- **d.** It prevents beneficiaries from contesting the will

5. Which assets are generally NOT controlled by a will?

- **a.** Property passing through probate
- **b.** Assets titled solely in the deceased person's name
- **c.** Assets passing by beneficiary designation or survivorship
- **d.** Personal property listed in the residuary clause

6. What happens when property is owned with a right of survivorship?

- **a.** The deceased owner's share passes under the will
- **b.** The court decides how the property is divided
- **c.** The property is split equally among heirs
- **d.** The surviving owner automatically receives full ownership

7. In the chapter's examples, why can joint ownership unintentionally defeat a person's wishes?

- **a.** Because joint owners must agree on beneficiaries
- **b.** Because survivorship rules override what the will says
- **c.** Because joint ownership increases estate taxes
- **d.** Because probate courts favor surviving spouses

8. Which quality is emphasized as most important in choosing an executor?

- **a.** Professional legal or financial training
- **b.** Living in the same household as the testator
- **c.** Organization, honesty, and willingness to follow through
- **d.** Being the largest beneficiary under the will

9. Why is it important to clearly state an intention to disinherit a child?

- **a.** To avoid paying estate taxes
- **b.** To prevent the child from serving as executor
- **c.** To eliminate the need for probate
- **d.** To avoid the child being treated as an omitted heir

10. What is a common consequence of dying without a will?

- **a.** Assets pass according to state intestacy laws rather than personal wishes
- **b.** Assets are distributed equally among all friends and relatives
- **c.** Charities automatically receive a portion of the estate
- **d.** Minor children receive inheritance only through trusts

Answers

1. **C** – A will coordinates decisions about property distribution, executors, and guardians.
2. **B** – Every will must name an executor to carry out its instructions.
3. **D** – The executor gathers assets, pays debts and taxes, and distributes property under the will.
4. **C** – A self-proving affidavit simplifies probate by confirming proper execution in advance.
5. **C** – Assets passing by beneficiary designation or survivorship bypass the will.
6. **D** – With survivorship ownership, the surviving owner automatically receives full title.
7. **B** – Survivorship rules override the will, even when the result wasn't intended.
8. **C** – Reliability, organization, and follow-through matter more than technical expertise.
9. **D** – Clear language prevents a disinherited child from claiming an unintended share.
10. **A** – Without a will, state intestacy rules, not personal wishes, control distribution.

CHAPTER 4

LIVING TRUSTS

> ***"By failing to prepare, you are preparing to fail."***
>
> **– *Benjamin Franklin,***
> *American statesman, inventor, and Founding Father*

By now, you've seen what a will can do for you and where its limits are. A will is powerful, but it usually brings the court into the picture through **probate**, with its forms, deadlines, and public records.

A **living trust** works differently from a will. Instead of relying on a court process after death to transfer assets, you create the trust during your lifetime and transfer certain property into it. The trust document explains how those assets should be managed if you become incapacitated and how they should be distributed after your death.

When the trust is properly created and funded, the assets held in the trust can pass to beneficiaries with little or no court involvement.

Now the real question is: *Does this tool fit you*?

If you live in a state where probate is long, expensive, or both, a trust can save your family a lot of time and frustration. Even in states where probate is relatively short, some people strongly dislike the idea that their will, their debts, and the broad outline of their estate could end up in a public file at the courthouse. A trust, by contrast, is usually a private document. Your beneficiaries are entitled to information, but strangers are not.

So, when you think about trusts, try asking yourself two things: How much do I want my family to deal with the court after I die? And how much does privacy matter to me? Your honest answers will tell you whether this chapter deserves a careful read or just a skim.

What a Living Trust Actually Is

Despite the mystique that sometimes surrounds them, a **trust** is really nothing more than a "**legal container.**" You place certain assets inside it, you decide who holds the keys, and you write the rules for how everything inside should be managed and eventually handed out. One person manages what's inside, another benefits from it, and the trust document spells out exactly how the whole system should work.

In every trust, there are three roles:

- The **settlor** (or grantor), who creates the trust and puts property into this legal container,
- The **trustee**, who holds the keys and manages what's inside, and
- The **beneficiaries**, who are allowed to benefit from the contents.

The trust document is the written instructions. It explains which assets belong in the container, who is in charge, how that property may be used, and who receives it when everything is finished.

Trusts come in many forms. Some are created to last for generations and are **irrevocable**, meaning the person who created them cannot easily change the terms or pull the assets back out. Others, like the ones we're focusing on here, are **revocable**. A **revocable living trust** is a trust you create while you're alive, which you can change or cancel while you still have capacity. During your lifetime, it holds your property for your benefit. After your death, it becomes a road map for how that property should be handled and who should receive it.

"Living" and "Revocable"

The word "*living*" simply means you create the trust now, during your lifetime, instead of having it spring into existence through a will at your death. The word "*revocable*" means you keep the steering wheel firmly in your hands.

As long as you remain mentally capable, you can amend your trust, change beneficiaries, replace a trustee, add or remove assets, or revoke the trust entirely. You're not locking your assets into a box and throwing away the key. You're putting them into a labeled, organized container that can adapt as your life changes.

It's equally important to be clear about what a revocable living trust does **not** do. From a legal and tax perspective, you and your trust are treated as essentially the same person while you are alive. You still report the income on your own tax return. Your creditors can usually reach the assets. The trust, by itself, does not act like a shield against lawsuits or debts, nor is it a magic tax shelter.

Its real job is more *practical*: to make it easier to manage your assets if you become incapacitated, and to pass them on after your death without needing a full-blown probate proceeding.

The Three Roles – Often Played by One Person

As we said, the three characters in any trust are the settlor, trustee, and beneficiary. In most everyday living trusts, especially for individuals or couples, you often begin by playing **all three parts**.

Imagine Elena, who creates the "Elena Rivera Living Trust." She signs a trust document and transfers her home, her main investment account, and some savings into the trust.

In that moment:

- She's the settlor because she created the trust and moved her property into this legal container,
- She's also the trustee because she keeps the keys and remains in charge of managing those assets, and
- She's the current beneficiary because the trust terms say the assets are to be used for her benefit during her lifetime.

On a day-to-day level, very little changes. She still lives in her home, she can still sell it, refinance it, or move. She still decides how to invest her money. She can still spend her savings. The big difference is that, on paper, those assets are now titled in the name of her trust rather than in her own name.

The trust document then explains what happens later: What if Elena becomes incapacitated? What if she dies? Who takes over as trustee, and who receives the remaining property?

How a Living Trust Works Together With a Will

Many people assume that if they create a living trust, they no longer need a will. In reality, a trust-based plan still needs a will, just a different kind.

When you build your estate plan around a living trust, your will usually becomes a short document known as a **pour-over will**. Instead of containing all your detailed instructions, it acts like a safety net. It says that anything still in your individual name at your death should be "poured over" into your trust, to be handled under the trust's terms. The will is also the document where you nominate guardians for minor children.

So, think of the living trust as your main instruction manual and the pour-over will as the backup system that catches anything you forgot to place inside the legal container while you were alive.

What You Keep When You Use a Trust

People often worry that once they "put everything into a trust," they're giving something up. With a well-drafted revocable living trust, that is not true.

You will still be able to do all the things with your property that you could do before: live in it, sell it, borrow against it, change investments, even give assets away if you wish. The trust terms can and should make this clear. You also keep the power to change your mind. As long as you're mentally competent, you can adjust beneficiaries, change trustees, or revoke the trust entirely.

The real shift is not in control, but in organization. By placing assets inside this legal container now, you make things much easier for the person who will one day have to step in for you, whether because of incapacity or death.

Let's make it concrete with an example.

David and Priya are married and in their early sixties. They have one home, a rental condo, some savings, and a brokerage account. They create a joint revocable living trust and retitle the house, the condo, and their main investments into it. They stay on as trustees and use the assets as they always have: paying bills, reinvesting, and enjoying life.

Their trust states that while either of them is alive and capable, the assets are for their benefit. When one dies, the survivor continues as trustee and beneficiary. When both die, their niece, Sara, becomes successor trustee. At that point, Sara's job is to pay any final bills and taxes and then divide what's left between three named beneficiaries.

Because the major assets are already inside the trust's legal container, Sara does not need to run a full probate for those assets. With some professional help, a lawyer for guidance, and perhaps an accountant, she gathers statements, arranges appraisals, settles obligations, and follows the instructions in the trust. The work is real, but it is usually less formal and less public than running everything through a probate court.

When You No Longer Want to Be the One Managing Everything

Another advantage of a living trust is how it handles the possibility that you might not always have the capacity needed to manage your own finances.

In your trust, you name one or more successor trustees, people who will take over if you can no longer act on your own behalf from a mental or physical capacity. You also say when that handover can happen. Some people require a written letter from their doctor; others prefer a more flexible standard. The key point is that you decide in advance who can step in and how that decision is made.

If you become seriously ill or lose mental capacity, the successor trustee can begin paying your bills, managing your investments, and taking care of the trust property for your benefit, without a court having to appoint a conservator or guardian of the estate for you. The trust becomes part of your disability planning, not just your death planning.

Trust Administration: What Happens After You're Gone

It's important to be honest: a living trust does not mean that nothing has to be done after you die. There is a process called **trust administration**. Your successor trustee must still identify what the trust owns, pay your final bills and taxes, and then distribute or retitle assets according to your instructions.

Many successor trustees hire a lawyer for guidance, especially at the beginning. The trust usually pays for professional fees, appraisals, and any other necessary costs. Even so, trust administration is often simpler and faster than probate because it does not have the same rigid court deadlines, mandatory hearings, and public filings.

Compare that to a typical probate case, where an executor may have to file petitions, inventories, notices, and periodic reports, all according to a statutory schedule. The end result, beneficiaries receiving property, might look similar, but the path to get there can feel very different.

Creating a Living Trust

By the time you reach this section, you already have a solid idea of what a trust is and why so many people choose it as the backbone of their estate plan. Now the focus shifts from understanding *what* a trust does to deciding *how* yours should be built. Creating a living trust is really about designing the "legal container" that will hold your assets, choosing the people who will manage it, and deciding who ultimately benefits from what's inside.

Just as you did in the chapter on wills, you'll need to make several decisions, some simple, and some requiring a bit more reflection. The Trust Worksheet included in this chapter will help you capture your choices clearly, and the more you prepare before drafting anything, the easier the entire process becomes. It's completely normal to jump ahead to other chapters when needed, especially those on blended families, international assets, taxes, or naming non-citizens in key roles. A trust impacts many parts of your financial life, and each part deserves its moment of attention.

Clarifying the Purpose

Every trust begins with intention. Yes, the primary goal of a **revocable living trust** is to avoid probate, but most people have additional reasons for creating one: ensuring a smooth transfer of wealth to children, supporting a partner, helping a friend, protecting a vulnerable family member, or even planning responsibly for a pet. Being clear about your goals at the outset makes the rest of the planning process much easier.

Choosing the Trustee and Successor Trustee

Once you know why you're creating the trust, the next step is determining who will manage it. During your lifetime, that's almost always you. After all, this container is holding *your* property for *your* benefit, and nothing about transferring assets into the trust takes control away from you.

But you do need to name a **successor trustee**, someone who steps in when you no longer are able to manage your affairs. This person becomes responsible for paying bills, making financial decisions, handling taxes, and ultimately distributing the assets inside the trust to your beneficiaries. If you were to become ill or lose capacity before death, the successor trustee would temporarily manage the trust for you, while your **agent under a durable power of attorney** handles anything that remains outside the trust, such as retirement accounts or insurance policies.

Choosing a successor trustee is less about technical expertise and more about character. You want someone dependable, organized, communicative, and capable of staying calm when others are not. A good trustee doesn't need to be a financial expert; they only need the judgment to seek professional help when appropriate. They will represent you when you're no longer able to speak for yourself, so trust, real, personal trust, is essential.

Beneficiaries

After you have decided on your trustees, it's time to decide who your beneficiaries are. During your lifetime, you are the primary beneficiary, which is why you continue to use and control everything in the trust exactly as before. The trust simply holds the container; you decide what happens inside it.

When you die, the container opens to others. If you're married, your spouse often steps in as beneficiary. If you have children, they typically become the final recipients. If you're single, your list might include parents, siblings, friends, or charities. The structure can be simple, with assets paid out immediately, or more layered, held in trust for a child until they reach a certain age or for a partner during their lifetime.

How Many Trusts?

Another decision involves the number of trusts you'll need. Single people and unmarried partners often create separate trusts because each person owns property individually. In community property states, married couples frequently create one joint trust, while blended families or couples with significant separate property sometimes choose additional, separate trusts to keep certain assets distinct.

The goal isn't to make things more complicated than necessary. It's to create a structure that reflects reality and protects everyone's interests fairly.

Here are five variations showing how couples with 20-year relationships might approach the decision:

Example 1 – One Shared Trust for Community Property
Alan and Mirela, married for two decades and with two children together, own everything as community property. A single joint trust fits their needs perfectly.

Example 2 – Two Trusts for Separate Property
Married later in life, Cameron and Louise each brought property they want to keep separate. Their premarital agreement requires it, so each establishes their own trust.

Example 3 — One Joint Trust + One Separate Property Trust
Marla and Benson jointly own their home and investments, but Marla recently inherited property she wants to keep separate. They create one joint trust and one individual trust for her inheritance.

Example 4 — One Trust with Separate Paths for Each Spouse's Children
Grace and Robert have adult children from previous marriages. They create a joint trust, but when the first spouse dies, that spouse's share stays in trust for the survivor, and eventually flows back to their own children, not to their partner's children.

Example 5 — Two Trusts for a Long-Term Unmarried Couple
Sophia, divorced with three daughters, and her partner, Paul, each create a trust. They provide lifetime benefits for each other, then leave whatever remains to her daughters and to Paul's chosen charity.

Trustees

Once you've decided what the trust is for and who benefits from it, choosing the people who hold the keys, the trustees, becomes the next natural step.

During your lifetime, you typically play both roles: **settlor** (who creates the trust) and **trustee** (who manages it). You retain the ability to buy, sell, invest, or give away assets exactly as before. If managing things becomes difficult, your successor trustee can step in temporarily, still using trust assets for your benefit.

After your death, the successor trustee becomes fully responsible for settling the trust. This usually involves appraisals, taxes, paying final bills, and distributing the remaining property. While some costs are unavoidable, such as legal advice, tax preparation, and property sales, trust administration almost always takes less time and money than probate.

Here are a few examples of how trustees step into their roles:

Example 1 — A Smooth Family Transition
Daniel and Riley create a trust and name Riley's brother, Marcus, as successor trustee. When they eventually pass away, Marcus pays their final bills, settles the estate, and distributes everything to their children without involving the court.

Example 2 — Joint Trustees After a Parent's Death
Anita funded her trust with her home and a brokerage account. After she dies, her daughters, Rachel and Tessa, act as co-trustees. They work with an attorney, sell the house, pay expenses, and divide the remaining assets.

Example 3 — Equal Shares for Adult Children
Omar names his daughter, Isabel, as successor trustee. After Omar's death, she pays expenses, then divides the trust assets equally among herself and her brothers. They decide to keep the family home as a rental, each owning a one-third interest.

As you can see from these examples, a successor trustee isn't a magician; they're simply the individual who steps in with enough structure and authority to carry out the wishes you laid out in your trust. To make that work in real life, the law gives trustees specific responsibilities, and it helps to understand these expectations and responsibilities.

Over your lifetime, most living trusts operate in two stages. First, while you're alive and able, you manage the trust assets for your own benefit. Later, after you die or become incapacitated, someone else (your successor trustee) steps in to manage and distribute those assets for the people you've named. The rules below mainly apply to that later stage, but it helps to understand them from the start.

What Trustees Are Expected to Do

A **trustee** is held to a higher standard than an ordinary helper. Legally, they have what's called a *fiduciary duty* to the beneficiaries. In plain terms, that means they must put the interests of those beneficiaries ahead of their own whenever they act for the trust.

That high standard has a few practical consequences.

First, a trustee must manage trust assets **carefully and honestly**. They should keep careful and accurate records, pay attention to important deadlines, *and safeguard trust property*. If there is more than one beneficiary, the trustee must also be **impartial**, they can't play favorites unless the trust itself authorizes different treatment for different people.

Second, the trustee must always act **for the benefit of the beneficiaries**, not themselves. That means they can't use trust assets as a personal checking account, make loans to themselves from trust funds, or mix trust money with their own accounts. If they do, and the beneficiaries are harmed, they can be held personally responsible.

Third, trustees are allowed, and often expected, to **get help**. A careful trustee might hire a *lawyer* to explain the trust document, an *accountant* to handle tax returns, or a *financial advisor* to manage investments. The reasonable cost of this help is usually paid by the trust itself, not out of the trustee's own pocket. The law doesn't require brilliance; it requires prudence and good judgment.

In many situations, the trustee will also be responsible for **filing tax returns for the trust itself**, particularly after your death. A revocable living trust normally uses your own Social Security number and doesn't file a separate return while you're alive. But if the trust later becomes irrevocable, for example, at the death of the settlor in the case of a single settlor trust, new tax reporting rules may apply. In those cases, a tax professional can be invaluable.

Finally, in most states, trustees have a duty to **keep beneficiaries informed**. That often includes providing periodic statements or accountings that show what the trust owns, how it has been invested, and what has been spent. When you are both settlor and trustee during your own lifetime, you don't have to report to yourself, but it's still wise to keep organized records. Whoever comes after you will be very grateful you did.

All of this can sound daunting on paper, but in practice, many family trustees handle their duties successfully with a mix of common sense and professional support.

Beneficiaries

Once the stage is set and you've named your trustee and successor trustee, the focus naturally shifts to **beneficiaries**, the people or organizations who will benefit from the container you've built.

During your lifetime, you're the main beneficiary. The trust exists so that your assets can be used for your needs, such as housing, food, medical care, travel, charitable contributions, and anything else your life requires. If you're married or have a partner, you might structure your trust so that both of you are beneficiaries while both of you are alive.

Your trust then answers the question: *What happens next?*

Often, the answer is straightforward: when you die, your spouse, partner, or children inherit what remains. In other cases, the plan may be more complex, perhaps because there are young children, a loved one who needs care, or a desire to support a charity or a close friend alongside family members.

Here are a few examples with different family situations to show how these choices might play out.

Example 1 — Young Children and a Delayed Inheritance

Liam and Nora have two daughters in elementary school. They decide a living trust is right for them and transfer their home, a savings account, and an investment portfolio into it. During their lifetimes, they are both trustees and beneficiaries, using the assets to support their family as they always have.

Their trust says that when both parents have died, the assets will be divided into equal shares for each daughter. If a daughter is at least 30 at that time, she receives her share outright. If she is younger, her share stays in trust for her, with Nora's sister, Emma, acting as successor trustee. Emma will use the funds for the girls' education, health, and reasonable support until each reaches age 30, then distributes what's left.

Here, the trust balances two goals: giving the children full control when they are old enough to know how to manage it and making sure the money is still there to support them while they are younger

Example 2 — Providing for a Parent, Then a Charity

Marcus is single and doesn't have children, but he has a close relationship with his mother, Clara, who lives on a modest pension. He creates a living trust, moves his condo and investments into it, and names his long-time friend, Zoe, as successor trustee.

Marcus's trust says that if he dies before Clara, all of the trust assets should be held for Clara's benefit during her lifetime. Zoe, as trustee, can use the funds to supplement Clara's income: paying medical costs, improving her housing, or simply giving her more comfort and security. When Clara passes away, or if she doesn't survive Marcus, the trust directs Zoe to distribute anything remaining to a nonprofit organization that supports cancer research.

In this way, Marcus uses one container to take care of a parent first and a cause he cares about second, without leaving Clara to navigate a complicated estate herself.

Example 3 – Equal Shares for Adult Children

Elena is divorced and has three adult children. She owns a small house, a checking account, and a mutual fund portfolio. Wanting to keep things simple but avoid probate, she creates a living trust and names her oldest son, Daniel, as successor trustee.

Her instructions are straightforward: when she dies, Daniel should pay any remaining bills and taxes, then divide what's left into three equal shares. The children can choose whether to sell the house and split the proceeds or keep it together as a rental, each owning one-third as tenants in common.

This structure doesn't try to control her children's choices in detail; it simply gives them a clean, organized starting point.

Funding the Trust

Once the living trust is drafted and signed, there's one last step that makes all the difference: you must actually **move your assets into it**. Lawyers call this *funding the trust*, and despite sounding technical, it's simply the act of changing the legal owner of certain assets from *you* to *you-as-trustee*.

This is very different from creating a will. A will sits quietly in a drawer until the day it's needed. Nothing "moves" into it during your lifetime. A trust, however, is only useful if you place assets inside the "container" while you're alive. If you don't, the trust remains empty, and an empty trust is worse than useless, because it creates the illusion of planning without accomplishing anything.

It's surprisingly common. People sign a beautifully drafted trust, put it in a folder, and never take the final step. Then, years later, their families discover that every major asset is still titled in the person's individual name. As a result, the trust cannot control those assets, and probate becomes unavoidable.

> ***Example:*** *When Beatrice created her living trust, she intended to spare her three adult children the delays and costs of probate. Unfortunately, she never transferred her home, her investment account, or her checking and savings accounts into the trust. She passed away assuming everything was handled. Her sister, Elaine, named as successor trustee, brought the documents to an attorney, only to learn that nothing had been funded. Before the trust could distribute anything, the entire estate had to go through probate, defeating Beatrice's main purpose for creating the trust in the first place.*

What Belongs Inside a Living Trust?

Funding a trust requires some paperwork, but once you understand what actually needs to be moved, the task becomes manageable. Not everything you own belongs in the container, only certain kinds of assets.

The general rule is simple:

Assets that would otherwise go through probate are often good candidates to place in your trust. Assets that already have a built-in way to transfer automatically, such as beneficiary-designated accounts or jointly owned property with right of survivorship, often pass outside probate and may not need to be retitled into the trust.

However, "often" doesn't mean "always." Some people intentionally retitle assets into a trust or name the trust as a beneficiary to achieve specific planning goals (for example, to manage inheritances for minors, provide continuing management, coordinate distributions, or handle blended-family planning).

So, you *do not* transfer:

- Retirement accounts,
- Life insurance policies,
- Accounts with "payable-on-death" or "transfer-on-death" designations,
- Property held with a right of survivorship, or
- Your everyday checking account (unless it holds a large balance).

Those assets already travel on their own "track," guided by beneficiary forms or survivorship rights, not by your trust.

Everything else is fair game.

That usually means:

- Your home and any rental properties,
- Non-retirement investment accounts,
- Valuable bank accounts,
- CDs without beneficiary designations,
- Partnership interests,
- Stocks or bonds held in your own name, and
- Any significant asset that would otherwise require probate.

How to Transfer Property into the Trust

The mechanics depend on the type of asset. Think of it as retitling something: the asset doesn't change, just the legal name on the ownership line.

For financial accounts, brokerage accounts, savings accounts, or large bank accounts, you simply inform the institution that you now want the account titled in the name of your trust. They'll provide forms asking for the trust's name, its date, and the trustees' names. Even though your trust doesn't file its own tax return, the institution still needs a Social Security number for reporting purposes, usually one of the trustee's.

Real estate requires a "recorded deed." If you own a home, a second property, or land, the ownership must be formally deeded from you as an individual to you "as trustee" of your living trust. If an attorney prepared your trust, their office may handle the deed for you. If not, the recorder's office in your county can guide you on the correct format.

> ***Example:*** *After signing their Gonzalez Family Trust, Eduardo and Marisol transferred their home by recording a new deed listing them as "Eduardo Gonzalez and Marisol Gonzalez, Trustees of the Gonzalez Family Trust dated March 4, 2026." Next, they contacted their brokerage firm, requested the trust-ownership form, and retitled their investment account. Finally, they updated their large savings account at the credit union. They left their day-to-day checking account alone because it rarely held more than a few thousand dollars, and it wouldn't trigger probate anyway.*

The important thing to remember is that *you can't fund a trust before it exists.* Institutions won't move assets into an unsigned or un-notarized document. A helpful strategy is to gather all the forms you'll need ahead of time, sign your trust, and finish the transfer paperwork while the project is still fresh in your mind.

Pour-Over Will

Even with a living trust, a **will** remains necessary, just a different kind of will. This version is called a **pour-over will**, which works hand-in-hand with your trust. It acts as a safety net for any assets that, for one reason or another, didn't make their way into the trust during your lifetime.

Think again of your trust as a cup holding your major assets. The pour-over will is the saucer underneath. If any assets spill into the saucer, because you forgot to transfer them, acquired something late in life, or simply overlooked an account, the will directs the executor to "pour" those assets into the trust after your death.

The trust then handles the distribution using the instructions you already wrote.

But don't rely on the saucer. A pour-over will only works efficiently if the value of the assets left outside the trust are small enough to qualify for your state's small-estate transfer rules. If they exceed that amount, those assets must go through probate before they can be poured into the trust. If this happens, the whole point of using a trust, to avoid probate, has been lost.

Consider these two scenarios:

Parker transferred his house and investment accounts into his trust but overlooked a small savings account. After his death, his successor trustee used a simple small-estate affidavit to claim the account and add it to the trust. No probate was required.

Now compare that to Beatrice's situation, the empty trust described earlier. Almost all of her assets were left outside the trust, and their combined value far exceeded the small-estate limit. Her successor had no choice but to open a full probate case, wait through the court deadlines, and pay lawyers and filing fees before the assets could be transferred.

Guardian Nominations Still Require a Will

A living trust can't name guardians for minor children. Only a will can do that. If you're a parent, your pour-over will includes your guardian nominations, ensuring that the court knows exactly who you want to care for your children if the unthinkable happens.

Executors Still Have a Role

Finally, your pour-over will must name an **executor**, even if most of your assets are handled through the trust. The executor deals with tasks that relate to *you personally*, not to the trust, for example: filing your final income tax return, paying any last medical bills, canceling contracts, and handling personal logistics.

Often, people name the same person as both trustee and executor for simplicity, but this is not required. The roles can be divided if that makes more sense for your situation.

Should You Create a Living Trust Yourself?

After outlining your decisions, the next question is whether you want to draft the trust on your own or hire a lawyer. The basic steps never change: you need to sign a trust agreement, then transfer the appropriate assets into it. And over time, whenever you acquire new property, whether it's a house, a bank account, or a brokerage portfolio, you'll need to make sure ownership is placed in the trust so the container remains full.

On paper, the steps sound simple. But, like buying a home or filing a tax return, the mechanics can get tricky once you're in the middle of them.

Some people prefer to draft their own trust using reputable software or guided online platforms. For individuals with straightforward lives, one home, a couple of bank accounts, and uncomplicated beneficiaries, DIY tools can work well. They walk you through the process, ask the right questions, and generate documents that follow your state's rules.

But online tools have limits. And life, as you know, doesn't always fit neatly into predefined boxes.

If you are wealthy, if your family includes children from past relationships, if you're married to a non-U.S. citizen, if you own a small business or an interest in one, if your assets include privately held stock, partnerships, or other complex property, or if you're caring for a child with lifelong needs, a lawyer can help ensure your trust holds up in real life, not just on paper.

A good estate planning lawyer helps you think through questions that don't always show up in worksheets: How should gifts to a guardian be structured? When should a child's trust end? What happens if a beneficiary struggles with addiction or unstable finances? How do you plan for parents and children at the same time? How do you protect a disabled child without jeopardizing public benefits?

Hiring a lawyer also means having someone manage the process. They keep you moving forward, help you avoid steps you may have overlooked, and make sure your trust aligns with the rest of your estate plan, including powers of attorney, health directives, and your pour-over will.

Most attorneys charge a flat fee for this work. The cost varies by region, but many trusts take around 10 hours of lawyer time from start to finish. Someone billing $300 per hour might charge roughly $3,000; someone billing $400, closer to $4,000. Higher fees often reflect complex tax planning intended for high-net-worth clients. Lower fees can sometimes indicate minimal attorney involvement.

If professional guidance is needed, or if your situation simply feels too important to risk a drafting mistake, the investment is usually well worth it.

Trust Mills

At some point, you may come across a flyer or postcard advertising a "Living Trust for $499!" or inviting you to a *free seminar* promising to reveal probate secrets the legal system doesn't want you to know.

Exercise caution.

While some seminars are genuinely educational, many are run by companies known as **trust mills**, businesses that sell low-cost, one-size-fits-all trusts with little or no attorney oversight. Their materials often exaggerate the dangers of probate and gloss over the responsibilities involved in trust administration.

Worse yet, some of these operations gather your financial information and pass it on to insurance salespeople who may pressure you into buying products, such as annuities, that aren't appropriate for you, especially if you're a senior.

If a trust is dramatically cheaper than the typical rate in your area, ask hard questions. Does an attorney review the documents? Will your data be shared with third parties? Is funding assistance included? Are powers of attorney and a will part of the package?

Estate planning isn't a place for shortcuts. If something sounds too good to be true, it probably is.

Preparing a Trust-Planning Worksheet

The purpose of the Trust-Planning Worksheet is to help you organize the key decisions that must be made before a trust can be drafted. It's not a legal form and it doesn't ask you to write trust language. Instead, it gives structure to your thinking, so those decisions are clear, complete, and consistent.

The worksheet walks you through a few core areas: the basic structure of the trust, who will serve as trustee and successor trustees, how the trustee should be compensated, which assets you intend to place in the trust, and who should benefit from each of those assets. You're also asked to think about alternate beneficiaries and about when the trust should distribute its property and close.

As you work through the worksheet, you may notice that the same names appear more than once. That's normal. Most estate plans rely on a small group of trusted people, and this worksheet simply makes those relationships visible.

Once this worksheet is complete, drafting the trust, whether on your own or with professional help, becomes far more efficient because the essential decisions have already been made.

https://drive.google.com/file/d/1M9G4Acs77dXQ5OVgZSRkrRKaeaUUY-0Ry/view?usp=sharing

Chapter | 4 | Assessment Test

1. **What is the primary reason many people choose a living trust instead of relying only on a will?**

   a. To reduce income taxes during life
   b. To avoid probate and keep estate matters private
   c. To eliminate the need for beneficiaries
   d. To protect assets from creditors

2. **Which description best explains what a revocable living trust is?**

   a. A trust that cannot be changed once signed
   b. A trust created only after death through a will
   c. A trust that acts as a legal container you can change or cancel during life
   d. A trust that transfers ownership immediately to beneficiaries

3. **In most living trusts, who often serves simultaneously as settlor, trustee, and beneficiary during life?**

   a. The estate planning attorney
   b. The person creating the trust
   c. The successor trustee
   d. The primary beneficiary named after death

4. **What does a revocable living trust generally NOT do while the settlor is alive?**

   a. Allow the settlor to manage and use the assets
   b. Help with incapacity planning
   c. Shield trust assets from the settlor's creditors
   d. Avoid probate after death

5. **How does a living trust help if the settlor becomes incapacitated?**

   a. It automatically appoints a court guardian
   b. It allows a successor trustee to step in without court involvement
   c. It transfers assets immediately to beneficiaries
   d. It replaces the need for a healthcare directive

6. **Why is funding the trust considered a critical step?**

a. Because unfunded trusts are automatically invalid
b. Because assets not transferred into the trust remain subject to probate
c. Because funding determines tax rates
d. Because beneficiary designations are created during funding

7. **Which of the following assets is generally NOT transferred into a living trust?**

a. A non-retirement brokerage account
b. A rental property
c. A checking account with a large balance
d. A retirement account with a named beneficiary

8. **What is the main function of a pour-over will in a trust-based estate plan?**

a. To eliminate the need for an executor
b. To name beneficiaries for retirement accounts
c. To move overlooked assets into the trust at death
d. To replace the trust document

9. **Which role does a successor trustee typically play after the settlor's death?**

a. They rewrite the trust based on family needs
b. They supervise the probate court
c. They manage, settle, and distribute trust assets
d. They serve only as a symbolic representative

10. **When is professional legal help most strongly recommended for creating a living trust?**

a. When assets consist of only a home and a checking account
b. When probate is simple in the state
c. When family and assets are complex or unusual
d. When the trust will hold only cash

Answers

1. **B** – Living trusts are commonly used to avoid probate and maintain privacy.
2. **C** – A revocable living trust is a flexible legal container that can be changed or revoked during life.
3. **B** – Most people initially act as settlor, trustee, and beneficiary of their own trust.
4. **C** – Revocable living trusts do not shield assets from the settlor's creditors during life.
5. **B** – A successor trustee can manage trust assets during incapacity without court involvement.
6. **B** – Assets not transferred into the trust remain outside it and may require probate.
7. **D** – Retirement accounts usually pass by beneficiary designation and are not placed in the trust.
8. **C** – A pour-over will acts as a safety net for assets left outside the trust.
9. **C** – After death, the successor trustee handles administration and distribution.
10. **C** – Complex families, assets, or situations often require professional guidance.

CHAPTER 5

How to Pass Property Without a Will or a Trust

> ***Simplicity is the ultimate sophistication.***
>
> **— *Leonardo da Vinci,***
> *Italian polymath of the Renaissance*

Until now, we've focused on the big tools of estate planning: **wills**, **trusts**, and how property ownership shapes what happens when someone dies. Those tools create the structure of your plan; they tell the law who should inherit, who's in charge, and how young or vulnerable beneficiaries should be protected.

But there is an entire set of *lighter*, faster, and surprisingly powerful tools that work on a completely different principle. Instead of building a long-term management plan (like a will or trust), these tools simply let property **jump over probate** and land directly in the hands of the person you choose.

Just a form, a signature, and a beneficiary. No court. No delay. No drama.

For some people, especially those with uncomplicated lives, few assets, or only adult beneficiaries, these tools can do all the heavy lifting. For others, they become the finishing touches on a larger estate plan, filling small gaps or adding privacy where you want it. Either way, they're worth understanding.

Later, in Chapter 10, we'll look at retirement accounts, which transfer by beneficiary designation too. But for now, let's look at the tools you can use on ordinary bank accounts, investments, and similar assets.

Payable-on-Death (POD) and Transfer-on-Death (TOD) Designations

A **POD** or **TOD** designation is one of the simplest ways to allow an account to pass directly to someone else after your death. Banks, credit unions, and most brokerage firms offer beneficiary forms for their accounts. Once completed, the designation creates an automatic transfer process that takes effect after the institution receives proof of death and the beneficiary completes the required steps.

During your lifetime, nothing changes. You're still the only owner. The beneficiary can't access your money, can't view your balances, and can't interfere in any way. The designation simply waits in the background.

Imagine it as a sealed envelope sitting in a drawer, invisible to everyone until the day it matters.

How POD/TOD Accounts Work

When you open a POD or TOD account or add a beneficiary to an existing one, the financial institution records your beneficiary in its internal system. That's it.

After you die, the beneficiary shows:

- Their ID, and
- Your death certificate

and the account becomes theirs, completely outside probate.

Example: *Carlos has a savings account holding $42,000. He wants that money to go to his niece, Talia, who has always helped him with errands and doctor visits. Carlos fills out the POD form at his bank, naming Talia as beneficiary upon his death. She has no control over the account while Carlos is alive. When he dies, the bank transfers the account to her directly. His executor doesn't have to touch it, and the account never enters probate.*

Brokerage accounts work the same way, though the form is usually called a **TOD (transfer-on-death) registration**. Most states permit TOD transfers for securities, but some brokerage firms still choose not to offer them. If yours doesn't, you may be able to transfer the account to a firm that does, but don't assume it's automatic or hassle-free.

Note: *Moving a brokerage account can involve paperwork, processing time, possible fees, and temporary limits on trading while the transfer is under way. In some situations, the best approach is simply to weigh the convenience of TOD registration against the practical and tax or administrative considerations of switching firms.*

Example: *Miriam keeps her investments at a broker that doesn't support TOD designations, but she wants her younger brother to inherit that account* *cleanly. She transfers her portfolio to a different brokerage that allows TODs, fills out the form, and the account is now set to bypass probate entirely.*

TOD designations also work for U.S. savings bonds and Treasury securities if you hold them electronically at **TreasuryDirect**. For anyone still holding paper bonds, the Treasury will convert them into digital form before allowing you to add or change beneficiaries.

POD and TOD designations can be helpful for many reasons, but two stand out.

First, **privacy**. A will becomes a public document once filed with the court. Trusts must be disclosed to the beneficiaries. But POD and TOD designations remain entirely private. Only the beneficiary ever knows they exist.

> ***Example:*** *Adrian and Leilani are both widowed and remarried later in life. Adrian worries that his adult children, whom he loves but who can be contentious, may challenge his estate plan or try to influence Leilani when he dies. Because nearly all of their wealth sits in joint investment accounts, they decide to name Leilani's grandchildren as the TOD beneficiaries of those accounts. The children never see the beneficiary forms, and when the surviving spouse dies, the accounts pass to the grandchildren.*

Second, POD and TOD designations are extremely useful for **giving a specific asset to a specific person**, even when the rest of your estate goes elsewhere.

> ***Example:*** *Aiden inherited a $95,000 brokerage account from his father years ago. He wants his son from his first marriage, Jonah, to receive that particular account, even though all his other assets will go to his current partner through a trust. Aiden names Jonah as the TOD beneficiary on that single account, ensuring Jonah receives it directly and without probate.*

Sometimes, a POD designation recognizes the person who did the heavy lifting.

> ***Example:*** *Harriet's daughter, Lynn, lives close by and handles most of the caregiving as Harriet ages. Her other three children live out of state. Harriet keeps her will simple and leaves her estate equally to all four children, but she names Lynn as the sole POD beneficiary on one investment account, her way of acknowledging Lynn's day-to-day support.*

Because beneficiary designations are private, the other children may never even know.

A Note on FDIC Insurance

Adding POD beneficiaries can increase FDIC coverage, but only if the account is properly titled and the beneficiaries qualify under FDIC rules. In general, FDIC insurance is up to **$250,000 per depositor, per insured bank, per ownership category**. POD accounts are typically treated as a type of revocable trust account for FDIC purposes, which may provide additional coverage based on the number of qualifying beneficiaries, but the coverage is **not unlimited** and depends on the account's structure. If you're relying on POD designations to protect balances above standard limits, confirm coverage with the bank and consider professional guidance.

> ***Example:*** *Marcus keeps $520,000 in a savings account. He names his two adult sons as POD beneficiaries. Now $500,000 of that account is FDIC-insured. Without beneficiaries, only $250,000 would have been protected.*

This doesn't matter for everyone, but for people holding large cash reserves, it's a rare instance where estate planning improves financial safety today.

When a Beneficiary Designation Might Be All You Need

For people with simple lives, no minors, and no need for long-term financial management, relying almost entirely on POD and TOD designations can be enough.

> ***Example:*** *Julia's estate consists of one investment account and two bank accounts. Her children are grown, financially stable, and responsible. She names both children as equal beneficiaries on all her accounts. When she dies, everything transfers directly to them automatically. Julia's executor only has to handle her final bills and personal items. No probate, no trust, and no court involvement at all.*

For Julia, it isn't just good planning, it's the whole plan.

When POD and TOD Accounts Are Not Sufficient

As we said, designating beneficiaries on an account works beautifully when the situation is straightforward: one asset, one adult beneficiary, and no strings attached. The moment life becomes even slightly more complex, these forms begin to show their cracks.

The **first** limitation appears when you try to split things evenly among children. A POD or TOD designation applies to a single account, and you won't know its balance at your death. If one child receives the account and the others receive something else, keeping everything "fair" becomes more art than math. And if your children are young, you still need a guardian and a plan for managing their money, which are needs that a beneficiary form can't address. For that, you need a will, and often a trust.

A **second** limitation is that a beneficiary form can't supervise money. If someone you care about has special needs, struggles with spending, or simply needs a guardrail, only a trust lets you structure how the money can be used, and who should oversee it. A POD/TOD designation gives full ownership to the beneficiary immediately, with no strings attached.

A **third** limitation arises when you want to shape what happens *after* your beneficiary's own lifetime. Once they inherit, it becomes their property, and they can leave it to whomever they choose, even someone you would never have selected. If you want a second spouse to use funds during their life, but ultimately leave the remainder to your children from a prior marriage, you can't do that with a simple designation. A trust is the only instrument with the flexibility to say, "First to you, then to them."

More than anything, the problem with beneficiary forms is that they can't do "what-if" planning. Real life is full of what-ifs. Wills and trusts anticipate them; simple processes like the POD and TOD do not.

Let's look at some common cases here.

If Beneficiaries Don't Outlive You

A common complication arises when you leave an account to several individuals and one of them dies. To know what will happen, you must read the fine print on the form. If you see **per stirpes**, the deceased beneficiary's children inherit their parent's share. If you see **per capita**, all surviving beneficiaries inherit equal shares. This leads to vastly different outcomes.

And if *all* of your named beneficiaries die before you, the account falls back into your estate and ends up in probate, the very process you were trying to avoid.

> ***Example:*** *Herman named his daughter Lily as the POD beneficiary of a $900,000 investment account. Lily died unexpectedly. Herman never updated the designation. When he later passed, the bank had no beneficiary on file, and the account was forced into probate. Only after a lengthy proceeding was the money finally given to Lily's two children.*

When You Want Unequal Gifts

Another limitation is the inability, in many institutions, to assign different percentages to beneficiaries. Some banks insist on equal shares. Others don't permit multiple beneficiaries at all. If you want to leave more to one child and less to another, or add layers of protection, you may need a will or trust.

> ***Example:*** *Caroline and Thomas have three adult children with very different circumstances. One is financially thriving, one is barely scraping by, and one is raising a large family while battling a serious illness. They initially hoped to keep things simple by using a TOD registration for their brokerage account, but the firm offered only equal shares. Their attorney steered them instead toward a living trust, which let them assign specific percentages and build a safety net for the grandchildren should their ill daughter die first.*

When the Beneficiary Is a Minor

POD and TOD designations work poorly when the person inheriting is a minor. A bank isn't permitted to distribute funds directly to a child, so the court must appoint a property guardian. That process freezes the money until the child becomes an adult, and a guardianship can be expensive and restrictive.

A better method is to name an adult custodian under your state's Uniform Transfers to Minors Act, which gives flexibility and avoids court intervention.

Example: *Nate and Olivia want to leave an investment account to their niece, Maya, who is six. On the beneficiary form they write:* ***"Angela Rivera, as custodian for Maya Rivera under the [STATE] UTMA, until age 21."***

If Nate and Olivia die while Maya is young, Angela can manage the funds freely for Maya's benefit, without court supervision, and Maya receives the money outright at age 21.

When Your Estate Still Needs Cash

Naming a beneficiary doesn't automatically protect an account from creditors or taxes. If you die owing medical bills, legal fees, or final income taxes, those obligations may have to be paid before the estate can be fully settled. In many cases, POD or TOD accounts pass directly to the beneficiary and are not used to pay debts. But if the probate estate doesn't have enough cash to cover valid debts, expenses, or taxes, state law may allow the estate (or creditors or a taxing authority) to seek payment from non-probate transfers, including, in some situations, funds that went to POD/TOD beneficiaries. How (and whether) that happens varies widely by state, and it can create real family tension if one beneficiary is asked to "give back" money so the estate can pay its bills. If there's a realistic risk your probate estate could be illiquid, consider planning options that leave sufficient liquid assets available for expenses, or avoid POD/TOD designations on accounts that the estate may need to use.

Most families won't face federal estate tax, but if they do, POD/TOD accounts are generally still included in the taxable estate. Even when an account passes outside probate, beneficiaries may need to contribute toward an estate tax bill or other required costs, depending on the overall plan and applicable law.

When Marital Rights Step In

Spouses often have legal rights to a portion of your assets, whether in community property states or in states with elective-share laws. For certain assets, especially many employer retirement plans, a spouse may be the default beneficiary, and naming someone else may require the spouse's written, witnessed consent. For other accounts, a financial institution may still allow you to name a non-spouse beneficiary, but your spouse could later assert marital rights to some or all of the asset (for example, if the funds are treated as marital or community property). A simple, written consent, obtained in the right situations, can prevent delays, disputes, and years of conflict.

In community-property states, half the money earned during the marriage legally belongs to each spouse, even if the account is titled in one name. You can't give away what you don't own. You may need a prenuptial/postnuptial agreement or your spouse's notarized consent.

In non-community-property states, the rules differ, but spouses often have a right to a portion of the deceased spouse's estate. POD and TOD assets may or may not be included in that share, depending on state law. When in doubt, it's safer to obtain spousal consent.

> ***Example:*** *Dina, who lives in California, keeps a savings account under her name only. She wants the funds in the account to go to her niece, Mia, who is a school counselor. Because the account contains marital earnings, Dina must obtain her husband Mark's notarized consent to name Mia as the beneficiary. Without that consent, Mark could later claim half the account after Dina's death, undoing Dina's intention.*

Joint Bank Accounts

Joint bank accounts can seem like the simplest way to make sure money passes to the right person. And in one sense, they are. When two people hold an account together with **right of survivorship**, the surviving owner automatically becomes the full owner when the other dies. Nothing needs to be filed in court. No probate judge needs to get involved. The transfer happens purely because of how the account was titled, by what lawyers call **"operation of law."** This means the transfer is automatic and requires no secondary action from a court or an executor; the survivor simply becomes the owner the moment the first person passes away.

Recovery from a POD or TOD beneficiary is not routine. It generally occurs only if the probate estate does not have enough assets to pay debts or taxes, and the specific rules vary by state.

If you look at a statement and see *"JTWROS,"* that's short for "joint tenants with right of survivorship." Some married couples may instead see *"tenants by the entirety,"* a similar form used in roughly half the states. Either way, the effect is the same: once one owner dies, the surviving owner instantly owns the entire balance.

But the story doesn't end there, and this is the part many people overlook. The surviving co-owner can do anything they want with the account, including changing any beneficiary designation you both agreed on.

> ***Example:*** *Bob and Richard shared a savings account and added Bob's son, Seth, as the POD beneficiary. Their intention was simple: Seth would inherit the account, but only after both of them were gone. Bob died first, leaving Richard as the sole owner. Years later, after Richard and Seth had a falling-out, Richard changed the beneficiary to a charity. When Richard eventually died, Seth inherited nothing.*

If Bob had wanted to **guarantee** that Seth eventually received the account, a joint tenancy was the wrong tool. He and Richard could have placed the account into a **living trust** instead. The trust could have allowed Richard to use the money for life, while still ensuring the account passed to Seth when Richard died. Joint accounts are excellent at handling the *first* transfer, but they offer no protection at all for the *next* one.

This is why many people who rely on joint accounts for simple convenience still need a will or trust in place to handle the rest of their estate.

> ***Example:*** *After Bob died, Richard found himself owning the couple's home, their savings, and their investment account. He lived in Washington, where probate is relatively painless, so he created a simple will leaving everything to his nieces and nephews. Had he lived in a state where probate is slow or expensive, he almost certainly would have used a living trust instead.*

Transfer-on-Death Deeds

A **Transfer-on-Death (TOD) deed** is essentially a beneficiary designation for real estate. You stay in full control while you're alive, and you can revoke or change the deed whenever you want. When you die, the person you named becomes the new owner, usually after recording a death certificate and signing a simple affidavit.

It sounds wonderfully straightforward. In practice, TOD deeds vary dramatically from state to state. Some states have smooth, simple procedures; others impose extra safeguards to prevent fraud or exploitation.

In California, for example, a TOD deed must be notarized, signed by two witnesses, and recorded within sixty days, requirements that apply to no other deed. After the owner dies, the beneficiary must mail formal notices to *all* heirs (even those who inherit nothing) and inform them of their right to challenge the transfer. These additional steps make a TOD deed feel a little like a mini-probate for the house.

Your state may be more relaxed or more strict. That's the real lesson here: the idea is simple, but the execution depends entirely on local law.

TOD deeds also come with practical limitations. Because creditors have first priority, the beneficiary's interest isn't truly secure until any claims have expired. Title companies may refuse to insure the home during that period, which can delay any sale. And if other family members believe the beneficiary pressured or influenced the homeowner, they can try to challenge the deed in court.

On top of that, TOD deeds struggle with "what-if" scenarios. If one of your named beneficiaries dies before you, their share usually disappears rather than passing to their children. If your only beneficiary dies before you, the house falls back into your probate estate, exactly what you were hoping to avoid.

For people who own little besides a house, and whose wishes are straightforward, a TOD deed can be a helpful tool. But for more layered plans, such as giving a spouse lifetime use of the home while preserving the remainder for children, a **living trust** offers far more flexibility and protection.

Small-Estate Affidavits and Simplified Probate

Even with the best planning tools available, many people die without using any of them. When that happens, states often provide a simpler process for modest estates.

One option is a **small-estate affidavit**. Instead of opening a probate case, an heir signs a sworn statement confirming that the estate is below the state's "small-estate" limit and that they are entitled to the property. After a short waiting period, a bank or institution can release the asset directly.

Some states offer a second shortcut: a **simplified probate procedure**. The court is technically involved, but the process is much faster, with almost no hearings or complicated filings. These procedures are usually available only for relatively small estates and often only when no real estate is involved.

These aren't exactly "planning" techniques, they're fallback options. But they can make a world of difference for families who inherit from someone who never got around to formal estate planning.

Chapter | 5 | Assessment Test

1. **What is the defining feature of POD and TOD designations?**

   a. They transfer ownership during life
   b. They require court approval after death
   c. They automatically move assets to a named beneficiary at death
   d. They replace the need for all other estate planning tools

2. **During the account owner's lifetime, what rights does a POD or TOD beneficiary have?**

   a. Full access to the account
   b. The right to view balances
   c. The ability to block withdrawals
   d. No rights at all

3. **One major advantage of POD and TOD designations discussed in the chapter is:**

   a. Creditor protection
   b. Privacy
   c. Tax elimination
   d. Guaranteed fairness among heirs

4. **When might POD or TOD designations alone be sufficient as an estate plan?**

   a. When beneficiaries are minors
   b. When the estate includes complex assets
   c. When the owner has adult beneficiaries and a simple estate
   d. When unequal gifts are desired

5. **Why are POD and TOD designations often inadequate for young beneficiaries?**

   a. They expire when the beneficiary turns 18
   b. Banks refuse to honor them
   c. They trigger automatic probate
   d. Banks cannot manage or delay distributions for minors

6. **What happens if all named POD or TOD beneficiaries die before the account owner and no update is made?**

   a. The account is split among extended family
   b. The funds escheat to the state
   c. The account passes under intestacy rules
   d. The account falls back into the estate and may go through probate

7. **Why can joint bank accounts create unintended consequences in estate planning?**

   a. They are taxed at higher rates
   b. The surviving owner can later change beneficiaries
   c. They always require probate
   d. They cannot be closed after death

8. **What is a key limitation of transfer-on-death (TOD) deeds for real estate?**

   a. They transfer ownership immediately
   b. They cannot be revoked
   c. They vary significantly by state law and may be challenged or delayed
   d. They are available in every state

9. **Which situation most strongly calls for a trust instead of relying only on beneficiary designations?**

   a. Leaving one account to one adult beneficiary
   b. Holding modest cash balances
   c. Wanting property to benefit one person for life, then others later
   d. Avoiding privacy concerns

10. **What are small-estate affidavits and simplified probate procedures best described as?**

   a. Advanced planning strategies
   b. Alternatives to beneficiary designations
   c. Tools only available through trusts
   d. Fallback options for modest estates

Answers

1. **C** – POD and TOD designations cause assets to transfer automatically to a named beneficiary at death.
2. **D** – Beneficiaries have no rights or access while the owner is alive.
3. **B** – Beneficiary designations remain private and do not become public court records.
4. **C** – For simple estates with adult beneficiaries, these tools may be sufficient.
5. **D** – Beneficiary forms cannot manage or delay distributions for minors.
6. **D** – Without a living beneficiary, the account reverts to the estate and may require probate.
7. **B** – The surviving joint owner can change beneficiaries, defeating earlier intentions.
8. **C** – TOD deeds depend heavily on state law and may be challenged or delayed.
9. **C** – Trusts allow "first to you, then to them" planning that forms cannot accomplish.
10. **D** – These are fallback procedures for small estates, not proactive planning tools.

YOUR CHILDREN

> ***"Children are the living messages we send to a time we will not see."***
>
> **– Neil Postman,**
> *American author, educator, and cultural critic*

For parents, estate planning stops being an abstract legal project the moment the conversation turns to **guardianship**. Nothing asks more of your heart, or your imagination, than choosing the adults who would raise your children if you couldn't. It's the most important decision in your entire plan, and often the hardest one to face.

The hardest part of the entire planning process is simply getting past the emotional weight of guardianship choice. It's uncomfortable, even heartbreaking, to picture a world where you aren't there to raise your children. The mind naturally resists going down that road.

But something interesting happens once the decision is finally made and written down. The background anxiety, the quiet "what if" that hovers in the mind of every parent, starts to ease. Putting a plan in place doesn't invite tragedy; it shields your children if life ever takes an unexpected turn.

Doing this now gives you the one thing the law can't provide on its own: control. You're the person who knows your children, your family dynamics, and you and your family's values. If you don't write down your wishes, a judge, however kind and well-intentioned, will be left to guess.

And unlike many estate decisions, this one isn't permanent. You can change your will at any time as your children grow and your relationships evolve. The important thing is simply to start.

Think of this step the same way you think about installing smoke detectors or buying car insurance. You hope they'll never matter. But you rest easier knowing they're there, doing their work in the background, protecting the people you love most.

What Happens If You Don't Choose Anyone?

If parents leave no instructions, a judge steps in. Usually a relative comes forward and asks to be appointed, and if that person appears capable, the court approves them. But if no one volunteers, or if your family doesn't know who you would want, the judge has to pick based only on the limited information before them. You lose the opportunity to steer the decision toward the person who actually shares your parenting style, your values, your stability, and the emotional world your child knows best.

That's why skipping this step leaves a larger question mark than any parent ever intends to leave.

What Personal Guardians Actually Do

A **personal guardian** (sometimes called a *guardian of the person*) steps into the legal and practical role of a parent. They make sure your children are fed, safe, educated, treated when sick, and guided in daily life and big decisions. They handle school meetings, doctor appointments, bedtime routines, curfews, friend groups, and moral boundaries. They decide what movies your kids watch, what they eat, and how they spend summers. In short, they become the adults responsible for shaping childhood into adulthood.

But one thing guardians *don't* have to do is pay for your children out of their own pocket. A guardian is responsible for care, not financing that care. Ideally, your estate plan includes a **trust or custodial arrangement** (Chapter 7) so the guardian has funds to use on your child's behalf.

If no trust exists, the court may appoint a separate guardian of the estate to manage significant assets until the child reaches adulthood. Many parents avoid this by creating a trust, either during life or through their will, so a court-appointed financial guardian and ongoing court supervision are not required.

> ***Example:*** *Shae becomes guardian for her 10-year-old niece, Shelby, after Shelby's parents pass away. Shae moves Shelby into her home, enrolls her in school, meets with teachers when Shelby struggles, makes medical decisions, and ensures day-to-day stability. But Shae doesn't pay out of her own income. Shelby's inheritance, managed through a trust, covers her expenses.*

How Courts Appoint Guardians

When a guardian is needed, the person you named in your will typically files a petition with the probate court. The judge reviews your nomination and must confirm that appointing the nominee is in the child's best interest. **In most states, a parent's choice is given strong priority**, so courts generally start with the assumption that your nominee should serve. In practice, judges almost always honor the parents' selection unless there is a compelling reason not to, such as serious health issues, instability, an inability to provide appropriate care, or credible evidence of past problems.

When evaluating a potential guardian, courts look at things like the relationship between the guardian and the child, the stability and safety of the proposed home, the adult's physical and mental health, and general moral fitness. In many states, children around age 14 or older have the right to express a preference, and courts are required to consider it.

If someone in your family disagrees with your choice, they can formally object, which is why putting your nomination in writing is so important. If there is someone you do not want considered, you can say so in your will and briefly explain why. Because a will becomes public after your death, some parents choose to keep especially sensitive details in a separate, private letter, often addressed to the person they nominated as guardian, so it can be shared with the court **if a dispute arises**. A letter can help explain your reasoning, but it is not a substitute for naming the guardian in the will, and its impact in a contested case can vary by state and by judge.

Once appointed, the amount of court involvement depends on the type of guardianship and on state law. A guardian of the person may have relatively limited day-to-day supervision in some places, but a guardian of the child's property (often called a guardian of the estate) commonly faces ongoing court requirements, such as posting a bond, filing an inventory, submitting periodic or annual reports and accountings, and obtaining court approval for certain major financial decisions. In other words, some guardianships are fairly streamlined, but many involve meaningful, continuing oversight.

RESOURCE: *For state-by-state guardianship rules,* **Justia.com** *maintains a "Guardianship Legal Forms: 50-State Survey." Bridging Refugee Youth & Children's Services (BRYCS) also offers state-specific guides for guardianship procedures.*

Choosing the Right Guardian

Every parent knows, deep down, that no one on the planet can truly replace them. Still, estate planning asks you to do something brave: choose the people who would raise your children if you no longer were able to do so. You're not trying to find a clone of yourself; you're simply identifying adults who could provide a loving home, carry your values forward, and get your kids safely to adulthood.

Because life is unpredictable, it's wise to name not just one guardian, but at least one or two backups. A first choice may move, become ill, or simply be unable to step into the role years from now. A short list gives the court options that you have preapproved.

At the end of this chapter, you'll find a dedicated worksheet designed to help you identify which values matter most to you in a guardian, so you can make your choice with greater clarity and confidence.

The "Ideal Guardian" Exercise

Before completing the worksheet, a helpful way to begin is by defining, on paper, what your *ideal* guardian would look like. This isn't about searching for perfection; it's about identifying the qualities you care about most. Some parents prioritize stability. Others prioritize shared values, emotional closeness, or geographic proximity. Some care deeply about religious upbringing; others about education or parenting style.

When two parents are involved, each should make their own private list first. Only afterward should you compare notes. At first, those lists might look wildly different, which is normal. Most couples eventually discover that, underneath the details, they want the same core things for their kids.

Even divorced parents, when communication is possible, are better off naming the same guardians in their separate wills. If the worst happens, it prevents a painful tug-of-war between two sets of well-meaning adults.

Children themselves can sometimes provide valuable insight, especially older ones. You don't have to present it as a catastrophe scenario. A gentle version might be: *"We're making a plan, just in case someone else has to help take care of you one day. How would you feel if Aunt Carla was that person?"* Their reactions can help guide your choices, or at least highlight practical considerations like school, friends, and routines.

Of course, these decisions aren't permanent. What works when your kids are toddlers may not make sense when they are teenagers. You can revisit your choices any time by updating your will.

And remember: if both parents don't die together, the surviving parent will control what happens next. But choosing the same guardians still avoids confusion and a potential courtroom clash after the second parent dies.

> **Example:** *Imagine a single mother, Laura, who has three kids aged six to 12. Their father has died. When Laura sits down to make her "ideal guardian" list, she ranks things like emotional closeness, parenting style, stability, and educational values. She knows no one will score a perfect 10 in every category, but the list reveals what matters most to her.*
>
> *Once she understands her priorities, she lists the people in her life who come closest to those qualities. At this stage, she doesn't eliminate anyone, she simply brainstorms. Later, she'll narrow that list down to a primary choice and one or two alternatives.*

Making Your List of Potential Guardians

When you begin listing possible guardians, think about individuals rather than couples. You can name a couple if you want, but it's safer to choose one person as the legal guardian, with the understanding that their partner or spouse will likely help with daily care. If the couple later separates, you avoid the nightmare of your child becoming part of their custody dispute.

What About Godparents?

Many families treat godparents as important figures in a child's spiritual or emotional life. Godparents have **no automatic legal priority** to serve as guardians. If you want a godparent to act as guardian, you must name them in your will; otherwise, they are legally no different from any other adult in your child's orbit.

Special Considerations for Same-Sex Parents

For same-sex couples, the best safeguard is ensuring that **both parents are legal parents**. A step-parent adoption, usually simple and cost-effective, creates equal parental status. Without it, the surviving partner sometimes has to petition the court just to adopt the child after their spouse dies.

If legal adoption isn't possible yet, the biological or adoptive parent should explicitly name their partner as guardian in their will. Otherwise, the partner may have no legal path to raise the child, regardless of their real-life role.

In the example above, when Laura completes her brainstorming, she ends up with a short list of trusted adults, each with strengths and weaknesses. Perhaps her sister has the emotional bond but lives across the country. Maybe her best friend shares her parenting style but has limited space at home. Seeing everything on paper helps her make calm, thoughtful decisions instead of relying solely on instinct.

Narrowing Your Choices

Once you've identified the values that matter most to you and pulled together a list of people who could serve as guardians, the next step is the difficult but necessary work of narrowing that list. This usually begins by crossing off the individuals whose limitations are simply too serious to ignore.

> ***Example:*** *Elena initially considers her brother and two close friends as guardians. But her brother's spouse has values she would never want shaping her children's daily lives, so she removes him from the list. She also eliminates her beloved godparents, who are wonderful people but who are now in their late seventies and are unlikely to have the stamina required to raise two energetic kids. She hesitates over a cousin she loves deeply, but who lives across the country, and uprooting her teenage son from his school and social life would feel like piling one loss on top of another.*

By now, your own list may shrink, along with your confidence. This is the moment many parents feel the urge to quit, thinking, *"No one is perfect, so I can't choose anyone."* But perfection isn't the standard. Your goal is to choose an individual who can provide safety, affection, routine, and stability, not a person who's a mirror image of yourself.

Return to your list of values and consider the traits you marked as essential. Focus on the ones that truly matter. Then look again at the remaining names. Which person brings at least one or two of those important values into the room? Who has the temperament your children respond to? Who feels steady?

If you still feel torn, simplify the decision:

Whose love feels most genuine to your children?

Who do they trust without effort?

Those answers are often the clearest guide.

> ***Example:*** *In trying to choose a guardian, for years Marisol and Daniel couldn't commit to anyone. One sibling lived across the country. Another had a demanding job. A close friend had three kids of her own. Every potential guardian had a drawback. The result was paralysis: no will, no nominations, nothing written down.*
>
> *Everything changed the morning Marisol went into labor with their youngest child. A family friend, someone their children adored, arrived to take the older kids for the night. The children ran to her, hugged her tightly, and settled into her car with complete ease. As she buckled them in and drove away, waving, Marisol and Daniel realized, without needing to say a word, that she was the person who could step into that role if life ever required it.*
>
> *They finished their estate plan a week later.*

Once you've made your own choices, record them in your planning worksheet. But don't finalize anything until you've confirmed that your nominees are actually willing to take on this responsibility if the need ever arises. (We'll talk about how to approach that conversation later on.)

Your Choice Is Not Set in Stone

A guardian nomination isn't a lifelong contract. The person who's right today may not be right in five years, and that's normal. A choice that works for the next few years is vastly better than leaving the space blank. Children grow. Relationships change. People change jobs, move homes, or go through challenging seasons. You can update your will any time to reflect those changes.

If you've thought and rethought this question and still can't make a decision, pause and read through the section "Common Problems and Some Solutions." If none of those ideas help loosen the knot, here is the most practical piece of advice you'll ever receive about guardianship:

Choose someone anyway.

A thoughtful, imperfect choice you make *yourself* is far better than leaving the decision to a judge who's never met your child.

You can always revise your choice later; however, what you can't revise is silence.

Common Problems and Some Solutions

If you've tried your best and every potential guardian still feels wrong, you may have run into one of the classic obstacles below. These are more than small imperfections; they're real barriers. But often there are simple solutions.

Your First Choice Is Older Than You Are

Often, the person who feels like the most natural guardian is a parent, an aunt, or a family friend who has known your children since birth. They may be the most loving and emotionally grounded choice right now, even if you know they might not be the right person 10 years from today.

This is perfectly fine. Guardianship planning doesn't have to extend 20 years into the future. Many parents find clarity when they frame the decision in shorter windows: Who could give my children stability and affection for the next three to five years? As children grow into adolescence, their needs change; your nominees can change with them. What matters is that someone appropriate is named now.

> ***Example:*** *Riley and Mateo have a toddler and a kindergartner. The people their children run to at every holiday gathering are Riley's parents, energetic 60-somethings who adore them. Riley knows that, long-term, her parents might age out of the role. But today, for little kids, they're the obvious choice. She and Mateo decide to name them now and revisit the decision once the kids are older and more settled into school and extracurricular life.*

Your preferred guardian is terrible with money.

It's common to find someone whose emotional connection to your children is perfect, yet whose financial habits make you uneasy. Parenting and financial stewardship are different skill sets, and good estate planning can separate them.

To do that, you typically need a **trust-based plan**. You can name one person as the child's guardian (to handle day-to-day care), and name a different person, such as a financially savvy relative, a professional fiduciary, or a corporate trustee, to serve as **trustee** and manage the child's inheritance. This way, the caregiver can focus on stability, routines, school, and emotional support, while the trustee handles budgets, investments, and long-term planning, making distributions for the child's benefit under the rules you set.

Without a trust (or another legally recognized management structure), money left to a minor may trigger a court-supervised arrangement. In that situation, the court may appoint a guardian or conservator of the child's property, require a bond, and require ongoing reports or accountings, meaning you may not have full control over who manages the funds or how much court oversight is involved.

> ***Example:*** *Ash chooses his lifelong friend, Mara, as the person he trusts most to raise his son. Mara is patient, hands-on, and deeply involved in the boy's life. But Mara also jokes openly about her total inability to handle a*

savings account. Ash solves the dilemma by naming Mara as the personal guardian and appointing his financially meticulous cousin, Lior, as trustee. Mara can focus on parenting; Lior ensures the inherited money lasts as long as the child needs it.

You Like the Guardian, But Not Their Spouse

It's also very common to feel confident about one person but uneasy about their partner. Maybe the spouse is simply someone you don't know well. Maybe your parenting philosophies clash. Maybe your gut tells you your child wouldn't thrive in that household dynamic. Whatever the reason, you're not obligated to appoint a couple just because they're married.

You can nominate only the individual you trust. As long as the couple stays together, your child would still live in their shared home, but legal authority rests solely with the person you named. And if the relationship were to end, your child would remain with the guardian you chose.

If, however, the spouse is someone you would absolutely not want involved in raising your child, that can be a signal to consider another candidate.

> ***Example:*** *Naomi wants her brother Ellis to be her daughter's guardian. Ellis is warm, dependable, and already deeply involved in the child's daily life. But Ellis's husband, Patrick, has a volatile personality that makes Naomi uneasy. Instead of abandoning Ellis as an option, she names only Ellis in her will. This preserves the relationship Naomi values while ensuring that, if the marriage ever ended, custody wouldn't automatically shift to someone Naomi never intended to entrust with her child.*

Your First Choice Lives Far Away

It's very common today for the person you most trust to raise your children to live in another state, or even on another continent. The law does **not** require your chosen guardian to live where you live. Courts look first at whether the person is a suitable caregiver, not their ZIP code.

That said, distance adds some practical issues. In many states, when a guardian lives elsewhere, the court may require them to post a **bond**, a kind of insurance, to guarantee they'll carry out their responsibilities properly. An out-of-state guardian may also need to ask the court handling your estate to transfer the guardianship case to the state where they live. That means more paperwork, more time, and usually more legal fees, but courts regularly approve such transfers when they're clearly in the child's best interests.

If the guardian lives in another country, the process usually has two steps: a court in your state appoints them as a **temporary guardian** so they can act legally and collect the child, then a court in their home country appoints them as **permanent guardian**. Once that's done, the original court can close out the temporary guardianship.

Because distance can slow things down, if your chosen long-term guardian lives far away, it's wise to also nominate a **local temporary guardian** in your will. This is someone nearby who could step in quickly in an emergency, helping your child stay in familiar surroundings and maintain routines while the longer-term guardian travels and the necessary court steps are completed. The goal is speed and continuity, not bypassing the court entirely.

> ***Example:*** *Elena lives in Denver with her eight-year-old twins. The person she fully trusts to raise them is her brother Julian, who lives in Montreal. In her will, she names Julian as the guardian, but she also names her close friend and neighbor, Rosa, as a temporary guardian. If Elena died unexpectedly, Rosa could care for the twins right away, get them to school, and keep them in their neighborhood while Julian travels to Colorado, deals with the courts, and gets formally appointed where he lives.*

You Have Children From Previous Relationships

Blended families make guardianship decisions more complicated because not all children share the same history or the same legal parents. Some parents decide that all children should stay together no matter what. Others decide that different children need different guardians, especially where relationships with their other biological parent may be very different.

There's one key point to keep in mind: **if a child still has a living legal parent, guardianship may never come into play for that child.** In most cases, if one parent dies, the other legal parent automatically gains custody, unless a court finds them unfit.

> ***Example:*** *Caroline has a 15-year-old son, Mason, from her first marriage, and with her current husband Noah, she has two younger children, Eva and Leo. Mason spends summers and some holidays with his father, who is very involved in his life. If Caroline and Noah die, everyone expects Mason to live with his father.*
>
> *In her will, Caroline names her friend* ***Nadia*** *as a backup guardian for Mason, but only "if Mason's father is unable or unwilling to take custody." For Eva and Leo, she names Noah's sister,* ***Iris****, who lives nearby and sees the children weekly. Noah's will matches this: he names Iris for Eva and Leo and names Mason's father as Mason's primary guardian. They don't name a guardian for Mason in Noah's will, because Noah is a step-parent, not a legal parent.*

The underlying principle is simple: look at each child's reality, who they are bonded to, where they are rooted, who their legal parents are, and build your plan around that.

You Don't Want Your Ex to Get Custody

For many divorced or separated parents, the hardest part of guardianship planning is the fear that, if they die first, their ex will gain custody by default. The law generally gives the **surviving legal parent** the first right to custody, unless a court has a strong reason not to, such as serious neglect, abuse, or total abandonment.

If you are deeply concerned about your ex's ability to parent safely, you can't simply "skip" them by naming someone else in your will. But you **can**:

- Nominate the person you believe should be guardian; and
- Clearly explain why you believe your ex should not have custody, and keep this updated.

You can do this directly in your will, or in a separate letter. The will is legally powerful but will become a public document after your death. A private letter, kept with your estate plan and given to your chosen guardian, can spell out more personal or sensitive details and include supporting documents, such as court orders, police reports, medical records, or written findings from prior custody cases.

If a court ever has to decide between your ex and your chosen guardian, these written reasons are a road map showing the judge what you saw, what you feared, and what you wanted for your child.

> ***Example:*** *Nate has full custody of his seven-year-old daughter, Holly. Her other parent, Riley, has a long history of substance abuse and has repeatedly failed to show up for visits. Nate worries Holly would not be safe in Riley's care. In his will, Nate names his cousin, Tara, as the person he would want to serve as Holly's guardian* ***if a court decides a guardian is needed****, and he briefly explains his concerns. Nate also keeps a private file with his estate documents that lists key facts and dates and identifies where supporting records can be found (for example, court orders, treatment records, or police reports). If a dispute ever arises, Tara can share that information with Nate's lawyer so it can be presented to the court* ***in the proper form****.*

Important reality check: *Even if a will names someone else, courts generally give strong priority to a surviving biological parent unless there is proof the parent is unfit or that placing the child with that parent would cause serious harm.*

Your Family Doesn't Like Your Choices

Sometimes the friction isn't with an ex, it's with your extended family. Maybe you've moved away, changed religious traditions, or built a life with a partner your relatives don't fully accept. You might know in your bones that your chosen guardian is right for your child, but also suspect that a parent, sibling, or in-law would be furious, and might even try to fight your decision.

The law is on your side more than you might think. Courts take a parent's written choice of guardian very seriously. To overturn it, a relative would need to show a **strong, concrete reason** why your nominee is unfit, such as serious crime, abuse, or neglect. Mere disagreement, distance, or disapproval is not enough.

Still, conflict can be painful for your child, especially if it erupts right after losing a parent. To reduce the risk of an ugly fight, you can prepare the ground now:

- You can gently **talk with key family members** about your choice and why you made it, if that feels safe and constructive.
- You can **write a letter to your family**, to be opened only if you die, explaining the values behind your decision and asking them to respect it.
- You can **write a separate, more detailed letter to your chosen guardian**, giving context about any relatives who might object and why you don't think they're the right choice.

You can also put some or all of your reasoning directly into your will, knowing that it will be public later. The right approach depends on your family, your relationships, and your tolerance for awkward conversations.

> ***Example:*** *Imani and her wife, Rachel, are raising their son, Micah. They want Micah to stay with Rachel's brother, Aaron, and his partner, who live in the same city and share their approach to parenting. Imani's father, however, is very traditional and has never fully accepted their marriage. Imani is fairly sure that if she and Rachel died, her father would want Micah to live with him.*
>
> *Imani decides not to confront her father now, but she does write a clear letter to him, to be opened only if she and Rachel both die. In it, she explains that they love him but want Micah to grow up in a home that fully supports his family story, in the city and community he already knows. She keeps the letter with their wills, along with a separate memo to Aaron explaining that, if a dispute ever arises, that letter can be used to show the court exactly what they intended.*

If you truly expect a fight, it's wise to speak with an **estate planning attorney**. They can help draft your documents in a way that anticipates and withstands challenges.

When You're Worried Your Children Won't Like Your Choice

Sometimes the resistance isn't from adults at all; it's from your kids. Teenagers especially may already have strong opinions about where and with whom they would want to live. Even younger children can feel reassured, or unsettled, by the idea that a plan exists.

In many states, children around age 14 and older have the right to tell a judge their preference for guardian, and courts will take that into account along with everything else. If you think your child would strongly disagree with your choice, or simply be worried about the unknown, it can be helpful to talk about it now, gently and age-appropriately.

You're not asking your child to make the decision. You're helping them understand that you have a plan, that they won't be left adrift, and that the people you've named are chosen because they are safe and loving.

Sometimes, just knowing *who* they would go to is enough to quiet the fear.

After You've Chosen a Guardian

Once you've narrowed your list to the two or three people who genuinely feel right, there's one final step before putting anything in writing: *you have to talk to them.*

Think of this conversation as part of the planning, not a test or a negotiation. You're inviting someone you trust to take on a role you hope will *never* be needed. Most people understand this instinctively, and the honesty of it tends to soften the awkwardness.

Pick a calm moment, tell them you're working on your estate plan, and share that you would like to name them as guardian. Explain why you chose them, whether it's their values, their bond with your children, their stability, their kindness, or simply the way they've shown up in your life. People appreciate being told that they are trusted with something that important. It also helps them understand your reasoning, which can prevent confusion years later.

At the same time, be clear that this is a big responsibility, even if the likelihood of it becoming real is extremely small. Let them know you will not be offended if they decline. Sometimes people have commitments you don't know about, elder care, health issues, financial limitations, or simply the recognition that their life would be stretched too thin. It is better to find out now.

These conversations often reveal practical details you haven't considered. Your chosen guardian may mention that their home is too small to add more children without significant upgrades, or that they would need a second car. That's when you can revisit your planning, maybe increasing life insurance, structuring your trust to allow the guardian to remain in your home, or earmarking funds for specific needs.

You may also discover that the guardians you've chosen haven't done their own estate planning and appreciate the nudge. In some cases, they will share that they were hoping to ask *you* to serve as *their* children's guardian. There is no downside to this conversation; it either confirms your choice or gives you clarity you couldn't get any other way. And if having the conversation feels impossibly uncomfortable, that's often a sign that the person might not be the right choice after all.

Some parents even take a short trip with their chosen guardian before finalizing anything, a weekend at the beach, a cabin in the mountains, even a simple overnight visit. When you're imagining someone raising your children, you start to notice how they interact, set boundaries, and handle stress. Countless parents have changed their nominations after one difficult weekend that revealed something they hadn't seen before.

Giving Guardians Some Written Guidance

After you've chosen your guardians and spoken with them, you may want to give them something more personal, such as a letter or recorded message that explains your intentions and offers insight into your hopes for your children. This isn't required, and it's not legally binding, but many parents find comfort in it. Think of it as a road map, not a rulebook.

If writing such a letter makes you emotional to the point of paralysis, skip it. Choosing a guardian is already a monumental step; you don't need to pile on more emotional weight. But if the idea brings you peace, or if your choices might confuse or surprise relatives, a letter can prevent conflict and provide clarity at a moment when your family will need it most.

Many parents include their reasons for choosing the guardian, especially when the choice involves a friend rather than a relative. They also record traits about each child that might help the guardian support them: temperaments, routines, sensitivities, favorite traditions, or long-term dreams you hope they'll be encouraged to explore. Parents sometimes share their thoughts about education, faith, community, extended family ties, or values they want passed down.

These letters can be incredibly meaningful, but they are not required. They're simply an offering, your voice preserved in a moment when your children may need it.

Guardian Worksheet

Choosing a guardian is one of the most personal decisions you'll make in your estate plan, and the process is much easier when you can see your thoughts laid out clearly. That's what this worksheet is designed for. It gives you a place to gather your priorities, name the qualities that matter most to you, and compare potential guardians in a structured, thoughtful way.

Many parents find that once their values and candidates are written down, ranked, compared, and weighed, the right choice becomes far more obvious. You may surprise yourself by seeing patterns you hadn't noticed, or by realizing that someone you hadn't considered seriously actually aligns best with the life you want for your children.

https://drive.google.com/file/d/1IwGmbq7GxZk8pJiwAcjP38da7jFKuRYL/view?usp=sharing

This is the moment to take a breath. Choosing a guardian is, without question, the hardest emotional task in estate planning for parents of minor children. You've confronted fears, sorted through complicated relationships, and made thoughtful decisions that put your children's safety and well-being first.

The hardest part is behind you. Everything that comes next, structuring the inheritance, choosing trustees, filling out forms, is far more straightforward. But don't lose momentum. Your decisions only have legal force once they're written into a properly executed will or trust. Until then, they are just intentions.

You've done something brave and profoundly loving. Now let's finish the plan that protects those choices.

Chapter | 6 | Assessment Test

1. **Why does the chapter emphasize that choosing a guardian is the most important decision for parents?**

   a. Because it permanently locks in your children's future
   b. Because it determines who will manage the inheritance
   c. Because it decides who will raise your children if you are no longer able to
   d. Because courts rarely review guardian choices

2. **What usually happens if parents die without naming a guardian in their will?**

   a. Children automatically stay with godparents
   b. A judge must decide based on limited information
   c. The oldest relative gains custody
   d. The children enter foster care

3. **Which responsibility belongs to a personal guardian rather than a trustee?**

   a. Investing inherited assets
   b. Filing tax returns for the estate
   c. Managing trust distributions
   d. Making day-to-day parenting decisions

4. **Why do many parents separate the roles of guardian and financial manager?**

   a. To avoid probate
   b. To reduce taxes
   c. To match caregiving skills and financial skills
   d. To satisfy court requirements

5. **How do courts generally treat a parent's written guardian nomination?**

   a. They ignore it entirely
   b. They treat it as binding in all cases
   c. They consider it but may override it if clearly not in the child's best interest
   d. They require unanimous family approval

6. **Why is it recommended to name backup guardians?**

   a. Because courts require at least three options
   b. Because a guardian's circumstances may change over time
   c. Because backup guardians automatically inherit property
   d. Because children must choose among them

7. **What is the legal status of godparents if they are not named in a will?**

   a. They automatically have priority over relatives
   b. They are treated as default guardians
   c. They must be approved by a religious authority
   d. They have no special legal standing

8. **What additional complication can arise if a chosen guardian lives far away or abroad?**

   a. The guardian cannot be appointed
   b. The child must remain in the current state
   c. Additional court steps and delays may be required
   d. Guardianship automatically transfers to a local relative

9. **Why can naming the same guardians in both parents' wills be especially important?**

   a. It reduces drafting costs
   b. It prevents confusion and conflict after the second parent's death
   c. It eliminates the need for a trust
   d. It guarantees court approval

10. **What is the chapter's core advice for parents who feel unable to choose a "perfect" guardian?**

    a. Delay the decision until children are older
    b. Let the court decide
    c. Choose multiple guardians with equal authority
    d. Make a thoughtful choice now and revise it later if needed

Answers

1. **C** – Guardianship determines who will actually raise your children if you are no longer there.
2. **B** – Without instructions, a judge must choose based on limited and imperfect information.
3. **D** – A personal guardian handles daily parenting and major life decisions for the child.
4. **C** – Estate planning allows caregiving and financial management roles to be separated.
5. **C** – Courts strongly favor parents' choices but must still act in the child's best interest.
6. **B** – Life changes, and backups ensure your wishes can still be followed.
7. **D** – Godparents have no automatic legal role unless named in a will.
8. **C** – Distance can require extra court procedures and cause delays.
9. **B** – Consistency avoids confusion and potential disputes later on.
10. **D** – An imperfect but thoughtful choice is better than leaving the decision blank.

Personal Notes

CHAPTER 7

Leaving Property to Your Children

> "*The best inheritance a parent can give his children is a few minutes of his time each day.*"
>
> ***— O. A. Battista,***
> *American author and business consultant*

Two Roles to Think About

When you imagine the children in your life and try to plan for their future, two different questions quickly emerge. One is emotional and immediate: who would actually raise them if you were suddenly gone? The other is more technical but just as important: who would manage any money they inherit? In legal terms, the person who raises the child is often called a ***guardian of the person***, while the person who oversees the child's money is sometimes referred to as a ***guardian of the estate***. They sound similar, but they play very different roles. One guides a child's daily life; the other protects the financial resources that will support that life.

These roles can be given to the same individual, but that may not be the best choice if you want to ensure accountability. Someone who is nurturing, patient, and grounded in the day-to-day realities of caring for a child may not be equally comfortable making investment decisions or handling large sums of money. By separating the responsibilities, you create a supportive team instead of placing all the pressure on one person. It allows each adult to do what they do best, which is exactly what you want for a child who has already experienced a major loss.

Why Children Need Adult Oversight

As we shift from the emotional to the practical side of planning, it helps to remember that the law views children as needing protection in financial matters. As minors, children can't sign binding contracts, take responsibility for major assets, or directly receive more than a minimal amount of money without adult supervision. Each state sets its own threshold. In some places, even a gift of a few thousand dollars requires an adult to step in; in others, the amount may be higher. But the purpose is always the same: to make sure a child isn't left alone to handle decisions for which they're not yet prepared.

Even when a child turns 18, the milestone that marks adulthood on paper, the transition doesn't magically turn them into seasoned financial managers. An 18-year-old might be perfectly capable of handling the balance from a summer job but still overwhelmed by the responsibility of an inheritance. This is why many families choose to delay full access to funds until a child is older and more mature. It isn't about limiting them; it's about guiding them toward financial independence at a pace that fits their stage of life and encouraging responsible decision-making.

Understanding What You're Leaving

Before deciding who will manage the money, it's helpful to understand what the child might actually inherit. Many people assume they have very little to pass on, but a quick review often tells a different story. A ***life insurance policy,*** alone, can transform a child's financial picture. Equity tucked away in a home can add more. Retirement accounts, 401(k)s, 403(b)s, and IRAs may have grown over time. When you add these pieces together, the total can be surprisingly substantial.

A rough estimate, rounded to the nearest $10,000, is enough to guide your choices. Once you see the full picture, your decisions shift. Leaving a 25-year-old $50,000 outright may feel perfectly reasonable. Leaving that same young adult $500,000 might make you pause. Larger inheritances tend to benefit from greater structure, not because the young person is untrustworthy, but because money of that size can shape the rest of their life.

Finding the Right Money Manager

Once you have a sense of the scope of your estate, you can consider who should manage it. Start by thinking about the people in your life who are prudent with money and comfortable making long-term decisions. They don't need to be professional investors. They simply need to understand the responsibility and feel capable of handling it with care.

Parents of young children often choose the same person to raise the children and manage the money. That can work beautifully, especially when the caregiver is already handling similar responsibilities in their own home. But it isn't the only option. If the person who would be the perfect caregiver is less comfortable with financial matters, overwhelmed by paperwork, or prone to impulsive decisions, you can choose someone else for the financial role. In families where former partners share parenting, splitting these responsibilities can reduce conflict. The surviving parent might naturally raise the children, while another trusted adult handles the money you leave behind.

Whomever you choose, what matters most is reliability. This person will be making decisions meant to serve the child for years. They will need to invest the funds thoughtfully, treat the beneficiaries fairly, and communicate with the caregiver so the child's needs are always understood. If the roles are split, cooperation is essential. One knows the child's everyday needs; the other knows the financial boundaries.

When the Child Isn't Yours

Planning becomes especially delicate when you're leaving money to a child who isn't legally your own. A simple gift, say, $25,000, left directly to a 10-year-old nephew, can create consequences you never intended. Because minors cannot legally control that amount, a court may require the parents to petition for a guardian to be appointed to oversee it. This process usually involves background checks, hearings, and ongoing reporting to the court. It turns a heartfelt gift into an administrative nightmare that can last for years.

Fortunately, it's easy to avoid this. If you name an adult *custodian* or *trustee* in advance, the money passes directly into responsible hands without involving the court. This small step spares the family significant stress at an already emotional time.

This becomes especially important with retirement accounts. A minor who inherits an IRA generally can't control it directly. The inherited funds must be held in an inherited IRA (often called a beneficiary IRA), and the financial institution typically needs a legally authorized adult to act on the child's behalf to establish and manage the account. Without an authorized adult, such as a court-appointed guardian or conservator, a UTMA/UGMA custodian (where available and appropriate), or a trustee, the family may have to go to court to obtain the necessary authority, which can be time-consuming and expensive. Thoughtful beneficiary planning, such as naming an appropriate trust or custodial arrangement when suitable, can help the transfer happen smoothly and keep management in the right hands.

> ***Example:*** *Imagine Samuel, who named his grandchildren, ages 9 and 11, as direct beneficiaries of his IRA. After he died, his daughter tried to open inherited IRAs on their behalf, only to learn that she lacked the authority to do so. The financial institution required a court-appointed guardian. What followed was a round of forms, delays, and hearings that Samuel never intended. If Samuel had instead named his daughter as custodian for the accounts under his state's UTMA, the transfer likely would have been far more straightforward and could have avoided the need for court involvement.*

Do Not Name a Minor as a Direct Beneficiary

It is very common for parents and other relatives to think, "I'll just put my child's name on this account or policy so it goes straight to them." That instinct comes from a good place, but in legal terms, it usually creates more problems than it solves. Financial institutions generally cannot release funds directly to a minor child, even if that child is listed as the beneficiary on a bank account, retirement plan, or life insurance policy. If you name a minor outright, a court may have to appoint someone to manage the funds, adding delay, cost, and ongoing court supervision at exactly the time your family needs things to be simple and calm.

Instead of naming a minor directly, your estate plan should steer those funds into a legal structure that can hold and manage money for the child on clear terms. In this book, that structure is usually either:

- A living trust you create during your lifetime, or
- A testamentary children's trust created under your will, which only comes into being at your death.

In practical terms, this means that beneficiary forms and POD or TOD designations should not list a child under the age of majority by name. Instead, they should point to the trust that will hold the funds for that child. For example, your beneficiary designation might say "to the Smith Family Living Trust dated March 10, 2026" or "to the children's trust under my Last Will and Testament," using the exact wording your attorney or financial institution requires.

This same idea applies across the major types of accounts and policies you may own:

- Bank and investment accounts with POD or TOD instructions;
- Retirement accounts, such as IRAs, 401(k)s, 403(b)s, and similar plans; or
- Life insurance policies and annuities.

By sending these assets into a living or testamentary trust rather than to a minor directly, you give your chosen trustee, not the court, authority to manage the funds, invest them prudently, and use them for the child's health, education, and support on the timeline you decide. You also avoid putting a large lump sum into an eighteen-year-old's hands all at once unless that is truly what you want. The trust terms can allow the trustee to hold and distribute money gradually, or to delay full control until the child reaches an age at which you feel more comfortable.

Later, in Chapter 10, you will see how this same principle applies when you update beneficiaries on retirement accounts and life insurance policies. When a potential beneficiary is a minor, the safest practice is almost always to name a trust, either your living trust or the testamentary children's trust under your will, rather than naming the minor child directly.

Choosing the Right Structure

Now that the people are in place, the next step is choosing how the money will be held. Most families use one of two structures: a ***custodial account*** or a ***trust***. Both achieve the same basic purpose of ensuring that a child's money is managed responsibly. However, they operate differently and suit different situations.

A **custodial account** is often the simpler choice for most situations. It places the child's property under the supervision of a custodian until the child reaches the age of majority set by the state, usually 18 or 21. In some states, the age may be 25. During that time, the custodian can invest the money, use it for the child's needs, and must keep it separated from their own assets. This works well when the inheritance is modest or when you expect the child will be ready to manage their own finances in early adulthood.

A **trust**, on the other hand, offers far greater flexibility. Instead of relying on a fixed legal age, you decide exactly when and how the child should receive the money. You can allow the trustee to pay for education, medical care, housing, or other essentials, and you can delay full access until the child reaches an age you consider mature, perhaps 25, 30, or even later. Some parents choose to distribute the money gradually, giving small portions at set ages, so the child gains experience managing finances without being overwhelmed.

A trust can be created for each child individually or designed as a single, shared fund, sometimes informally called a *"pot trust,"* which allows the trustee to support each child according to their needs. This can be especially helpful when children are different ages or when one has substantially higher expenses than the others. While trusts may require more drafting and more thoughtful management, they provide long-term stability and a degree of customization that custodial accounts simply can't match.

Children with Special Needs

There's one situation where neither a custodial account nor a standard trust is enough: when a child has a disability that may prevent them from managing money independently. Many of these children rely on government programs, such as Medicaid or Supplemental Security Income, for essential services. These programs have strict financial limits and eligibility requirements. If a child receives money directly, even a modest inheritance, it can make them temporarily ineligible for program benefits.

To avoid this, families often use a ***special needs trust***. This type of trust allows a trustee to manage money for the child throughout their life. Because the child doesn't legally own the assets, the inheritance doesn't interfere with program eligibility. The trustee can pay for therapies, equipment, education, recreation, and other needs that improve the child's quality of life without disqualifying them from government support.

Families may also use an ***ABLE account***, which is a tax-advantaged savings account designed for individuals whose disabilities began before a certain age. Money in an ABLE account can be used for a wide range of disability-related expenses, including housing, transportation, education, and everyday living needs. When used properly, these accounts generally do not affect eligibility for Medicaid or Supplemental Security Income. Many families combine the two tools, a special needs trust for long-term protection and an ABLE account for everyday flexibility.

Custodial Accounts

When you're thinking about how to leave money to a child, it helps to start with the simplest tool available. A ***custodial account*** is exactly that: a straightforward way for an adult to hold and manage money on behalf of a minor. These accounts look and feel like ordinary bank or investment accounts, but each is held in the name of the child, and the authority to make decisions rests with an adult who serves as the ***custodian***.

You can open one of these accounts while you're alive, or if it's part of your estate plan, the executor named in your will can open it later. Either way, the structure is the same: the money legally belongs to the child, but a responsible adult handles it until the child is old enough to assume responsibility.

Most states follow the UTMA, which lays out the rules for how custodians must act and when their role ends. Although every state tweaks the details slightly, the general pattern is familiar: the account remains under adult supervision until the child becomes a legal adult, usually at age 21, though some states allow a delayed handoff up to age 25.

Because these age limits vary from state to state, this is a good moment to pause and check the age limit where you live. If you scan the QR code below, you'll find a complete table summarizing the UTMA rules for all 50 states. This is an easy way to get oriented before choosing whether a custodial account fits your goals.

If you're reading this digitally, you can click here instead:

https://drive.google.com/file/d/1gLE-cez5JIVEjGTQzdfJ7-a1U3v550F7/view?usp=sharing

That built-in ending point is important. If you're comfortable with a child taking full control of their inheritance sometime between 18 and 25, a custodial account can fit beautifully. But if the amount is large, or if you feel strongly that the money should support particular goals, such as education or a first home, then this type of account is too rigid. Once the child reaches the legal cutoff age, the custodian must turn over whatever is left, with no strings attached.

Setting Up the Account

Creating a custodial account doesn't require legal execution. You can simply state in your will or living trust that any money going to a specific child should be placed in such an account, and then name the custodian who will manage it. If the child is inheriting more than just cash, perhaps a small home, a rental property, or company stock, the custodian can manage those assets as well, buying or selling property or making investment decisions in a way that supports the child's needs.

One important rule catches some families by surprise: each child needs their own account. You can't create a single pot of money to be shared among siblings. A custodial account, by definition, is tied to one beneficiary. This separation sometimes becomes a burden when children have very different needs. If one child faces unexpected medical expenses, for example, the custodian cannot use a sibling's account to help.

The upside is that custodial accounts are familiar to banks and brokerage firms. The rules are standard, the paperwork is simple, and financial institutions know exactly how to handle the funds when the child reaches the termination age. Most institutions don't charge for setting one up, and the custodian can usually open the account with minimal delay.

Families often appreciate the clarity of these accounts, but simplicity comes with trade-offs. Here is a clear summary you can refer to as you consider whether this path fits your situation:

Using Custodial Accounts for Children's Assets

Pros	Cons
Easy to set up	No ability to restrict spending to certain purposes (e.g., education only)
Low or no cost	Assets cannot be shared across siblings
Universally recognized by banks and brokerages	Must end at age 21 (or up to 25 in some states), even if the child isn't ready
Straightforward to manage	Remaining funds must be handed over with no restrictions

Choosing the Right Custodian

Choosing the custodian is often the simplest and most personal part of the process. You're looking for someone who's steady with money, organized with paperwork, and genuinely motivated to act in the child's interest.

If the same person you've chosen to care for the child also manages money well, naming them for both roles can make life easier. But it's perfectly acceptable, and sometimes wise, to separate caregiving from financial oversight. If you're leaving money to children who aren't your own, you might name their parent as custodian, or perhaps a close relative or friend who has a knack for financial matters.

If you're divorced, you can still name someone other than your former partner to manage the money. Just keep in mind that the custodian will likely need to stay in contact with your ex, since that person may be raising the child day-to-day. To prevent future complications, it's helpful to name an alternate custodian in case your first choice is unable or unwilling to serve when the time comes.

What the Custodian Actually Does

Once the executor or trustee transfers the inheritance into the custodial account, the funds legally belong to the child. But until the child reaches the designated age, the custodian makes every financial decision. Their responsibility is to act prudently, meaning they must invest in a way that is sensible, moderate, and aligned with long-term benefit. Speculative choices, like risky start-up ventures or penny stocks, don't meet this standard.

The money can be spent on anything that genuinely benefits the child. This covers much more than bare necessities. Funds might be used for housing, school tuition, laptops, sports programs, summer camps, or even a first car. If the child travels for educational programs or cultural exchanges, those expenses can be paid as well.

Custodians must maintain careful records, tracking every investment and every withdrawal. They also file tax returns for the child when needed. Despite this responsibility, there is no ongoing court supervision. The custodian is trusted to act honestly, keep the account separate from personal funds, and make decisions that support the child's best interests. If concerns arise, relatives can bring issues to court, but doing so is stressful and expensive, one more reason to choose a custodian thoughtfully.

The Kiddie Tax

A concept that sometimes surprises families is the **Kiddie Tax**, a federal rule designed to discourage shifting income-producing assets to children just to take advantage of a child's lower tax bracket. In plain English, it aims to prevent a parent from reducing taxes by transferring, for example, dividend-paying stock to a child. But it doesn't apply to all income or all amounts**.** It generally applies only to certain children (typically, under age 18 and, in some cases, under age 24 if a full-time student), and only when the child has unearned income above an annual threshold. For 2026, unearned income over $2,700 may be taxed at the parent's marginal rate under these rules.

When choosing between a custodial account and a trust, keep this in mind: placing high-income investments in a child's name can trigger the Kiddie Tax and reduce the tax benefit you might have expected.

Under this rule, unearned income, such as interest, dividends, and investment earnings, may be taxed at a higher rate for children under 18 and for full-time students who are still dependents up to age 24. It affects investment-heavy custodial accounts more than those used for short-term expenses. Anyone using a custodial account for substantial assets should understand the rule or seek advice from a tax professional.

When Custodial Accounts Work Well

Custodial accounts shine when the goal is simplicity. If you're making a modest gift, something you expect the child will use before adulthood, they can be a perfect fit. They cost little to create, nearly every financial institution knows how they work, and they don't require a trustee, a trust document, or an attorney to administer them.

But custodial accounts fall short in two important ways for many parents. First, they end too soon. Most families don't want a 21-year-old to inherit everything at once, especially if the amount is significant. Second, these accounts can't be customized. You can't direct the funds to be used only for tuition, saved until the child buys a first home, or divided unevenly among siblings to reflect different needs. For that level of personalization, a living trust is almost always the better tool.

To better understand these rules, let's see two examples.

> ***Example 1:*** *Elias left his niece and nephew a block of company stock he had bought decades earlier. Over time, the value had grown dramatically. He named his brother, Martin, as custodian. When Elias died, Martin realized that if he simply held the stock until the children turned 25, each would receive well over $100,000 all at once, far more than Elias had ever anticipated. Guided by an estate attorney, Martin began gradually using the custodial funds for meaningful expenses: school activities, technology, tutoring, and summer programs. By the time the custodianship ended, the children still received money, but in an amount they could handle responsibly.*
>
> ***Example 2:*** *Serena, an eight-year-old, inherited her parents' estate and the proceeds of a life insurance policy. Her aunt, Maribel, was named custodian. She invested most of the funds in a balanced portfolio inside a custodial brokerage account, keeping a separate custodial bank account for everyday expenses, everything from school supplies to medical bills. Maribel worried that, as Serena approached 21, she might not be ready to manage whatever remained. But custodial rules are strict: once Serena reached the age defined by state law, the money became fully hers. All Maribel could do was offer guidance and hope Serena accepted it.*

Children's Trusts

When a gift to a child becomes more than pocket money, and especially when you want that gift to support their future rather than their impulses, a ***children's trust*** gives you the structure you need. Unlike custodial accounts, which end automatically and hand everything over at a fixed age, a trust lets you stretch guidance into the years when young adults are still finding their footing. It's a way of saying, "I want this money to help you grow, not overwhelm you."

At its heart, a trust is simply a set of instructions wrapped around a bucket of assets. You choose a ***trustee***, which is the adult who will step into your place and manage the money with the same blend of practicality and care that you would use yourself. Some people want the trustee to be extremely hands-on, approving every school bill or medical cost; others prefer a broader approach that allows the trustee to respond to real-life needs as they come up. Either style can work. The key is that the trustee always acts for the child's benefit and follows the road map you've provided.

Because life doesn't follow neat categories, trustees often have to exercise judgment. Maybe a teenager wants money for a "necessary" upgrade that is more about status than schoolwork. Or maybe a young adult is choosing between graduate school and a full-time job. A well-written trust gives the trustee enough flexibility to recognize the difference between a wise step forward and an impulse that could drain the funds too quickly.

Trusts can also protect beneficiaries who face adult challenges early on. If a beneficiary struggles with addiction, impulsive spending, or simply hasn't had much experience managing money, you can build guardrails into the trust itself. For example, you can authorize (or direct) the trustee to pay for certain expenses, such as housing, treatment, therapy, education, or basic living costs, while keeping the remaining funds invested. The key is that the trustee's power isn't unlimited; it comes from the standards you write into the trust, such as "health, education, maintenance, and support," specific permitted expenses, or staged distributions tied to milestones. In many families, this structure feels less like punishment and more like relief, a clear plan that protects the beneficiary while they get onto more stable ground.

Setting Up a Trust

A children's trust isn't something you set up and fund ahead of time. It only comes to life if you pass away while a child is still too young to handle the inheritance. Until that moment, it's just a set of instructions tucked safely inside your will or living trust, ready to be used if it's needed, but completely dormant while you're here and in charge. This timing can surprise people. If every beneficiary is already older than the "distribution age" when you pass away, there's no trust to manage at all. The assets go out directly, exactly as if the trust language were never used.

Here are two examples that show how that works:

> ***Example 1:*** *Monica and Eli want their daughter and son to receive their inheritances outright at age 28. When Monica dies, both children are already in their thirties. Because the age requirement has been met, the successor trustee distributes everything immediately, no trust is created, and no long-term management is needed.*
>
> ***Example 2:*** *Diego has three grandchildren. His plan says that anyone under 26 keeps their share in trust until they reach that age. When he passes away, one grandchild is 30, one is 24, and one is 19. The 30-year-old adult grandchild receives an outright distribution. The other two receive their distributions in trusts tailored to their ages and needs, and the trustee opens separate accounts for each one.*

Key Decisions You'll Need to Make

When you set up a trust, you're really answering four practical questions:

1. **Who will manage the money?**
   Your trustee should be someone steady, reliable, and fair, not necessarily wealthy or financially sophisticated. Many parents choose a sibling or close friend; for more complicated circumstances, some choose a professional.
2. **Will children share one pot or have separate slices?**
   A shared trust, sometimes called a "family pot," can be helpful while children are young because their needs may not be equal; one child may have higher medical costs, while another may need tutoring or childcare. As children grow, many parents prefer to divide the trust into separate shares so each child's long-term plans can unfold independently.
3. **How can the money be used?**
   Most families choose a broad standard such as *health, education, maintenance, and support*, which gives the trustee enough room to respond to real circumstances. Others add more tailored instructions, perhaps help with buying a first home, funding a study-abroad semester, or supporting a career transition. You're designing the guardrails that reflect your values.
4. **When does the trust end?**
   This is one of the most personal decisions. Some parents choose a single age, like 28 or 30, when everything is handed over. Others spread it out, releasing portions over several milestones. What matters is choosing an age when you believe the beneficiary will have enough maturity to use the assets to build a stable adult life.

What Trustees Actually Do

Understanding the trustee's role helps you choose wisely. A trustee's primary obligation is loyalty and managing the trust solely for the beneficiaries' benefit. They must invest and spend prudently, avoid conflicts of interest, and keep trustworthy records.

Being fair doesn't always mean treating everyone identically. Suppose you set up a single trust for three children. If one child develops a chronic illness and the trust permits medical support, the trustee can pay for treatment, even if that reduces the amount available to the others. Fairness means meeting needs according to the rules you've set, not pretending every situation is the same.

Trustees also have strict boundaries. They can't use trust money for themselves, live rent-free in trust property unless you explicitly allow it, or steer investments toward their own businesses. Their role is to act as a steward, not a beneficiary, and act in the best interests of the beneficiaries.

The ***Uniform Prudent Investor Act***, which nearly every state follows, gives trustees a road map for investing: look at the portfolio as a whole, balance risk and reward, and choose investments that match the trust's purpose. So a trustee could hold some growth-oriented stocks as long as the overall portfolio remains balanced and appropriate.

Taxes and Annual Reports

Every **irrevocable** trust generally has to file its own tax returns with the IRS (and often the state) each year. A **revocable living trust** typically does **not** file a separate return while the person who created it is alive; instead, the trust's income is usually reported on that person's individual tax return. Trust taxation follows slightly different rules than personal taxes, particularly when it comes to capital gains, so many trustees hire accountants who specialize in fiduciary accounting to keep the numbers clean and compliant.

Most states also require trustees to provide periodic updates to the beneficiaries (or their guardians). These updates can be simple or formal depending on the trust's terms and state law, but they should clearly show how the trust is being managed.

Trustee Compensation

While trustees are often entitled to reasonable compensation, the standard may be set by the trust document, state law, or court review. Many family members choose not to take payment unless the work becomes substantial. If they do accept compensation, it's often based on an hourly rate or a fee schedule (sometimes a small percentage of trust assets), similar to what professional trustees charge.

Whatever approach is taken, transparency is crucial. Trustees should be prepared to explain their fees and show that they reflect real work performed, and it can help to disclose the fee arrangement to beneficiaries in advance when possible. Overcharging, or even the appearance of overcharging, can lead to friction or legal challenges, so careful documentation protects everyone.

Naming a Trustee

Choosing someone to manage money for a child is a very personal decision. The good news is that it's rarely a complicated one. Most people already know, almost instinctively, who in their life is both **steady with responsibility** and **sensible with money**. That person is usually a natural fit for the role of ***trustee***, which is the adult who steps in to handle the funds held in a **children's trust**.

Sometimes the right person is the same adult you've chosen to raise your children if you die while they're still young. Many parents feel comfortable keeping those roles together because that's how they manage things in real life: one person caring for the children and their finances. But it's just as common to split the responsibilities. Maybe one sibling is wonderful with kids, while another is great with spreadsheets. Or maybe you want both sides of the family to stay connected if something happens to you. These are all perfectly valid reasons to separate the roles of the trustee.

> **Example:** *Imagine a couple, Nora and Will. They want Will's brother, Sam, to raise their kids if needed because he already spends every other weekend helping with soccer carpools. But when it comes to handling money, Nora's cousin, Elise, is the clear choice. She works in finance and has always been*

the "family organizer." Nora and Will decide that Sam should handle the parenting and Elise should manage the trust. The two get along well, and everyone knows exactly what their role would be.

This kind of division works beautifully **as long as the trustee and guardian can communicate openly**. If the guardian asks for money to cover private school or summer tuition and the trustee doesn't believe that expense fits the trust's rules, the trustee's decision controls. That balance of power is intentional; the trustee's job is to follow the instructions you leave, even if others disagree.

When Beneficiaries Are Already Adults

Even when the people you're leaving money to are legally adults, you may still want to provide some supervision. Turning 18, or even 25, doesn't magically give someone the skills to manage an inheritance. If you want the money protected until a later age, a **trust** is the only tool that lets you stretch that supervision beyond the limits of a custodial account.

Example: *Jonas wants to leave a gift to his partner's two college-aged kids. They're smart and responsible, but still figuring out adulthood. Jonas leaves each of them a modest inheritance, but he asks that their trustee hold onto the money until they turn 30. During that time, the funds can only be used for things that genuinely move their lives forward, such as graduate school, medical needs, or certifications that help them launch a career.*

That structure gives the kids room to grow without dumping too much responsibility into their laps too soon.

What About Co-trustees?

Families sometimes think it's safer to appoint two trustees to share the job. On paper, it sounds balanced: two perspectives, two sets of eyes, no one making decisions alone. In practice, it can be tricky.

Two trustees often must agree before anything major happens, including investments, withdrawals, and big decisions. If both trustees genuinely trust and respect each other, this can work smoothly. But if there's tension, or if one person tends to move faster or slower than the other, even everyday tasks can start to drag. And if they truly can't agree, the trust may end up stuck. Some trusts solve this by building in a tie-breaker or dispute-resolution mechanism (for example, giving one trustee final say in limited areas, naming a neutral third party to break deadlocks, or allowing replacement of a trustee), but if there's no workable solution, a court petition may be the only backstop, which is exactly the kind of headache a well-designed estate plan tries to avoid.

There's also a practical side: getting two signatures on the same paperwork can be a hassle, especially if they live in different cities. Some documents even require notarization, which can add extra friction.

None of this means co-trustees can't work. They just work best when the two people already have a strong, easy relationship and a similar approach to money and decision-making.

Should a Sibling Be the Trustee?

Parents often assume the oldest child should "step in" as trustee for younger siblings. While this works for some families, it often creates tension.

Picture a teenager asking her older brother, now trustee, for money to start a small business. If he says, "No," even for a perfectly good reason, it feels personal, not procedural. No matter how carefully he tries to be fair, disagreement can turn into a sibling argument rather than a trustee decision.

That's why many estate planners recommend choosing someone outside the group of future beneficiaries when possible.

What About Grandparents as Trustees?

Grandparents are loving and devoted, but trusteeship is a long-term role. If your child is three years old today and the trust lasts until they're 30, the trustee must be able to serve for nearly three decades.

If your preferred trustee is elderly, you can still name them, but be sure to name a younger successor. Your plan should work even if the first trustee steps aside either voluntarily or involuntarily.

And remember, your choice isn't permanent. Life changes, and so can your estate plan. If someone you've named goes through a major shift, health issues, divorce, or relocation, you can update your trustee list at any time.

If Your Family Is Complicated, Get Advice Early

Every family has its dynamics. Some are calm and cooperative; others have long-standing tensions or very different personalities. If you sense that choosing a trustee might stir up conflict, or if your estate includes complicated assets, such as a family business, it's wise to ask an estate-planning attorney for guidance. A solid plan can prevent misunderstandings, resentment, or even lawsuits later on.

A trustee who is careless, overwhelmed, or perceived as "playing favorites" can unintentionally cause lasting damage in a family. The reverse is also true: the right trustee can help preserve relationships by making decisions transparent and fair.

Professional Trustees

Some families decide that the most reliable choice is a *professional trustee*, which can be a trust officer at a bank, a private fiduciary, or a financial institution that handles trusts full-time.

Professionals bring experience, objectivity, and financial skill. They're also helpful when family relationships are strained or when you're leaving behind investments that require careful oversight. Because trustees are paid for their work, they treat the trust like a real ongoing responsibility, not a favor squeezed between their own work and family life.

Fees vary, but most professionals charge a percentage of the assets they manage, often somewhere around 0.75%–1.25% per year. Larger trusts usually come with lower percentage fees (but naturally higher dollar amounts). Some institutions only accept trusts above a certain size, so it's worth asking about minimums.

Still, professional trustees aren't perfect for every family. They may not have the personal insight needed for sensitive decisions, like whether a young adult is ready to handle a lump sum or should stick to getting support in smaller steps. And financial institutions can merge, move, or consolidate departments, which can make the relationship feel less personal over time.

If you're considering a professional trustee, a short conversation can tell you a lot about whether they're a good fit. You don't need a formal interview; just cover a few practical points:

- **Minimum requirements:** Ask whether the firm has a minimum trust size before they accept the role.
- **Fees and structure:** Clarify their annual fee, how it's calculated, and what the cost would look like for a trust roughly the size you expect.
- **Investment approach:** Have them describe their general strategy and how they balance risk and return for long-term beneficiaries.
- **Past performance:** You can ask for a broad sense of how their trust portfolios have performed over recent years compared with typical market benchmarks.
- **Communication:** Find out how beneficiaries will receive updates, quarterly statements, online dashboards, or something else, and ask to see a sample.
- **Who handles the account:** Confirm whether you'll be dealing with a local manager or a regional office.
- **References:** If you want insight from real clients, ask whether they can connect you with a few people who've worked with their trust department.

Structure the Trust

Now that you've chosen a *trustee*, the person who will actually run things, the next question is how you want to structure the trust itself. If you're planning for more than one child, you essentially have two choices: keep everything together in one shared arrangement or divide the money into individual pieces from the start.

Pooled Trust

A **pooled trust** (informally called a "pot trust") works a bit like a shared family budget managed by the trustee. Everything goes into one pot, and the trustee uses the money for whichever child needs it most at any given time. If your children are close in age and likely to hit major milestones around the same period, this structure can feel very natural.

> **Example:** *Imagine one child needs orthodontic treatment that insurance won't cover, and two years later, a sibling gets accepted to a specialized school with higher tuition. With a shared fund, the trustee can simply support each child when those expenses arise, without worrying about keeping each child's balance perfectly even. When the trust eventually ends, whatever is left is divided equally among the beneficiaries.*

This is a flexible approach, but it's not for every family. If a parent feels anxious that early expenses for an older child might drain the pot and leave a younger child with very little, then separate trusts tend to offer more peace of mind.

> **Example:** *Leila and Marcus set up a pot trust for their three kids, ages 4, 6, and 8. They choose Marcus's brother, Trey, as trustee, and tell him to use the funds for the children's health, education, and support. Each child will receive a $15,000 distribution after college, but the trust won't fully end until the youngest turns 27. By that time, the oldest will be in her early thirties, but all three will share equally in whatever remains. The structure lets Trey focus on the children's real needs, not on keeping a spreadsheet perfectly symmetrical.*

Create Separate Trusts

Separate trusts work well when the children are **far apart in age** or when you want each child's ultimate inheritance to reflect their own choices, such as the cost of their education or the timing of major life events.

With individual accounts, a trustee doesn't have to juggle competing requests. Each child has a clear starting balance and a clear spending rhythm. An older child can head off to college knowing exactly how much support they have. Younger siblings won't worry that someone else is "using up" their share.

> **Example:** *Samira and Devin have four children between the ages of 3 and 14. They decide that when the second parent dies, the trust will split into four equal shares. The same trustee will manage each share, but distributions come only from the individual account tied to that child. Each child receives a small distribution at age 24 to start building financial habits, then gains full control at 28. This means the oldest will receive their funds long before the youngest is grown, but each child has a fair and predictable structure.*

How Long Should a Trust Last?

Deciding when a trust should end can feel surprisingly emotional. Parents of toddlers often picture calm, sensible future adults; parents of teenagers sometimes picture… something else entirely.

A helpful way to think about it is to look back at your own life: *At what age would you have been ready to manage a meaningful amount of money?* That age, whether it's 25, 30, or later, is usually a reasonable ending point for your children, too.

And yes, **trusts should end**. Unless a child has *special needs* or serious challenges like addiction or chronic debt issues, most young adults eventually want (and deserve) full ownership of their inheritance. Many beneficiaries do appreciate guidance, but few enjoy feeling financially tethered into their thirties without a good reason.

Giving Out Money Along the Way

Instead of making your children wait until the very end, you can build in **interim distributions**, small amounts released at certain ages or after certain milestones. These aren't mandatory gifts; they're confidence-building moments that let kids practice managing money while a trustee still oversees the rest.

For example, you might let each beneficiary access 20% of their trust at age 25, with the remaining 80% staying in the trustee's hands. If the first chunk gets blown on a disastrous business idea or a fast car, the rest of the inheritance is still safe.

In a pot trust, you can even restrict interim distributions for older kids until you're sure enough money remains to support the younger ones through school.

> ***Example:*** *Jordan and Mateo have two children, ages 7 and 9, and about $1.4 million in combined assets. They create a pot trust because the kids are close in age. They decide that each child should receive $10,000 at 22, 30% of what remains at 26, and full control at 32. This gives their kids time to grow into responsibility without handing everything over during the whirlwind of early adulthood.*

How Much Control Is Too Much?

One of the hardest parts of setting up a trust is resisting the urge to control every detail from beyond the grave. A trust *can* be packed with rigid instructions, but that doesn't mean it *should* be.

You can certainly share your hopes: maybe you'd love to see your niece pursue a science degree, or maybe you dream of your son avoiding high-risk investments. Those wishes can go into a **letter of intent**, which is a gentle, nonbinding document your trustee can read after your passing.

What you should avoid is forcing the trustee into inflexible rules that might not make sense years from now. Life changes. Markets change. Kids grow in unexpected directions. A trust that's too specific can trap your trustee into outdated conditions or require a costly court petition to fix it.

A better approach is to give your trustee **clear goals** and **room to use good judgment**. Let them decide whether supporting a wedding makes sense or whether helping with a down payment is wise for a particular child at a particular moment.

Trustees are there to make thoughtful, case-by-case decisions. Giving them the freedom to do that is the best gift you can build into your plan.

The Property Guardian

After thinking through trusts, custodial accounts, and all the different ways an adult can manage money for a child, there's one last piece worth putting in place: a safety net that hopefully never gets used, but smooths everything out if it does. That safety net is the **property guardian**.

A *property guardian* steps in only when a child ends up owning something that isn't already covered by your trust or custodial arrangement. Most parents never run into this situation, especially if their estate plan is tidy and everything funnels through the structure they chose. But life doesn't always follow the blueprint. A child might be named directly on a life insurance policy by a grandparent, for example, or receive stock from a relative who wasn't thinking about legal technicalities. When a minor receives property this way, and it's worth more than a token amount, a court appointment is often required to authorize an adult to manage it until the child becomes a legal adult. In some cases, though, the asset can be moved into a custodial (UTMA/UGMA) account or transferred into an existing trust, avoiding a formal guardianship.

Naming a property guardian in your will doesn't create extra paperwork today; it simply tells the court, "If this unlikely scenario happens, please start with this person." And because you've already put careful thought into who can responsibly handle your children's money, most people choose the same person they selected as **trustee** or **custodian**. Keeping these roles aligned keeps things simple for the family and avoids confusion if the court ever needs to get involved.

If the amount in question is small, the court may allow your executor to avoid a full guardianship and, instead, may appoint a custodian under your state's **Uniform Transfers to Minors Act**. But this is handled case-by-case, which is another reason it's wise to have a trusted name written down ahead of time.

A property guardian's job is more rigid than that of a trustee or custodian. Because the court is supervising, everything the property guardian does must be documented: a full inventory of the child's assets, detailed records of every expense, and formal reports to the court at regular intervals. Many guardians hire a lawyer to help with the filings. And yes, the cost of that legal help comes out of the child's own funds. For all these reasons, a property guardianship is really a **last resort**, not a primary plan, which is exactly why naming one, just in case, is so important.

> ***Example:*** *When Daniel passed away, he had arranged a custodial account for the life insurance money meant for his 11-year-old son, Cole. But he hadn't realized that Cole's grandmother had also named him directly on a retirement account without choosing an adult custodian. To handle that asset, Cole's aunt had to be formally appointed as property guardian until Cole became an adult. Everything Daniel had channeled through the custodial account ran smoothly, but the separate inheritance required court approval and reporting. A simple designation would have avoided that extra step.*

Pulling Everything Together

Once you've decided who will manage money for the children, and how that money will be held, your plan finally comes into focus. All these decisions flow straight into your will or living trust. This is where everything you've been working through earlier in the previous chapters starts to click into place.

Some people find it helpful to draft a short summary for themselves, listing:

- The money manager (trustee or custodian);
- The structure you've chosen (trust, custodianship, or both);
- The ages or milestones you want for access; and
- Your backup property guardian.

It's not a legal document but a personal reference that helps you communicate clearly with your lawyer or advisor when it's time to put everything into writing.

When You Don't Want Your Ex Handling the Money

If you're divorced or separated and uneasy about your former partner managing your children's inheritance, this is something you can plan around thoughtfully. If you leave no instructions at all, a judge will choose someone responsible, and that could very well be your ex.

If that idea makes you uncomfortable, the simplest solution is to ensure that **all money flows through a trust or custodial account** managed by someone you trust. You can also state in your will that you prefer your ex not to serve as property guardian, especially if you have concrete reasons (like unpaid child support or a history of financial recklessness). Just remember that wills become public documents, so any criticism written inside one can be read by anyone after your death.

If privacy matters, there's another way: a separate letter. For this, you address a confidential letter to your executor and explain, in more detail, why appointing your ex would be harmful. It stays private unless a dispute arises. If the issue goes to court, the letter can be presented as evidence. Some parents even set aside a small insurance policy to help cover any legal costs if the issue becomes contested.

Life Insurance

All these decisions, trusts, custodians, and guardians, work best when there's enough money available to support your children's needs. And this is where **life insurance** enters the picture. For many families, it becomes the engine that funds everything you've just planned.

If most of your wealth is tied up in a home or retirement accounts, it can be hard for your children to access that money quickly. Selling property takes time, and withdrawing retirement funds can create tax bills you can't avoid. Life insurance fills that gap by providing liquid cash relatively soon after death (once a claim is processed), often at exactly the moment your family needs it most.

Life insurance is essentially a contract: you pay a premium and, in return, the company promises to pay a death benefit to the people you choose. From the insurer's perspective, it's a statistical wager; they price the policy based on the likelihood that they'll have to pay out while it's active. That's why coverage is cheaper when you're young and healthy, and more expensive if you wait until later.

Buying a policy early lets you lock in a stable, lower premium, which can save thousands of dollars over the life of the contract.

> ***Example:*** *A 30-year-old might pay a few hundred dollars a year for the same coverage that could cost a 45-year-old more than twice as much. The risk profile changes, and the premium follows.*

Life insurance supports your plan in several important ways:

- **Liquidity when it's needed.** Your beneficiaries can often get cash **relatively quickly after a claim is processed**, without needing to sell property or tap retirement accounts.
- **Tax benefits.** Life insurance payouts are **generally** free of **income tax**.
- **Replacing income.** If you're the primary earner, the benefit can help your family stay afloat.
- **Childcare coverage.** Funds can pay for help at home so surviving partners can keep working.
- **Avoiding probate.** Policies usually pass directly to your named beneficiaries, bypassing the court process.
- **Supporting children with disabilities.** Benefits can be directed into a special needs trust to preserve eligibility for essential services.
- **Estate-tax planning.** In rare cases (mainly for very-high-net-worth families), life insurance is often used to **provide liquidity to pay an estate tax bill** and, in some plans, it may also be structured to help keep the death benefit out of the taxable estate.

For many families, life insurance becomes the backbone of the entire plan. It guarantees that the trust or custodianship you've created actually has the funding it was designed to manage.

Insurance Through Work

Many people receive life insurance through their employer, often one or two times their annual salary. It's a nice benefit, but temporary. If you leave the job or get laid off, the coverage disappears, and you'll be older (and therefore more expensive to insure) when you go to replace it. Work insurance is a great supplement, but rarely a reliable foundation.

Type of Policy

Once you've decided that ***life insurance*** needs to be part of your plan, the next question is what kind of policy makes sense for you. The answer depends mostly on two things: your stage of life and what, exactly, you want the insurance to do for your family.

Broadly, you're choosing between two families of policies:

- ***Term life insurance***, which covers you for a set number of years; and
- ***Permanent life insurance***, which is designed to last as long as you do, and often includes a built-in savings component.

Let's walk through both.

Term Life Insurance

Think of term ***life insurance*** as "pure" insurance. You pay a premium for a specific period: 10, 15, 20, or 30 years. If you die during that window, the company pays your beneficiaries the death benefit you chose. If you live past the end of the term, the coverage ends. There's no payout, no refund, no savings. You were paying for protection during those years, and that's exactly what you got.

Because term coverage doesn't try to be an investment, it's usually the most affordable way to buy a large amount of protection, especially if you're relatively young and healthy. Premiums are often level for the entire term (though some policies use increasing premiums), which means that buying earlier can let you lock in a lower price for many years.

Many term policies come with useful features. For example:

- Some are **renewable**, which means you can extend the coverage without a new medical exam (though at higher, age-based premiums); and
- Some are **convertible**, which means you can turn your term policy into a permanent one later on, switching from temporary coverage to lifelong coverage without restarting the medical underwriting process.

For families with young children, term insurance often fits perfectly. You can choose a term long enough to get the youngest child through school or into independent adulthood. After that, your priorities may shift. Instead of protecting young kids, you may be focused on supporting a spouse or evening out inheritances among adult children. Or you may find you don't need coverage at all.

> ***Example:*** *Mia and Oliver are in their mid-thirties with two kids, ages 4 and 7. Most of their money is in their home equity and retirement accounts; their emergency savings would cover only a few months of expenses. They decide they want enough insurance so that, if either of them dies, the surviving parent can stay in the house, keep the kids in the same schools, and cover basic living costs and college tuition.*

They choose 25-year term policies, long enough to get their youngest past college age. After talking with a financial planner, they settle on a $900,000 policy for Oliver and a $500,000 policy for Mia, based on their incomes and goals. The premiums fit within their budget, and they know that if nothing terrible happens during those 25 years, they'll have raised their kids and built up savings in other ways. At that point, they may not need life insurance anymore, and that's a good outcome.

Permanent Life Insurance

While term coverage is like renting protection for a period of years, ***permanent life insurance*** is meant to be more like owning it for life. As long as the premiums are paid, the policy stays in force. These policies often include an ***investment or savings component***, commonly called ***cash value***. Part of your premium pays for the insurance itself; part is set aside and invested by the company.

Over time, the cash value can grow. You may be able to:

- Borrow against it;
- Withdraw some of it (with tax consequences in some cases); or
- Surrender the policy entirely and receive a **surrender value**.

The trade-off is cost. Permanent policies are significantly more expensive than term coverage for the same death benefit, especially in the early years because you're not just buying insurance, but also a long-term savings plan.

Within permanent insurance, there are several variations:

- **Traditional whole life**: You pay fixed premiums and receive a guaranteed death benefit. Cash value builds over time in a predictable way.
- **Universal life**: This is more flexible. You can often adjust your premiums and death benefit, within limits, and the cash value fluctuates based on interest credits or market conditions.
- **Variable and variable universal life**: These allow you to allocate the cash value among investment options, such as mutual fund-like subaccounts. Your cash value (and sometimes your death benefit) can rise or fall with investment performance.
- **"Second-to-die" or last-survivor policies**: These insure two people, often spouses, and pay out only after the second person dies. These are typically used in very large estates to provide liquidity for estate taxes.
- **Single-premium policies**: Here, you pay one large lump sum up front instead of ongoing premiums.

Most families with young children don't need to wade deeply into all these variations. Permanent policies often make sense when:

- You want coverage that will be available long after your children are grown;
- You like the idea of enforced saving through your premiums;

- You are planning for someone, such as a child with special needs, who may need long-term support; or
- You expect **estate-tax liability** (or other significant settlement costs) and want life insurance to create **liquidity** so assets don't have to be sold quickly.

In these situations, a permanent policy, or a term policy with a strong conversion option, can be a powerful tool.

How Much Coverage Is Enough?

Once you have a sense of *what type* of policy you want, the next question is how large it should be. This is where most people feel overwhelmed because every advisor seems to have a different formula.

There isn't a single "right" number. The goal is simple: to provide enough support so your loved ones can live the kind of life you'd want for them if you couldn't be there, with a premium you can actually afford.

If the "ideal" amount feels out of reach, remember this: **some coverage is always better than none**. A family with a $400,000 policy is still in a far better position than a family with no policy at all.

Let's look at three common ways people estimate their needs.

Income Multiples

One quick method is the **income multiplier**. Under this method, you take your annual income and multiply it by a number, often somewhere between 6 and 10.

For example, if you earn $70,000 a year, this method would suggest between $420,000 and $700,000 in coverage.

This method is simple and better than guessing, but it has limits. It doesn't account for:

- Whether your current income is actually enough for your family's goals;
- How long you expect your loved ones to rely on that income replacement; or
- The value of a stay-at-home parent's work.

So it's a starting point, not the final word.

Online Calculators

A more tailored approach uses online life insurance calculators. These tools ask about your income, debts, savings, planned college expenses, and how many years you want to provide support. They then estimate how large a death benefit would be needed to bridge the gap between what you already have and what your family would need.

If you're curious, a few widely used calculators, like the ones offered by **NerdWallet**, **Policygenius**, or **Life Happens**, can give you quick, free estimates in just a few minutes. Each uses its own assumptions about inflation, investment returns, and spending patterns, which means the numbers you get won't always match. Two calculators using the same inputs can easily suggest different coverage ranges. Treat them as helpful guides, not final verdicts.

Looking at Your Real Life

The most practical method is also the most personal: step back and think carefully about your **actual lifestyle** and how it would change after a death.

Consider questions like:

- Would the surviving partner need childcare to keep working?
- Would it be important to pay off the mortgage to keep the family home?
- Are there particular goals, like finishing college or avoiding major debt, that matter deeply to you?
- Would a part-time worker need to move to full-time, or vice versa?

From there, you can estimate the monthly cost of the life you'd want your loved ones to have. Once you know roughly what it would cost, you can work backward to figure out how much invested capital would be needed to support that spending, and, therefore, how big an insurance policy should be.

Many financial planners want your beneficiaries to have enough invested money, after paying off key debts, that the income it produces can cover ongoing expenses without quickly draining the principal.

For instance, if a family has $60,000 in debt and monthly expenses of $4,500, they might want enough insurance so that, after debts are paid, the remaining funds can be invested to generate at least $54,000 a year (roughly $4,500 per month). The exact numbers will vary with assumed returns, but the logic is the same: design the benefit to fund a realistic, stable life.

When Special Needs Change the Math

If you have a **child with special needs**, life insurance planning becomes more delicate and more important.

Many adults with disabilities depend on government programs like Medicaid for essential care. Receiving a large inheritance directly can unintentionally disqualify them from those benefits, at least until the money is spent down. That's why planners often use a ***special needs trust*** to hold the inheritance and keep eligibility intact. The trust can then use funds to supplement benefits, paying for therapies, equipment, travel, or other quality-of-life expenses, without replacing the core support the government provides.

In this situation, the question, "How much insurance do I need?" shifts. General rules of thumb, like "ten times your income," are designed for children who will eventually support themselves. A child with significant disabilities may never reach that point, and your goal is to support them over an entire lifetime.

This can mean:

- Purchasing **more** coverage than you otherwise would for a child without special needs; and
- Favoring **permanent life insurance** rather than term life insurance, so the policy is still there when you die.

A term policy that ends in your seventies or eighties may leave your special needs child without the extra resources you intended, precisely when they still need support. A permanent policy, by contrast, is designed to pay out whenever death occurs, as long as premiums have been maintained or the policy is otherwise kept in force.

Chapter | 7 | Assessment Test

1. **Why does the chapter distinguish between a guardian and a person who manages a child's money?**

   a. Because the law requires the same person to serve in both roles
   b. Because caregiving and financial management involve different skills
   c. Because guardians cannot legally handle money
   d. Because courts prefer separate appointments

2. **Why can leaving money directly to a minor create unexpected court involvement?**

   a. Minors cannot legally own any property
   b. Banks refuse to hold accounts for children
   c. Courts may need to appoint a property guardian to manage the funds
   d. Taxes increase when beneficiaries are under 18

3. **What is the main purpose of delaying a child's access to inherited funds?**

   a. To reduce estate taxes
   b. To ensure the child earns the money first
   c. To protect assets until the child is mature enough to manage them
   d. To comply with federal law

4. **Which situation is generally best suited for a custodial account rather than a trust?**

   a. A large inheritance meant to last a lifetime
   b. A modest gift expected to be used before early adulthood
   c. Assets intended to be shared flexibly among siblings
   d. Planning for a child with special needs

5. **What is a key limitation of custodial accounts highlighted in the chapter?**

   a. They require annual court approval
   b. They are difficult for banks to administer
   c. They end at a state-set age, regardless of the child's readiness
   d. They cannot hold investment assets

6. **Why are trusts often preferred for larger inheritances to children?**

   a. Trusts eliminate income taxes
   b. Trusts allow customized timing and conditions for distributions
   c. Trusts are always cheaper than custodial accounts
   d. Trusts avoid the need to choose a trustee

7. **What role does a trustee primarily play in a children's trust?**

   a. Raising the child day to day
   b. Managing and distributing trust assets according to the instructions
   c. Supervising the guardian's parenting decisions
   d. Acting as a court-appointed official

8. **Why is a special needs trust often necessary for a child with disabilities?**

   a. To increase eligibility for government benefits
   b. To avoid filing tax returns
   c. To allow the child to control investments directly
   d. To preserve eligibility for needs-based government programs

9. **What is the main reason life insurance is often used to fund plans for children?**

   a. It provides quick liquidity when it's needed most
   b. It guarantees investment returns
   c. It replaces the need for trusts
   d. It avoids all estate taxes

10. **What is the primary function of naming a property guardian as a back-up?**

    a. To manage all trust assets
    b. To replace the child's personal guardian
    c. To step in if a child unexpectedly receives property outside the main plan
    d. To eliminate the need for beneficiary designations

Answers

1. **B** – Caregiving and financial management require different skills and can be separated.
2. **C** – Courts may need to appoint a property guardian to manage significant assets left directly to a minor.
3. **C** – Delaying access protects assets until the child is mature enough to manage them responsibly.
4. **B** – Custodial accounts work best for modest inheritances and simple situations.
5. **C** – Custodial accounts must end at a legally defined age, even if the child isn't ready.
6. **B** – Trusts allow tailored distribution rules based on age, milestones, or needs.
7. **B** – Trustees manage, invest, and distribute trust assets according to the plan.
8. **D** – Special needs trusts preserve eligibility for programs like Medicaid and SSI.
9. **A** – Life insurance provides quick liquidity to support children immediately after a death.
10. **C** – A property guardian serves as a safety net for assets that fall outside the main plan.

CHAPTER 8

Estate Planning for Blended Families

"Fairness is not about everyone getting the same thing. Fairness is about everyone getting what they need."

— **Rick Riordan,** *American author*

Creating an estate plan is never simple, but when your family includes children from previous relationships, shared assets, or a new partner, the choices become more layered. Many people call this a *blended family*, but what really matters is this: you and your partner are bringing past lives, responsibilities, and, often, children into a new household. That mix deserves a thoughtful plan.

Blended families often face challenges that aren't present in a first marriage with mutual children. For example, you may want to make sure your partner is cared for and still ensure that certain assets eventually pass to your own children. Or you might have much older kids from a first relationship and toddlers with your current partner. Some people enter a second marriage owning a home they've purchased themselves and want to keep that home from becoming joint property. Unmarried couples face an additional layer of tax and legal concerns that married couples simply don't have.

None of these issues are impossible to solve, but they *do* require clarity, honesty, and sometimes a willingness to talk about topics everyone would rather avoid.

Married couples in blended households are usually trying to solve two big questions:

1. **What do we each own individually, and what do we own together?** Before you can decide who inherits what, you need to understand whether

your assets are separate, jointly owned, or (in community property states) automatically considered shared property.

2. **How do we control what happens to our property after one spouse dies?** This is especially important when each partner wants their own children to inherit something, or when one spouse has significantly more assets. You can't direct assets you don't legally own, so the first step is identifying ownership clearly.

Unmarried couples, instead, face a different set of concerns, and the law gives them far fewer automatic protections. Estate planning usually focuses on:

- **How property will transfer when the first partner dies** (because unmarried couples don't get the same tax benefits or treatment, and assets don't pass automatically);
- **Who will care for any minor children,** and how money will be managed for them;
- **How to balance each partner's children from previous relationships**, especially if both partners want their own children protected while also supporting each other; and
- **Planning for incapacity**, including powers of attorney and healthcare directives, because unmarried partners often must show legal proof before they're allowed to access medical information or make urgent decisions for each other.

Who Owns What

When two people form a blended family, they rarely start from zero. Each partner brings a personal history with them, including children, past commitments, and often property acquired long before the current relationship began. That alone doesn't make estate planning harder, but it does mean something very simple: **you can't plan what you don't understand**. Before any couple in a blended family can decide how to leave their assets, they need a clear picture of **who currently owns what**, and **why**.

Many couples postpone these conversations because finances can feel awkward or emotionally loaded. But the truth is that clarifying ownership early is a gift to the relationship. It alleviates confusion, avoids resentment, and prevents survivors (and children) from being forced to reconstruct the couple's intentions during a stressful moment of crisis.

Understanding ownership also means recognizing that different states apply different default rules that automatically decide how property is classified unless you intentionally provide for a different rule.

Community Property vs. Common Law

As we have explained in other chapters, in community property states, anything acquired during marriage generally belongs equally to both spouses, except gifts or inheritances. That's true even if only one spouse earned the income, or if an investment account is titled in one name only. When one spouse dies, the surviving spouse keeps the half they already own, and only the deceased spouse's half is transferred at death. The deceased spouse's half can be left to whomever they choose through a will or trust.

Community Property States
Arizona · California · Idaho · Louisiana · Nevada · New Mexico · Texas · Washington · Wisconsin (Louisiana and Wisconsin use slightly different legal frameworks but reach similar results.)

Other states, such as Alaska, Tennessee, South Dakota, Kentucky, and Florida, allow couples to **opt into** community property through a special agreement or trust, but unless a couple takes that formal step, their assets remain classified under **common law rules**.

In **common law states**, ownership follows the name on the title. If the bank account is in only one spouse's name, it's that spouse's property. If the home is jointly titled, both own it. This sounds simple, but there's a twist: even though each spouse technically owns their own property, **most common law states protect surviving spouses** by giving them a statutory right to claim a portion of the estate if they're left out.

So while community property states split ownership up front, common law states create a safety net on the back end.

Either way, you can't give away property you don't fully own, and you must plan with these rules in mind.

Conversations About Ownership

For blended families, ownership isn't just a legal category. It influences almost everything:

- Whether children from prior relationships will inherit anything;
- Whether a surviving spouse can remain comfortably in the family home;
- How stepchildren and partners interact after a death; and
- Whether the surviving partner will have the financial stability you intend for them.

These conversations can feel personal, but having them while everyone is healthy and cooperative is far easier than forcing loved ones to figure things out under pressure.

Here are some of the topics couples commonly need to address:

1. "Which assets are separate, and which do we consider shared?"

Many couples assume they have a mutual understanding, until they suddenly discover they don't. If you're unsure how to classify an asset, or if your views differ, a family law attorney can help clarify the rules in your state.

2. "How do we balance the needs of children from earlier relationships?"

You may want to support your spouse during their lifetime *and* ensure your own children receive an eventual inheritance. That can require careful structuring, sometimes even additional life insurance, to ensure that both goals are achievable without creating conflict.

3. "What happens to the house when one partner dies?"

This is one of the biggest stress points for blended families. Will the surviving partner live there for life? Will children need to sell the house to inherit? Can the survivor afford taxes, repairs, and mortgage payments? Clarity here prevents difficult and emotional disputes later.

4. "How should personal items be handled?"

Some personal items like furniture, artwork, family heirlooms, collections, and jewelry often carry more emotional weight than financial weight. Leaving informal expectations about these items is a recipe for tension. Written lists or trust instructions can spare the survivor from awkward conversations and prevent misunderstandings with adult stepchildren.

5. "Who should be named as beneficiaries on retirement accounts and insurance?"

These designations override your will. And in most states, a spouse must consent if you name someone else, which matters enormously if you want to leave assets directly to children from a previous marriage.

None of these topics should be rushed. Couples who work as a team will do well to treat these conversations as part of planning their future, rather than something grim or transactional.

Property Agreements

For couples, especially blended families, default ownership rules don't always reflect what they want. Fortunately, the law allows couples to rewrite the rules if they wish.

A **premarital agreement** (signed before marriage) or **postmarital agreement** (signed after marriage) can:

- Define which assets belong to whom;
- Prevent disputes about ownership after a death;
- Waive certain inheritance rights;
- Specify that certain assets stay in one person's family; and
- Reduce friction between stepchildren and a surviving spouse.

The agreements don't need to be complicated, but they **must** be clear, written, and consistent with state requirements. Each partner should always have the chance to consult their own attorney. After all, once an agreement is signed, you're legally bound by it.

When there is *no* written agreement:

- A spouse may claim statutory inheritance rights you didn't intend;
- Adult children may assert community property claims after one parent dies;
- The nature of property may be challenged during probate; and
- Families may face expensive legal disputes simply to clarify ownership.

With a written agreement:

- Ownership is clear;
- Beneficiaries know what to expect;
- The estate plan is easier to administer; and
- Emotional conflict is greatly reduced.

Example 1: Clarifying Ownership to Prevent Future Claims

Evan and Priya married later in life. Priya had a daughter from her first marriage, and Evan brought both a home and an investment account into the relationship. They lived in a community-property state. Over time, Evan continued contributing to his investment account, and the couple paid off the home's remaining mortgage.

Evan wanted Priya to inherit everything when he passed, but he worried that if Priya died first, her daughter might argue that part of the house or account belonged to Priya as community property, giving the daughter a legal claim.

To avoid this, Evan and Priya signed a simple written agreement confirming that the home and investment account were Evan's separate property. Their lawyers reviewed it, and the document was signed without conflict. Now, Evan can leave everything to Priya without worrying she'll unintentionally pass some of it to her daughter.

Example 2: Different State, Different Problem

Imagine the same couple living instead in a common-law state. Because titles control ownership there, the house and the investment account, both held in Evan's name, are considered entirely his. Priya's daughter has no rights to those assets unless Priya inherits them first.

If Evan's will tries to leave Priya nothing, state law won't let a surviving spouse be cut out entirely. Priya could still claim the state-mandated portion of Evan's estate, known as the statutory or elective share.

If Evan genuinely wants full freedom to leave all his property to someone else, such as his siblings or adult children, he and Priya would need to sign a written agreement in which Priya voluntarily waives her right to that statutory share. Without that agreement, Evan cannot completely disinherit her, even if everything is in his name.

Example 3: Protecting Property That Runs in the Family

Sandra inherited a cabin that had been passed down her family line for nearly a century. She and her husband, Leo, used the rental income for their shared expenses, but Sandra wanted absolute certainty that the cabin would stay in her family.

They signed a short agreement confirming the cabin, along with its income, would always be Sandra's separate property. Sandra's estate plan leaves the cabin to her children from a prior relationship, while other shared assets go to Leo. There's no ambiguity, no guesswork, and no tension about who will inherit what.

When Couples Aren't Married

Couples who live together without marrying *avoid* the legal presumptions of community or marital property; each partner owns what is in their own name. That simplifies ownership but doesn't eliminate planning needs. Unmarried partners still must decide:

- How to protect each other financially;
- What happens to shared property (especially real estate);
- How to support each partner's children from previous relationships;
- What rights the survivor has to live in the shared home; and
- Who will act financially or medically if one partner becomes incapacitated.

A well-written will or trust becomes essential here because unmarried partners **do not** inherit automatically.

Example 1: *Two partners, Maya and Rowan, each have children from earlier marriages. They own a home together and keep the rest of their finances separate. Their estate plans give each other the right to use the shared assets for life, but eventually the property returns to their respective children. Even without a marital bond, they used planning tools to ensure stability for each other and fairness for their families.*

Example 2: *Jon owns his home outright but lives there with his partner, Elise. Jon wants Elise to continue living in the home after he dies but eventually wants his children to receive it. His trust gives Elise the right to stay in the home for as long as she chooses, and he uses a life insurance policy to cover future taxes and upkeep so that she won't be burdened financially. When Elise no longer needs the house, Jon's children will inherit it without conflict.*

Planning the Estate in Blended Families

Once you look at how your family is set up today, the next step is building an estate plan that truly works for your situation. For blended families, that usually means building something that looks after a surviving partner **and** still stays true with children from earlier relationships.

The specific tools can vary a bit depending on where you live and how your assets are owned, but underneath all the legal language, you're mostly solving the same puzzle:

How do we take care of the person who's still here?

How do we make sure everyone else is treated fairly when they're gone too?

A big part of those answers, especially for couples with kids from prior relationships, is some form of ***irrevocable trust*** holding the first partner's share after they die. That sounds heavy, but in practice it's simply a way to say: *"My spouse or partner can use my money while they're alive, but they can't rewrite where it goes after they're gone."*

Whether you and your partner share one trust or each have your own, the core decisions are surprisingly similar. You'll need to work through four big questions:

1. Who steps in as ***successor trustee*** when one or both of you are gone or no longer able to manage things?
2. What happens in the trust at the **first** partner's death; how is the money split and what rules apply to the survivor?
3. What happens at the **second** partner's death; who actually inherits, in what proportions, and from which "bucket"?
4. How do your **beneficiary designations** (on retirement accounts, life insurance, and so on) line up with the plan in your will or trust?

Once those four pieces fit together, you usually have a solid framework. The rest is fine-tuning.

Successor Trustee

For blended families, choosing a ***successor trustee*** is often more delicate than choosing beneficiaries. You're not just picking who gets what, you're choosing who will act as the liaison to people who may already have mixed feelings about each other.

Many couples assume the surviving spouse or partner will act as trustee after the first death, and in most cases that makes sense. If your assets are being held in trust for your partner's benefit, it's natural (and emotionally kinder) for that person to control their own day-to-day finances rather than having a stepchild sign off on every decision.

The real pressure point usually comes *after both partners are gone*. That's when the children, stepchildren, or other beneficiaries deal directly with one another, and with whomever you've picked to manage and distribute what's left.

It's tempting to choose trustees for emotional reasons ("We don't want to hurt anyone's feelings"), but it's much smarter to think in practical terms:

- *Who is calm under stress?*
- *Who is reasonably organized with money?*
- *Who can speak plainly without attacking or withdrawing?*
- *Who is least likely to stir up old rivalries?*

If the honest answer is "None of the kids," it's better to recognize that now and consider a neutral ***professional trustee*** (like a private fiduciary or a bank's trust department) than to hand such a legally powerful role to an unsuitable trustee.

Example 1: One child from each side

Imagine Irene and Martin, who marry in their late fifties. Irene has two adult sons; Martin has an adult daughter. The three "kids" are polite but distant. Irene and Martin agree that each side of the family should feel represented when their estate is settled.

In their trust, they name Irene's older son and Martin's daughter as **co-trustees** *once both parents have died, and they specifically say that important decisions must be made by agreement. Before signing, they sit down with all three children and explain the plan: no one is being favored, and no one child has sole power. The kids may never vacation together, but at least everyone understands the rules.*

Example 2: Keeping things separate

Now picture Carl and Naomi. They each have two teenagers from prior relationships and live in a community-property state, but they have chosen to keep their finances separate. Each owns their own house, their own savings, and their own retirement accounts.

Their estate plan mirrors that separation. Carl names his brother and cousin as successor trustees for his trust; Naomi names a close friend and her sister for hers. They also sign a written property agreement confirming that what each brought into the relationship and what each accumulates in their own name stay separate. The goal isn't emotional distance; it's clarity. Each set of children inherits from their own parent, without needing to untangle mixed-up property later.

Example 3: When a neutral trustee is kinder

Sometimes the challenge isn't the structure of the family, it's one strong personality within it.

Take Linda, who has three adult children from a first marriage, and her husband, Patrick, with two daughters from his previous marriage. They create a single joint trust because almost all of their major assets are now jointly owned. Linda's oldest son, Eric, has a long history of conflict with everyone; he feels overlooked, resents his stepfather, and often presses his siblings for money.

Linda and Patrick realize that if Eric is ever given authority over the shared pot of family assets, he could make life miserable for everyone else. So instead of naming any of the five children as successor trustee, they hire a ***professional fiduciary*** *to take over after they both die. The professional will still have to deal with Eric, but will do so with legal training, insurance, and a duty to follow the trust's written instructions, not family politics.*

The Importance of an Irrevocable Trust

When a blended couple wants to provide for each other *and* make sure their own children eventually inherit their share, some form of ***irrevocable trust*** almost always appears in the design.

Think of it this way:

- While you're both alive, you usually keep a ***revocable living trust*** that you control together (or two revocable trusts if your property is separate). You can amend, restate, or revoke those documents whenever you agree to do so.
- At the first partner's death, the plan usually splits the money into at least two "buckets." One bucket stays revocable and fully under the survivor's control. The other bucket, funded with the first partner's share, locks into an irrevocable trust for the survivor's benefit. The survivor can *use* the assets, but can't change who will inherit them later.

Lawyers often label the deceased partner's bucket a ***bypass trust*** or "credit-shelter trust" and the survivor's bucket the ***survivor's trust*** or "A trust." The names matter less than the idea: your share is protected for your chosen heirs, while still available to support the person you love.

In a joint trust, this split happens inside that one document. In separate trusts, it happens inside the deceased partner's own trust document.

Let's look at some examples.

Example: *Owen and Lila each have children from prior marriages, two sons for him, one daughter for her. Together they've bought a home and combined most of their finances. They create a joint trust.*

Their plan says:

- *While both are alive, everything in the trust is available for their shared use.*
- *When one of them dies, the trust is divided. The surviving partner's half goes into a* ***survivor's trust*** *that the survivor can change or even leave entirely to charity if they want.*

- *The deceased partner's half goes into an* ***irrevocable trust*** *for the survivor's lifetime benefit. The survivor can use this money for* ***health, education, maintenance, and support****, but can't change the ultimate beneficiaries.*
- *When the survivor later dies, Owen's half goes to his sons and Lila's half goes to her daughter.*

For many blended couples, that structure feels like a balanced promise: "I'll make sure you're okay while you're here, and I'll make sure my kids are okay when we're both gone."

Taxes

Historically, these two-trust or three-trust plans were often written primarily to reduce federal estate tax. The logic was tax-driven: use the first spouse's ***estate tax exemption*** to fill a bypass trust, then use the ***marital deduction*** and a ***marital trust*** to defer any remaining tax until the second death.

Today, for most families, tax is *not* the main reason to use this structure. The federal estate and gift tax exemption is very high, about **$15 million per person in 2026**, or **$30 million for a married couple.** However, fewer than 1% of estates are expected to pay federal estate tax under current law.

So for a blended family of ordinary means, the real benefit of the "two-bucket" structure isn't tax savings; it's **control and clarity**. The first spouse's share is available to the survivor but can't be redirected away from the first spouse's children or other chosen heirs.

When an Irrevocable Trust Feels Like Mistrust

It's very common for the partner who didn't suggest using an irrevocable trust to feel a little stung at first. People in long second marriages often wonder, *"If my spouse loves and trusts me, why not just leave everything to me outright? Why put half of it in a trust that I can't change?"*

But the real issue usually isn't trust in the personal sense. It's the pressure that can fall on a surviving spouse or partner after the first one dies.

Without an irrevocable structure, the survivor can get caught between their own needs and the expectations of adult stepchildren:

"Mom would have wanted you to help me with a down payment."

"Dad promised this business would be mine."

"You're spending too much of our inheritance."

When the deceased partner's share is held in an irrevocable trust, the surviving spouse has a clear, truthful boundary to rely on:

"This is your parent's trust. I can use it for my support, but I'm not allowed to give out early inheritances or change who eventually receives it."

In practice, the structure becomes a **shield**, not a statement of doubt. It protects the survivor from being pressured or guilted, and it reassures the children that their parent's wishes will be honored without putting the surviving spouse in an impossible position. By using an irrevocable trust, you are not "locking away" money from your spouse; you are providing them with a legal shield. It allows the survivor to say to a persistent heir, "I cannot give you an advance because the trust terms don't allow it," preserving both the money and the family relationship.

Even in blended families that feel close and cooperative while both adults are alive, dynamics can change sharply after the first parent dies. Sometimes grief pulls people together; sometimes it cracks old fault lines wide open.

> ***Example:*** *Imagine a couple, Jonah and Elise, each of whom bring children from prior marriages into what seems like a happy combined family. When they set up their estate plan, they decided to be generous and simple: they split everything equally among all five children from both sides in* ***both*** *of their trusts. They also build in the two-bucket structure at the first death, more from habit than concern.*

Years later, Elise dies. In the months that follow, her three children start to feel protective of "their" mother's things. They pressure Jonah for keepsakes, argue over furniture, and insist on seeing account statements. Hurt and overwhelmed, Jonah eventually revises ***his*** *survivor's trust to leave his remaining assets only to his two daughters.*

Because of the way their plan was drafted, Jonah is free to do this. The irrevocable trust funded with Elise's share will still pass equally to all five children, just as she wanted. Jonah's own assets will pass only to his daughters, reflecting the reality of how relationships evolved after Elise's death.

Adding or Limiting Restrictions on the Survivor

Most blended-family plans give the surviving spouse or partner broad access to the deceased partner's irrevocable trust for **health, education, maintenance, and support**. Those four words are not accidental; they're a standard way to give meaningful access while avoiding tax problems.

Some couples, though, want tighter boundaries. For example, they might say that the surviving partner:

- Can live in the family home but **cannot** sell it and move to a more expensive property using trust funds;
- Can spend income freely but can touch the principal only for uninsured medical expenses; or
- Can use trust funds for normal living costs but not for major gifts to new partners or unrelated people.

These kinds of limits are possible, but each one is a trade-off between protecting children's future inheritance and giving the survivor enough flexibility to respond to real life.

Unmarried Couples

Unmarried couples with children from prior relationships face many of the *same* questions, just with slightly different legal mechanics.

Because unmarried partners don't get the automatic rights that spouses do, each person typically has their own **revocable living trust**, their own will, and their own set of beneficiary designations. When the first partner dies, their trust can:

- Hold that person's assets in an **irrevocable trust** for the surviving partner's lifetime;
- Allow the survivor to use those assets under clear rules; and
- Guarantee that, after the survivor dies, whatever is left goes to the first partner's children or other chosen beneficiaries.

The surviving partner's own trust stays revocable and changeable for as long as that person is alive and competent, just as with married survivors.

The main difference shows up at higher wealth levels. When one spouse dies, transfers to a **U.S.-citizen** surviving spouse generally qualify for the **unlimited marital deduction**, so federal estate tax is typically deferred at the first death.

For an **unmarried** partner, there is **no marital deduction**. The estate's taxable amount is calculated based on the estate as a whole, and federal estate tax is owed only to the extent the estate exceeds the **federal estate tax exclusion** for that year. In 2026, that basic exclusion amount is **$15,000,000** per person.

For almost all couples, that number is so high that federal tax is not the driving factor. The real question is still:

"How do I support my partner if I die first and still make sure my own kids or chosen heirs ultimately receive what I intended for them?"

For that, the same two-bucket model works very well: one **irrevocable** bucket for the deceased partner's share, guiding it to their children; one **revocable** bucket for the survivor's own property, fully under their control.

Planning for Children of Different Ages

When a blended family starts putting an estate plan together, one of the first challenges is figuring out **when** each child should receive an inheritance. And the truth is that not all children are in the same place in life.

Some may be adults with jobs, rent, and bills. Others may still be in elementary school and completely dependent on the surviving parent. Because of that, treating everyone exactly the same **at the same moment** doesn't always make sense.

This has nothing to do with loving one child more than another; it's simply about recognizing that a 28-year-old and a 6-year-old don't need the same things right now.

Imagine a parent with adult children from a previous relationship and much younger children with a new partner. If that parent dies first, the adult children might have to wait decades before receiving anything, especially if the surviving partner is young and expected to live many more years.

The parent may feel that this long delay is unfair. At the same time, the younger children still need to be raised, educated, and supported. So the solution can't be "give everything now," nor can it be "everyone waits forever."

A common way to handle this is to **split the timing**, not the family. The plan usually works like this:

- **Adult children receive something right away** when their parent dies, often a modest share or a specific account.
- **The rest of the assets stay in a trust** for the surviving partner, who uses them to run the household and take care of the younger children.
- **Whatever remains after the surviving partner dies** then goes to the younger children.

This approach gives the older kids a timely inheritance without putting the surviving partner in a financial bind.

There are two very practical ways families make this timing work smoothly:

- **Beneficiary designations**

  A parent can choose to send a particular asset, like a bank account, brokerage account, or retirement plan, directly to their older children. Meanwhile, the home, savings, and daily-use assets stay with the surviving partner, usually inside a trust.

- **Specific gifts**

  A parent can also use specific gifts to make sure certain people receive a defined amount or a particular item. For example, "If I die first, my children receive $____," or "When Jan dies, she leaves all of her jewelry to her daughter, Dena." This can provide clarity and reduce conflict over sentimental property.

- **Life insurance**

  Some families prefer life insurance because it keeps everything clean and uncomplicated. The adult children receive the insurance payout immediately, while the surviving spouse keeps the rest of the estate to raise the younger kids.

With this setup, everyone is included, but in a way that matches each child's stage of life and avoids financial strain on the survivor.

Chapter | 8 | Assessment Test

1. **Why is estate planning often more complex for blended families than for first marriages with shared children?**

   a. Because estate tax rules are stricter
   b. Because blended families usually own more property
   c. Because partners bring prior children, assets, and obligations into the relationship
   d. Because courts supervise blended-family estates more closely

2. **Why must couples clearly understand who owns what before making inheritance decisions?**

   a. Because ownership determines which assets can legally be given away
   b. Because courts automatically equalize ownership
   c. Because beneficiary designations override ownership rules
   d. Because ownership changes automatically at death

3. **In community-property states, what generally happens to community property at the death of one spouse?**

   a. All of it passes to the surviving spouse
   b. Half belongs to the survivor; the other half can be directed by the deceased spouse
   c. It is divided equally among children
   d. It automatically goes into probate

4. **What protection do common-law states typically provide to a surviving spouse?**

   a. Automatic ownership of all marital assets
   b. A statutory share that cannot be eliminated without agreement
   c. Guaranteed control of the family home
   d. Priority over all children as beneficiaries

5. **What is a primary benefit of premarital or postmarital property agreements for blended families?**

   a. They eliminate the need for a will
   b. They reduce federal estate taxes

c. They clarify ownership and reduce future disputes
d. They override beneficiary designations

6. **Why do unmarried couples need more deliberate estate planning?**
   a. Because unmarried partners inherit automatically
   b. Because tax exemptions are lower
   c. Because default legal protections for partners are limited
   d. Because trusts are unavailable to them

7. **What is the core purpose of using an irrevocable trust at the first partner's death in blended-family planning?**
   a. To reduce probate costs
   b. To prevent the survivor from using any assets
   c. To lock in who will ultimately inherit the deceased partner's share
   d. To eliminate income taxes

8. **Why can an irrevocable trust actually *protect* the surviving spouse emotionally?**
   a. It increases the survivor's legal authority
   b. It shields the survivor from pressure by stepchildren
   c. It avoids filing tax returns
   d. It prevents court involvement entirely

9. **When choosing a successor trustee in a blended family, what quality is most important?**
   a. Emotional closeness to the children
   b. Equal representation of both sides
   c. Practical judgment and ability to manage conflict
   d. Geographic proximity to beneficiaries

10. **How can life insurance help balance the needs of adult children and a surviving partner?**
    a. By avoiding probate
    b. By replacing the need for trusts
    c. By equalizing tax treatment
    d. By providing immediate funds to some beneficiaries while preserving assets for others.

Answers

1. **C** – Blended families combine prior children, assets, and responsibilities that require careful coordination.
2. **A** – You cannot direct assets you don't legally own.
3. **B** – Half belongs to the survivor; the deceased spouse controls the other half.
4. **B** – Most common-law states give surviving spouses a statutory share unless waived.
5. **C** – Written agreements clarify ownership and reduce conflict.
6. **C** – Unmarried partners receive few automatic legal protections.
7. **C** – The irrevocable trust preserves the deceased partner's inheritance wishes.
8. **B** – The structure gives the survivor a clear boundary against pressure or guilt.
9. **C** – Calm judgment and conflict management matter more than emotional ties.
10. **D** – Life insurance provides liquidity that can satisfy some heirs without straining the survivor.

CHAPTER 9

Taxes in Estate Planning

> ***"In this world nothing can be said to be certain, except death and taxes."***
>
> ***— Benjamin Franklin,*** *American statesman, inventor, and Founding Father*

Most people start an estate plan because they want to take care of the people or causes they love, not because they're excited to talk about taxes. And honestly, unless you're an accountant, tax discussions can make anyone's eyes glaze over. Still, taxes play a role in almost every estate plan, even if the impact is minimal.

Several different kinds of taxes can come into the picture: **estate tax, gift tax, income tax**, and depending on where you live, **state-level estate or inheritance tax**. This chapter doesn't try to turn you into a tax expert. Its purpose is to give you a solid overview, so you can spot issues that matter and know when getting professional help is needed.

If your estate is large or complicated, or if you own property outside the U.S. or have heirs who aren't U.S. citizens or residents, things get tricky fast. In these situations, it's important to work with an estate planning attorney and an accountant familiar with international tax rules. (See Chapter 11 for more on cross-border issues.)

Why Estate Taxes Are Rare

In earlier decades, estate-planning conversations revolved around avoiding the federal estate tax. Today, for most families, the more meaningful tax issue is

income tax, especially the kind triggered when children or other heirs eventually sell assets that have grown significantly in value, like long-held homes, stocks, or retirement accounts, which must be taxed when withdrawn.

This shift happened because the federal estate tax applies to far fewer estates than it once did. The exemption, the amount each person may leave tax-free, rose sharply under a 2017 law and continues to be adjusted for inflation.

For deaths in **2025**, the federal estate and gift tax exemption was **$13.99 million per person** (**$27.98 million** for a married couple with proper planning). This increased to **$15 million** per person and **$30 million for couples** in 2026. Under current law, this exemption level is set going forward and is adjusted for inflation starting in 2027.

Most families fall far below the threshold and will never owe federal estate tax, which is why focusing on income tax consequences is often more useful.

Your taxable estate includes essentially everything you own:

- Equity in real estate;
- Stocks, bonds, and other investments;
- Savings and cash;
- Retirement accounts; and
- Life insurance proceeds, if payable to your estate or if you owned the policy (or retained incidents of ownership) at death.

If you're married, the calculation includes **all of your separate property** and **half of your community property** (or half of jointly owned property if you live in a common-law state). Chapter 2 explains these ownership rules in clear detail.

If your total estate is below $15 million, you won't owe federal estate tax and typically won't need to file a federal estate tax return. If your estate exceeds that amount, your executor must file a return, and only the portion above the exemption is taxed. However, even estates below the threshold may choose to file a federal estate tax return (Form 706) to elect "portability," which preserves any unused federal exemption for a surviving spouse**.** Charitable gifts reduce the taxable part, and the top federal estate tax rate remains 40%.

It helps to put the numbers in perspective. Out of the millions of deaths recorded each year in the United States, only a tiny fraction, well under one percent, results in a taxable estate. Even as reporting thresholds shift, the pattern remains the same: only high-net-worth households ever encounter the estate tax.

For most readers, this is a reassuring reminder that estate planning should focus less on fear of a "death tax" and more on the tax issues heirs are far more likely to encounter, especially capital gains.

State Estate and Inheritance Taxes

Some states have chosen to create their own estate or inheritance taxes. These rules vary by location:

- An **estate tax** is paid by the estate before anything is distributed.
- An **inheritance tax** is paid by the individuals who receive the property.

Here are the states that currently impose these taxes. Because these thresholds are frequently adjusted, you should confirm current figures before relying on them.

State	Estate Tax Exemption
Connecticut	$15,000,000
District of Columbia	$4,988,400
Hawaii	$5,490,000
Illinois	$4,000,000
Maine	$7,000,000
Maryland	$5,000,000
Massachusetts	$2,000,000
Minnesota	$3,000,000
New York	$7,350,000
Oregon	$1,000,000
Rhode Island	$1,838,056
Vermont	$5,000,000
Washington	$3,076,000

State	Inheritance Tax?
Nebraska	Yes
Kentucky	Yes
Pennsylvania	Yes
Maryland	Yes (estate + inheritance tax)
New Jersey	Yes

Iowa eliminated its inheritance tax effective January 1, 2025.

If you live in one of these states or own property there, it's worth reviewing the specific thresholds; however, most families across the country remain unaffected. The **majority of U.S. states do not have either tax**, so they don't appear in the list.

Why Income Tax Planning Matters Most

For many families, the tax with the greatest real-world impact is **capital gains tax**, the tax on the difference between what an asset costs and what it sells for. That's why understanding how appreciated assets work, and when lifetime gifts help or hurt from a tax perspective, matters so much.

Passing property at death often provides significant tax benefits for your heirs, while gifting the same property during life can create avoidable tax burdens. With the right planning, you might even discover that you can be more generous than you thought.

And here's a surprising twist: in some situations, filing a federal estate tax return **even when you aren't required to** can create useful long-term tax advantages for a surviving spouse. This strategy can be extremely helpful for larger estates that fall below the taxable threshold but still want flexibility for the future.

Income Taxes & Estate Planning

Income taxes shape an estate plan in more ways than most people expect. They don't just show up at tax season; they influence the way you pass down property, when certain gifts make sense, and which assets create hidden costs for your heirs. Three situations appear again and again:

- When an asset has increased in value, selling it can trigger a sizable capital gains tax. But if that same asset passes at death, its tax value is *normally* reset, its **tax basis is typically increased to its date-of-death value**, often wiping out decades of taxable appreciation.
- Retirement accounts are taxed as beneficiaries withdraw the money, which means the value of those gifts can shrink depending on how quickly they're used.
- Appreciated assets, especially stocks and real estate, can become powerful charitable gifts because qualified charities don't pay capital gains tax when they sell them.

In this section, we'll look closely at how these rules affect real families making real decisions. Once you understand how income taxes work in the background, it becomes much easier to design an estate plan that protects the people you care about.

Capital Gains

Capital gains taxes apply to the difference between what you paid for something (its **cost basis**) and its sale price. If you purchased a share of stock for $10 and sold it for $110, the $100 increase is your gain, and that's the part taxed by federal and, often, state law.

Homes come with their own rules. If you've lived in your primary residence for at least two of the last five years, federal law lets you exclude up to $250,000 of gain from tax. Married couples who file jointly can exclude up to $500,000 if they meet the requirements. Unmarried co-owners don't share a single exclusion, but each owner may be able to claim up to $250,000 on their own share of the gain (if each meets the requirements), which can still total $500,000 overall.

In many parts of the country, that exclusion wipes out all taxable gain. But in states with extremely high housing prices, that buffer doesn't always go far enough.

Imagine a couple who bought a home decades ago for a modest amount, say $120,000, and sells it in 2025 for $2.2 million. They'll feel grateful for the growth, but even with the combined $500,000 exclusion, they still may owe capital gains taxes on well over a million dollars of profit. It's an unexpectedly large bill at a moment that is supposed to feel celebratory.

What happens to long-held property at someone's death turns this entire picture around.

When a person dies, most assets, houses, land, stocks, artwork, and more, are **revalued at the date of death**. This adjustment is called a "**step-up in basis**," and it can completely erase decades of taxable gain.

Here's how powerful this can be:

> ***Example:*** *Carla bought a small coastal home in 1980 for $60,000. By the time she passed away, that same home was worth $1.9 million. Her daughter, Elena, sold the property shortly after. Because Elena's tax basis was increased to the home's value on the date of Carla's death, she owed no capital gains tax on the sale.*
>
> *If Carla had sold the home while alive, her gain, almost $1.84 million, would have created a staggering tax bill even after using her $250,000 homeowner exclusion.*

The lesson is simple but important: **holding highly appreciated property until death often protects your heirs from steep capital gains taxes.**

Lifetime Gifts

Gifts given during life play by different rules. Instead of receiving a step-up, the recipient takes the donor's original tax basis. This can lead to large capital gains if the asset is sold later.

> ***Example:*** *Marcus bought shares of a growing tech company for $4 each. Years later, when each share is worth $30, he gives 300 shares to his niece as a graduation present. Because this is a lifetime gift, she inherits Marcus's original $4 basis. If she sells the shares, she'll owe tax on $26 of gain per share.*
>
> *Had Marcus held the stock until his death, and the shares were still worth $30 at that time, his niece's basis would have stepped up to $30, and she could have sold them tax-free.*

This is why most appreciated assets are better passed at death rather than given during life, unless the intended recipient is a charity.

Charity

Appreciated assets can be frustrating to hold. Sometimes people avoid selling them solely to dodge capital gains taxes. But for anyone with charitable intent, these same assets become powerful tools.

Qualified charities don't pay capital gains tax when they sell appreciated property. That means:

- **You** may claim a charitable deduction for the full market value (if you itemize and follow IRS rules).
- **The charity** receives the entire value, not reduced by tax.

Example: *Nadia owns $12,000 of appreciated stock she bought long ago for only $2,000. If she sells it, she'll owe tax on the $10,000 gain. Instead, she donates the stock directly to a literacy nonprofit.*

- *She takes a $12,000 charitable deduction (subject to IRS limits).*
- *The charity sells the stock for $12,000 and keeps every penny.*

It's one of those rare strategies where both sides benefit fully.

If you intend to support a charity, it's always worth asking whether the organization can accept stock, mutual funds, or real property. Most can, especially larger nonprofits.

How Your Own Property Affects Taxes

Another subtle but important factor is **how title to your home is held**. Married couples often discover that the way their deed is written affects how much of the property receives a step-up in basis at death.

- In **community-property states**, when one spouse dies, community property generally receives a full step-up in basis, often eliminating capital gains if the surviving spouse sells soon afterward. Separate property, or property not properly treated as community property, may not receive this full step-up.
- In **common-law states**, the result depends in part on how the property is titled, but in many cases, only the deceased spouse's share receives a step-up. The surviving spouse keeps their original basis on their share, which can lead to a sizable tax bill when the property is sold.

Example 1 – Community Property State

In the mid-1980s, Luis and Marisol bought a home for $150,000 in a community-property state. When Luis died years later, the home was worth $2.4 million. Because they held it as community property, Marisol's basis stepped up to the full $2.4 million. When she eventually sold it for $2.45 million, the small gain fell entirely under her $250,000 homeowner exclusion, *resulting in no capital gains tax.*

Example 2 – Common-Law State

Now imagine a similar couple, Eric and Dana, in a common-law state. They bought their home for $150,000 and held title as tenants by the entirety. When Eric passed, the home was worth $2.4 million. Only Eric's half received the step-up, leaving Dana with:

- *One-half basis of $1.2 million (Eric's half); and*
- *One-half basis of $75,000 (Dana's original half).*

If Dana later sells the home for $2.45 million, a very large gain remains taxable, even after using her $250,000 exclusion.

This is why understanding how your property is titled can make a meaningful financial difference for your surviving spouse.

If you're unsure how your home is owned, request a copy of the most recent recorded deed. Updating the form of ownership, when permitted, can sometimes provide significant tax benefits. Chapter 2 walks through how to read and correct your deed if needed.

A/B Trust

When people review an older estate plan, especially one created before 2012, one of the first surprises they often encounter is the **A/B trust**. For many couples, the structure was once essential; it helped protect families from federal estate taxes at a time when the exemption was much lower.

Today, however, while the higher exemption means many couples no longer *need* an A/B trust for federal estate tax reasons alone, A/B trusts are still very common and are often used for other planning goals, such as preserving a deceased spouse's share for children from a prior relationship, controlling how assets are used by the surviving spouse, or planning for possible future changes in tax law.

What an A/B Trust Is

An A/B trust is a type of living trust used by married couples. When the first spouse dies, the trust automatically splits into two parts:

- **A – The Survivor's Trust**

  Holds the surviving spouse's assets and remains revocable.

- **B – The Bypass (or Credit Shelter) Trust**

  Holds the deceased spouse's share of assets, up to the federal estate tax exemption. This portion becomes **irrevocable**, meaning the terms cannot be changed without a court order.

The original purpose of the B trust was tax-driven. Before the exemption grew to today's levels, many families risked paying estate tax when the second spouse died. The B trust solved that problem by letting the first spouse use their exemption. The assets held in the B trust stayed out of the surviving spouse's estate entirely, preventing double taxation.

The surviving spouse could usually access money in the B trust, but technically didn't own it, so the IRS couldn't tax it again later.

Why A/B Trusts Were Once Helpful

When the federal exemption was only **$1 million**, as it was in 2002, many middle-class families easily surpassed that amount through home equity, life insurance, and retirement accounts. Splitting assets into A and B trusts prevented widowed spouses from facing a surprise estate tax bill later.

> ***Example:*** *Daniel and Rosa had a trust containing $2.2 million in 2003. When Daniel died, his $1 million went into the B trust. Rosa's $1.2 million stayed in the A trust. When Rosa died two years later, the exemption had risen to $1.5 million. Because Daniel's B trust assets were not counted as Rosa's, her taxable estate was only $1.2 million, below the exemption. A/B planning saved the family thousands in taxes.*

Fast forward to 2026, when the federal estate tax exemption is **$15 million per person**, 15 times larger. Even so, *most* families will still fall far below that threshold.

That shift means: **the tax problem that A/B trusts were designed to solve has disappeared for the vast majority of couples.**

Worse yet, keeping assets in the B trust now often creates a **new** problem—capital gains tax—because the assets in the B trust do **not** receive a step-up in basis at the surviving spouse's death. Only the A trust assets do.

This can cost heirs a surprising amount of money.

No Step-Up in the B Trust

As we said, the step-up in basis is one of the most valuable rules in estate planning. When someone dies, most of their property is revalued at its current market value. If an heir sells soon after, they often owe **no capital gains tax** at all.

But the B trust interrupts this.

Assets placed in the B trust at the first spouse's death **keep** the older, lower basis. At the second spouse's death, they do *not* step up again. Only the survivor's trust assets do.

Example: *Lena and Marco bought a house for $80,000 decades ago. When Marco died in 2001, the home was worth $550,000. Under their A/B trust, half went into the B trust at a basis of $275,000; the other half stayed in the A trust. By the time Lena died in 2024, the house was worth $2.8 million.*

Their son sold it for the full $2.8 million:

- *The A trust-half stepped up to $1.4 million →* ***no gain****.*
- *The B trust-half kept its $275,000 basis →* ***huge taxable gain****.*

After subtracting Lena's $250,000 home-sale exclusion (which only applied to her half), their son still owed roughly ***$350,000 in capital gains taxes****, all because part of the house was trapped in the old B trust.*

This is why so many families with older A/B trusts now discover they're protecting themselves from a tax they will never face, while accidentally triggering a tax they *will have to pay*.

When Keeping an A/B Trust Still Makes Sense

Even though A/B trusts are less useful for tax purposes, they still matter for **family protection purposes**, especially when:

- The couple has **over $15 million** in combined assets (or expects significant future growth);
- There are **children from different marriages** and the couple wants to ensure inheritance for each line; and
- One spouse is concerned about the other spouse's future decision-making due to dementia or vulnerability.

In these cases, an irrevocable structure can still serve important non-tax goals.

But even then, many modern estate plans prefer a more flexible approach, such as a **marital trust using the "Clayton election"** or **portability**.

Note: What "Portability" and a "Clayton Election" Mean

Portability *is a rule that lets a surviving spouse use any unused federal estate-tax exemption from the spouse who died first. In practical terms, it means a couple can often protect both exemptions without locking assets into an irrevocable bypass trust. However, portability does not replicate all the benefits of a bypass trust, such as creditor protection, remarriage protection, or generation-skipping transfer (GST) planning. To use portability, the survivor must file a federal estate tax return after the first death, even if no tax is owed.*

A ***Clayton election*** *is a flexible trust option that lets the surviving spouse decide, after the first spouse dies, how the deceased spouse's assets should be treated. The survivor can choose to keep assets in a marital trust (so they receive a second step-up in basis later) or place them in a bypass-style* *trust for control or protection. This approach keeps options open instead of forcing a decision years in advance.*

For most families, those with under $10 million in total assets, the most efficient option is often a **single revocable trust** because:

- All assets remain under the surviving spouse's ownership;
- At the second death, **everything receives a step-up in basis**, eliminating unnecessary capital gains taxes; and
- Since the estate is below the taxable threshold, no federal estate tax is due.

When to Seek Expert Help

If your trust was created **before 2012**, and especially if it contains an A/B split, it's wise to meet with a knowledgeable estate planning attorney. Two common situations need attention:

1. Your spouse has just died and your trust forces a B trust funding

If there's no tax reason to fund it, an attorney might help petition the court to modify the trust due to changed tax circumstances. Not all attorneys pursue this option because the long-term federal implications of court-ordered trust changes are still unsettled.

2. You're in a blended family and want precise control

In this case, a modernized plan, often involving a marital trust and portability, can give the surviving spouse use of the assets while still ensuring the decedent's children inherit what was intended.

Inherited Retirement Accounts

While many assets step up in basis at death, **retirement accounts do not**. IRAs, 401(k)s, and similar plans are income tax-deferred, not income tax-free. Anyone who inherits them must eventually pay income tax on withdrawals.

Current law requires most beneficiaries to withdraw the entire account within **10 years** of the owner's death. Only a few beneficiaries, most notably surviving spouses and minor children, can stretch withdrawals over a longer period.

This matters because if you leave:

- A $500,000 home to your daughter and
- A $500,000 IRA to your son,

your son will ultimately receive far less because he must pay tax as he withdraws the IRA funds. A fairer approach is often to divide **each** asset proportionally so both children inherit an equivalent after-tax value.

And if you want to support a charity, naming a charity as beneficiary of part or all of a retirement account is incredibly tax-efficient because charities pay **no** income tax on withdrawals.

What About Roth Accounts?

Roth IRAs and Roth 401(k)s follow the same 10-year withdrawal rule, but the withdrawals themselves are **tax-free**, provided the account has been open for at least five years.

This makes them especially powerful assets to leave to younger beneficiaries who may need flexibility.

Gift Tax and Lifetime Giving

At first glance, lifetime gifts might seem slightly out of place in a discussion about estate planning. After all, estate plans deal with what happens after death. But in real life, many people want to help their children or grandchildren *now,* with a down payment on a home, tuition, or medical expenses, while they're still around to see the benefit. The good news is that the tax system largely supports that instinct. If you can afford to help, you can usually do so without triggering any gift tax at all.

There's also something deeply satisfying about seeing your generosity make a difference while you're still alive. Fortunately, the law does not punish that generosity.

In theory, the gift tax applies to almost anything of value you give away during your lifetime. Cash, real estate, stocks, forgiving a loan, even allowing someone to live rent-free, all of these can count as gifts. Long ago, lawmakers recognized that without a gift tax, people could simply give everything away during life and leave nothing behind to be taxed at death. To prevent that, the tax code treats gifts made during life and gifts made at death as part of the same system.

In fact, the gift tax and the estate tax are really **one unified tax**, separated only by timing. Gifts made while you're alive fall under the gift tax rules; gifts made at death fall under the estate tax rules. Both share the same exemption and the same maximum tax rate, which is currently **40%**.

The key word here, though, is *potentially*. Today, almost no one actually pays either tax.

As we said, for **2026**, each person has a combined lifetime gift and estate tax exemption of **$15 million**. Only gifts and bequests that exceed that total amount are subject to tax.

That means if the total value of everything you give away during your life **plus** everything you leave at death is less than $15 million, **no gift tax or estate tax is ever owed**. Not now. Not later.

For most families, this exemption is so large that gift tax planning becomes more about paperwork than payment.

On top of the lifetime exemption, there's an additional rule that makes gifting even easier. Each year, you may give up to **$19,000 per person** (2026 figure) without using *any* of your lifetime exemption and without reporting the gift to the IRS. This is called the **annual gift tax exclusion**, and it applies separately to each recipient.

Because the exclusion applies per person, the numbers can add up quickly. A parent can give $19,000 to each child every year. If those children are married, gifts to their spouses count separately. And if both parents are giving, the amounts double.

Over time, a consistent pattern of annual gifts can transfer hundreds of thousands of dollars to loved ones, entirely tax-free and without touching the lifetime exemption. And importantly, gifts are **not income** to the recipient, so the person receiving the gift doesn't owe tax either.

> ***Example:*** *Maria gives $19,000 each year to her two children and their spouses, a total of four people. That's $76,000 per year. After 10 years, Maria has transferred $760,000 to her family without filing a single gift tax return and without reducing her lifetime exemption at all.*

When Gifts Exceed the Annual Limit

If you give more than $19,000 to any one person in a year, you must file a **gift tax return** the following spring. Filing the return does *not* mean you owe tax. It simply documents how much of your lifetime exemption you've used.

Think of the lifetime exemption as a very large balance. Annual gifts under the exclusion don't touch it at all. Larger gifts subtract from it, but no tax is due unless the balance ever reaches zero.

> ***Example:*** *In 2026, Elena gives her son $85,000 to help him buy a condo. The first $19,000 is covered by the annual exclusion. The remaining $66,000 must be reported on a gift tax return. Elena owes notax, but her remaining lifetime exemption is reduced from $15 million to $14.934 million. Since her total estate is modest, this reduction has no practical impact.*

These returns work like a running record. When someone dies, the IRS looks at the filed gift tax returns to determine how much exemption remains.

One helpful way to picture the system is like a large prepaid card. Small purchases, annual gifts under $19,000, don't touch the balance. Bigger purchases, large lifetime gifts, reduce it slightly. But until the entire balance is used, no tax is charged.

For most people, the balance is so large that they never come close to using it.

Special Rules for Gifts to Caregivers

Gifts to non-relative caregivers deserve special care. Because older adults can be vulnerable to undue influence, several states have laws that presume certain gifts to caregivers are invalid, especially if they are large, involve real estate, or are made shortly after caregiving begins.

To protect both you and the person you want to benefit from, some states require an **independent review** by an attorney who confirms that the gift was made freely and without pressure. This review must be done privately, without the caregiver present.

If you plan to make a substantial gift to a non-relative caregiver, it's wise to work with an estate planning attorney. You may need a **certificate of independent review**, which should be kept with your will or trust to ensure the gift is honored.

The Education and Medical (Ed/Med) Exception

In addition to annual gifts, the tax code offers a powerful and often overlooked exception for education and medical expenses. If you pay **tuition or medical bills directly** to a school or healthcare provider for someone else, those payments do **not** count as gifts at all.

There's no dollar limit, and these payments do not use any portion of your lifetime exemption. The key requirement is that the payment must go straight to the institution; you can't reimburse the individual.

> ***Example:*** *Victor pays $32,000 directly to his grandson's private high school. He does not report the payment, and his lifetime exemption remains untouched.*

Using 529 Plans for Education

Another popular way to support education is through a **529 college savings plan**. These plans allow after-tax contributions to grow tax-free, as long as withdrawals are used for qualified education expenses. Funds can be used not only for college, but also for certain K-12 tuition, vocational programs, and trade schools.

If the original beneficiary doesn't use all the funds, the account can be reassigned to another family member. And under current rules, longstanding 529 plans can even be rolled into a Roth IRA for the beneficiary, *but only within strict limits*, including a lifetime cap, a 15-year holding requirement, and the annual Roth IRA contribution limits.

Contributions to 529 plans count as gifts, but they qualify for the annual exclusion. There's also a special rule that allows **five years' worth of annual gifts to be made at once**, known as "front-loading." In 2026, that meant:

- Up to **$95,000** from one person and
- Up to **$190,000** from a married couple,

without using any lifetime exemption, so long as no additional gifts are made to that beneficiary for the next five years.

Accounting for Lifetime Gifts in Your Estate Plan

If you've made significant gifts during life, your estate plan can easily take them into account. A will or trust can instruct the executor or trustee to "equalize" prior gifts when distributing what remains at death, or to ignore them entirely.

> ***Example:*** *Years earlier, Renee gave her daughter $60,000 to help her buy a home. Her son didn't need similar help. Renee's trust later directed the trustee to factor that gift into the final distribution. When Renee died, the trustee added the earlier gift back into the calculation and adjusted the shares so both children ultimately received equal value.*

Of course, not every family wants this approach. For some, past gifts are simply part of life and not something to be balanced later. Fairness looks different in every family, especially when children have very different needs. What matters most is clarity. When expectations are clear, surprises are less likely, and family harmony is easier to preserve.

The Estate Tax

Now that lifetime gifts are clearer, it's easier to see where they fit into the bigger picture because the **estate tax** is simply the other half of the same system. When a person dies, the question is whether their **estate** is large enough to trigger federal estate tax. If it is, the tax is paid by the estate itself, before anything is distributed.

That's why it's called an "estate" tax. It's **not** a tax charged to the people who receive the inheritance, that would be an **inheritance tax**, and only a few states impose one. And despite the political nickname "death tax," the truth is more ordinary: everyone dies, but very few estates pay this tax.

If an estate tax is due, the estate pays it first, and beneficiaries inherit what remains. Sometimes the estate pays the tax "off the top" before distributions. Other times, the executor or trustee allocates the tax proportionally across beneficiaries. Either way, the concept stays the same: the tax is settled at the estate level, then the remaining assets pass to loved ones. The top federal estate tax rate is currently **40%**, so when the tax applies, it applies heavily, but again, to very few families.

For deaths in **2026**, the federal estate tax filing threshold (the exemption) is **$15 million per person**. *(source: irs.gov)*

What Counts as Part of the Estate

When the IRS measures whether an estate exceeds the exemption, it generally looks at **the value of everything the person owns**. That includes cash, investments, real estate equity, business interests, and, importantly, **life insurance proceeds** payable at death. Retirement accounts like traditional IRAs and 401(k)s are also counted in the taxable estate (even though they follow separate income-tax rules when beneficiaries withdraw the money).

And if the person was married, the way the couple owned property matters. In a **community-property state**, each spouse is treated as owning one-half of community assets, regardless of whose name appears on the deed or account, unless a valid marital agreement changes that default. (That ownership question can affect both estate tax calculations and income-tax basis issues.)

The Unlimited Marital Deduction

Here's a rule that surprises people in a good way: if you leave assets to your spouse, and your spouse is a **U.S. citizen**, those transfers qualify for the **unlimited marital deduction**. In practice, this means the government generally does **not** collect estate tax when the first spouse dies and everything goes to the survivor.

But it helps to understand what this rule is really doing. It doesn't erase estate tax forever; it usually **postpones** it. That's why many professionals describe it as a kind of "marital deferral." The IRS typically waits until the **second spouse** dies and then applies the estate tax rules to whatever remains in that survivor's estate.

> ***Example:*** *Anthony died in 2026 owning his half of a home, a joint bank account, and retirement savings, altogether about $1.6 million. He left everything to his wife, Mira. Because the estate is far below the exemption, no estate tax is due. And because everything passes to a U.S. citizen spouse, the marital deduction means the transfer to Mira itself does not trigger estate tax at Anthony's death. Later, if Mira dies still owning a large estate that exceeds the exemption in effect at that time, the estate tax issue would be considered then.*

Portability

Once you understand the marital deduction, the next concept, **portability,** starts to make sense.

Portability allows a surviving spouse to preserve and later use the deceased spouse's unused federal exemption (often called the deceased spouse's unused exclusion amount, or DSUE). In simple terms, portability can let a married couple "keep" both exemptions, even if everything was left to the surviving spouse.

But portability isn't automatic. To claim it, the estate generally must file a federal estate tax return (Form 706) and make the portability election, even if no estate tax is owed.

A practical way to think about portability is to think of it like saving a coupon you might not need today, but it could be valuable later if the surviving spouse's assets grow significantly, real estate values surge, or tax laws change.

There's also a real deadline issue. Under IRS rules, the portability election is normally tied to the estate tax return filing timeline, but the IRS has provided a streamlined late-election procedure for certain smaller estates, allowing portability to be elected up to **five years** after death in many cases that qualify.

One more real-life wrinkle: if the surviving spouse remarries, the preserved exemption from the first spouse generally doesn't remain indefinitely in the same way. Because rules around remarriage can affect how the "deceased spouse" is defined for DSUE purposes, it's one of the reasons people with changing family situations often get individualized tax advice.

When Portability Is Worth the Paperwork

So when would a surviving spouse actually bother filing an estate tax return just to elect portability?

It tends to be most attractive when the survivor expects their assets to grow because of a long life expectancy, substantial investments, real estate that may appreciate, or simply because they already own significant assets.

On the other hand, if the surviving spouse expects to spend down most of what they inherit and their total estate is likely to stay comfortably below the exemption, they might reasonably decide the cost and paperwork isn't worth it.

If You're Single: Philanthropy as a Tax Strategy

Unmarried people don't have portability, so estate tax planning, when it's needed, often focuses on different tools. One of the most straightforward is **charitable giving**. Qualified charitable gifts made at death generally reduce the taxable estate dollar-for-dollar, and can even reduce it to zero.

> ***Example:*** *Suppose Daniel, unmarried, died in 2026 with a $16 million estate, above the $15 million exemption. If he left $2 million to a qualified public charity, that charitable gift reduces the taxable estate so that the amount subject to estate tax drops dramatically.*

> ***Note:*** *Estate tax rules and portability elections can be high-stakes for larger estates, blended families, and survivors deciding whether the paperwork is worth it. This is educational information, not legal or tax advice; for a decision like a portability filing, it's usually worth coordinating with a qualified estate planning attorney and tax professional.*

Chapter | 9 | Assessment Test

1. **Why does the chapter say federal estate taxes are rare for most families today?**

   a. Because estate taxes were repealed
   b. Because most assets are exempt from taxation
   c. Because the federal exemption is very high
   d. Because only probate assets are taxed

2. **Which assets are generally included when calculating the value of a taxable estate?**

   a. Only probate assets
   b. Everything the person owned, including life insurance and retirement accounts
   c. Only assets titled in the decedent's name
   d. Only assets located in the United States

3. **What is the key difference between an estate tax and an inheritance tax?**

   a. Estate tax applies only to real estate
   b. Inheritance tax applies only to spouses
   c. Estate tax is paid by beneficiaries
   d. Estate tax is paid by the estate; inheritance tax is paid by recipients

4. **Why does income tax planning often matter more than estate tax planning for most families?**

   a. Income tax rates are always higher
   b. Income tax applies every year, not just at death
   c. Income taxes can significantly affect heirs when assets are sold or withdrawn
   d. Estate taxes never apply

5. **What is a "step-up in basis"?**

   a. A tax deduction for heirs
   b. A reduction in estate tax rates

c. A revaluation of assets to current market value at death
d. A rule that eliminates probate

6. **Why are highly appreciated assets often better passed at death rather than given during life?**
   a. Gifts are always taxed immediately
   b. Heirs may avoid capital gains taxes due to a step-up in basis
   c. Lifetime gifts are limited to cash
   d. The gift tax rate is lower at death

7. **How does holding property in a community-property state affect the basis at the first spouse's death?**
   a. Only the deceased spouse's half receives a step-up
   b. No step-up applies
   c. The surviving spouse must sell immediately
   d. The entire property generally receives a step-up

8. **Why can older A/B trusts create unexpected tax problems today?**
   a. They increase estate tax rates
   b. They eliminate the marital deduction
   c. Assets in the B trust may miss a second step-up in basis
   d. They invalidate beneficiary designations

9. **Why are retirement accounts often inefficient assets to leave to individual heirs?**
   a. They are excluded from the estate
   b. Withdrawals are generally subject to income tax
   c. They cannot be inherited by children
   d. They are always subject to estate tax

10. **What is one major advantage of naming a charity as beneficiary of a retirement account?**
   a. Charities receive a step-up in basis
   b. The account avoids probate
   c. Charities pay no income tax on withdrawals
   d. The gift does not count toward the estate

Answers

1. **C** – The federal estate tax exemption is high enough that most families never owe the tax.
2. **B** – The taxable estate generally includes nearly everything the person owns.
3. **D** – Estate taxes are paid by the estate; inheritance taxes are paid by recipients.
4. **C** – Capital gains and income tax can significantly reduce what heirs ultimately receive.
5. **C** – Assets are revalued at their market value as of the date of death.
6. **B** – The step-up in basis can eliminate decades of taxable gain.
7. **D** – In community-property states, the entire property typically receives a step-up.
8. **C** – Bypass trusts often prevent assets from receiving a second step-up at the survivor's death.
9. **B** – Beneficiaries must pay income tax as they withdraw retirement funds.
10. **C** – Charities can withdraw retirement assets without paying income tax.

Personal Notes

CHAPTER 10

Beneficiaries for Retirement Accounts and Life Insurance

> ***"What you leave behind is not what is engraved in stone monuments, but what is woven into the lives of others."***
>
> **– Pericles,**
> *Athenian statesman and general*

Retirement Accounts Aren't Just "Retirement" Anymore

Retirement accounts exist for a practical reason: they reward you, through the tax code, for setting aside part of your paycheck so you'll have something to live on later. When these tax incentives were created, Congress wasn't really imagining them as inheritance tools. The unspoken assumption was that you would save during your working years, spend the money during retirement, and leave little or nothing behind.

That's not a bad plan at all. It's also not always what happens.

Many people work longer than expected, or live more modestly than they predicted. Others find that their non-retirement investments do so well that they can cover most expenses without tapping retirement accounts beyond what the law requires. And because withdrawals from traditional retirement accounts are generally taxed as ordinary income, there's a natural hesitation to pull out more than necessary. Over time, those accounts can shift from *"money I'll use someday"* to *"money my family will inherit."*

Once you see that shift, one thing becomes clear: retirement accounts don't behave like most other properties at death. They come with their own rules, their own timelines, and often their own tax consequences.

This is where the law took a sharp turn. In the past, many beneficiaries could "stretch" inherited retirement accounts over their own lifetimes, taking distributions gradually and spreading the income tax bill across decades. That approach created a real advantage: heirs could delay withdrawals until later in life, sometimes into their own retirement, when their tax bracket might be lower.

The SECURE Act (passed in 2019) and SECURE Act 2.0 (passed in 2022) largely pulled that strategy back. Today, **most non-spouse beneficiaries must withdraw the entire inherited retirement account within 10 years**.

There's an important nuance that helps the rule make sense. Under current guidance, whether beneficiaries must also take withdrawals during years one through nine often depends on whether the original account owner had already reached the age where required minimum distributions (RMDs) had begun. If the owner had started RMDs, annual distributions are generally required during the 10-year window, with the account fully emptied by the end of year 10.

In simple terms, this means the tax-deferral benefit usually belongs to the person who saved the money. For many heirs, what's left is still valuable, but it's no longer a long, gentle stream of taxable income spread over a lifetime. It's often a shorter, more concentrated tax event.

And once retirement accounts become "inheritance assets" in this way, the next question naturally follows: If the rules are different and the tax bite can be bigger, how do you make sure these accounts fit neatly into your overall estate plan?

Why Life Insurance Belongs Right Next to Retirement Accounts

Life insurance enters the conversation for the same reason: it often passes outside the will, and it can represent a surprisingly large transfer of wealth.

People sometimes forget to mention life insurance when listing their assets because it doesn't feel like money they "have." It feels like a contract sitting in the background. But at death, that contract can turn into immediate cash, money that can pay off a mortgage, stabilize a household, cover final expenses, or keep a family's plans intact.

Just as importantly, life insurance follows the same basic transfer system as retirement accounts: it goes to the people named on the beneficiary form, not your will or trust. The distribution of life insurance benefits is dictated by the beneficiary designation on the beneficiary form.

That shared feature is the reason this chapter treats them together. The heart of the work here is coordination. You want your estate plan, your retirement accounts, and your life insurance policies all pointing in the same direction, so that your loved ones receive what you intend, without delay, confusion, or accidental tax friction.

Three Reasons These Assets Deserve Extra Attention

First, **retirement accounts often carry an income-tax cost for the person who inherits them**. A traditional IRA that shows $400,000 on a statement is not the same as a $400,000 brokerage account. The brokerage account might be inherited with a step-up in basis; the IRA is generally inherited with an income-tax bill attached to future withdrawals. If you want gifts to feel equal, you usually have to think in after-tax terms, not just account balances.

Second, **timing matters**. Even with the 10-year rule, beneficiaries generally benefit when the money stays inside the inherited account longer because growth inside the account remains tax-deferred (or tax-free for Roth assets). Pulling money out immediately may be necessary in some families, but when it's not necessary, rushing withdrawals can shrink what the beneficiary keeps.

Third, when handled properly, these assets can **avoid probate**. That's a real advantage. Beneficiary-designated assets usually transfer faster and more privately than assets that must move through a court process. But that advantage only works if the beneficiary forms are accurate and up to date.

The Most Common Plans People Have

Before you can name the right beneficiaries, you need to know what you actually have. Most people use a mix of three basic retirement vehicles: **traditional IRAs**, **workplace plans like 401(k)s (and 403(b)s for schools and nonprofits)**, and **Roth IRAs**. Some employers also offer **Roth 401(k) or Roth 403(b)** options.

If you've changed jobs, it's common to have more than one plan of the same type. Old 401(k)s especially have a way of lingering in the background. That's why a little housekeeping matters. A simple organizational system, one folder or binder section per account, with the most recent statement, does two things at once. It helps you see what you own, and it makes it far easier for someone else to locate these assets if they ever need to step in during an emergency.

Once you can see the list, the plan types stop feeling mysterious. They start to look like variations on a small set of rules.

Traditional IRAs

A traditional IRA (Individual Retirement Account) is usually something you open yourself. The general bargain is that you may get a tax benefit now, the money grows tax-deferred, and you pay income tax when you withdraw it.

For 2026, the contribution limit is **$7,500**, or **$8,600** if you're age 50 or older.

You can generally take distributions without early-withdrawal penalties starting at **age 59½**. If you withdraw earlier, penalties often apply in addition to income tax (though there are exceptions). You must begin required minimum distributions at **age 73**, and that age is scheduled to rise to **75 in 2033**.

One change worth noting is that, under current law, people can continue contributing to an IRA as long as they have earned income, even past the RMD age. That's a subtle shift, but it matters for older workers who are still earning.

401(k) Plans and 403(b) Plans

A 401(k) is typically offered through an employer. Contributions often come out of your paycheck before tax, which can reduce your taxable income now, and the account grows tax-deferred. Employers may offer matching contributions, which is one reason 401(k)s can become large over time.

A 403(b) works similarly but usually applies to employees of nonprofits and schools. The structure feels the same to the account owner; it simply sits under a different part of federal law.

The most important estate-planning point is this: workplace plans, like IRAs, pass by beneficiary form. So even if you "meant" for a plan to go to the same people named in your will, that won't happen unless the plan's beneficiary designation actually says so.

Roth IRAs

A Roth IRA is, in a sense, the traditional IRA turned inside out. You fund it with money you've already paid tax on, so you don't get a deduction up front. But in exchange, qualified withdrawals are tax-free, including the growth, once the basic holding rules are met.

This feature makes Roth accounts especially interesting in inheritance planning. If you can afford to pay the tax up front and you qualify to contribute, a Roth IRA can be a very efficient asset to pass along.

The income phase-out range for taxpayers making contributions to a Roth IRA is increased to between $153,000 and $168,000 for singles and heads of household, up from between $150,000 and $165,000 for 2025. For married couples filing jointly, the income phase-out range is increased to between $242,000 and $252,000, up from between $236,000 and $246,000 for 2025. The phase-out range for a married individual filing a separate return who makes contributions to a Roth IRA is not subject to an annual cost-of-living adjustment and remains between $0 and $10,000.

Roth conversions can also come into the picture. Converting a traditional IRA to a Roth usually triggers tax at the time of conversion, but that tax payment can reduce the size of a taxable estate while potentially leaving heirs a cleaner, more tax-efficient asset later. It isn't right for everyone, but it's worth understanding as an option.

Roth 401(k)s and Roth 403(b)s

Some employers offer Roth versions of workplace plans. The basic idea mirrors a Roth IRA: contributions are made after tax, but qualified distributions can be tax-free. Unlike Roth IRAs, these workplace Roth plans generally don't have the same income eligibility limits for participation.

For estate planning, the key is consistency. If you have a mix of Roth and traditional retirement assets, you may want to think intentionally about who inherits which account because the after-tax value to each beneficiary can be very different.

The Beneficiary Forms You Already Signed

Now we arrive at the practical pivot point of the chapter: most people don't have a retirement account problem. They have a beneficiary form problem.

Every IRA, 401(k), 403(b), and annuity asks you to name at least one **primary beneficiary**, your first choice to inherit the account if you die with money still inside it. You can also name **contingent beneficiaries**, who are backup beneficiaries if the primary beneficiary does not survive you.

Many people sign these forms once, often years ago, and never look at them again. That's normal. Life changes faster than paperwork. Divorce, remarriage, births, deaths, and shifting relationships can leave an old beneficiary form pointing to someone who no longer makes sense.

The good news is that not remembering who you chose doesn't mean you made a mistake. It just means it's time for a checkup. Many institutions now allow you to view beneficiaries online. Others require a call to human resources or to the plan administrator.

This checkup matters because, again, **your will or trust does not control these accounts**. If the beneficiary form says one thing and your will says another, the beneficiary form usually wins.

Choosing Beneficiaries: People, Trusts, and Charities

For married people, naming a spouse as primary beneficiary and children as contingent beneficiaries is common. For unmarried people, you can name a partner, relatives, friends, or charities.

Naming a trust as beneficiary is possible, but it's usually a "when-needed" tool, not the default. Trusts can hit the top income-tax brackets much faster than individuals, so retirement account distributions kept in the trust may be taxed sooner at higher rates. However, many trusts are drafted so the trustee distributes the taxable income to beneficiaries, in which case the beneficiaries, not the trust, generally pay the income tax at their own rates. In simple terms, naming a trust can increase taxes, so it's typically used only when the planning benefits, such as protecting a minor, supporting someone with special needs, or controlling distributions over time, are worth the tradeoff.

Charities are a special case worth highlighting. A qualified charity generally does not pay income tax on distributions from inherited retirement accounts. So a retirement account can be one of the most tax-efficient gifts you can leave to a charity, especially when compared to leaving that same account to an individual beneficiary who will owe income tax on withdrawals.

If you name a charity, there's one practical step people often overlook: tell them. Beneficiary designations aren't public. If the organization doesn't know you named it, it may take longer for the gift to be discovered and claimed.

> ***Example:*** *Suppose Mariah names a local hospice nonprofit as the beneficiary of her traditional IRA. When she dies, the nonprofit can receive the full value and use it directly for services. If she had instead named her brother, he might inherit the same account balance, but he would keep less after income taxes as he withdraws the funds.*

Getting the "Right People," But the Wrong Result

Even when the names on your beneficiary forms are correct, there's still a second layer of planning: withdrawal rules differ based on who inherits. Spouses have options that most other beneficiaries don't have. Some beneficiaries face the 10-year rule with additional annual RMD requirements, depending on the circumstances. And trusts and charities can trigger their own unique sets of rules.

That's why this chapter doesn't stop at "name someone you trust." It aims to help you name the right beneficiaries in a way that fits the tax rules, the timelines, and your broader estate plan, so that what you intend on paper becomes what your beneficiaries actually experience.

A Quick Reminder About Minors as Beneficiaries

If any of your potential beneficiaries are under the age of majority, resist the urge to list them directly on retirement or life insurance beneficiary forms. As discussed in Chapter 7 ("Leaving Property to Your Children"), naming a minor outright usually forces a court to step in and appoint someone to manage the money. A more coordinated approach is to name either your living trust or the children's trust created under your will as the beneficiary, and then let that trust hold and manage the funds for the child under the terms you have already put in place.

Beneficiaries and Withdrawal

Once you understand what kinds of retirement accounts you have, the next step is making sure they end up in the right hands. At first glance, that sounds easy: you name a beneficiary, and the money goes to that person. For most people, it really is that simple.

But retirement accounts don't live in isolation. They sit alongside your will, your trust, and the rest of your estate plan. And that means the first question is not, *"Who do I want to inherit this account?"* but rather, *"Do my beneficiary designations actually line up with the rest of my plan?"*

If those instructions don't match, your plan won't work the way you expect.

When Plans Don't Match

It's surprisingly common for retirement accounts to tell a different story than the will or trust that came later. Often, that mismatch isn't intentional, it's just the result of time passing.

Imagine this:
A living trust leaves everything to a long-term partner. But an IRA, opened decades earlier, still names a sibling as beneficiary. Or a will is updated after a divorce, but an old 401(k) still lists a former spouse. Or someone carefully creates a trust to manage assets for a loved one, but forgets to name that trust as the beneficiary of a retirement account.

In each of those situations, the beneficiary form, not the will or trust, controls what happens to the retirement account.

Here's a more subtle example that shows how serious this can be. Suppose someone creates a trust designed to provide income to a partner for life, with the remainder going to close friends. But the retirement account names only the partner, not the trust. If that partner dies shortly after, and without a will of their own, the retirement account may pass to *their* relatives instead, people the original owner never intended to benefit at all.

The takeaway is simple but powerful: **retirement accounts follow their own paperwork**. If that paperwork doesn't match your estate plan, the retirement account will break ranks and go its own way.

What Happens After You Die

Once you're confident the right beneficiaries are named, the next question naturally follows: *"What choices will those beneficiaries have when they inherit the account?"*

The answer depends on **who** the beneficiary is and **what type** of retirement account they inherit.

If the beneficiary is a qualified charity, the answer is easy. Charities can withdraw the money without paying income tax, so the entire balance can be put to use.

For most individuals, however, the rules are stricter. Under current law, almost all beneficiaries, other than a narrow group, must withdraw the entire balance of an inherited retirement account within **10 years** of the owner's death. In simple terms, this means inherited retirement accounts are no longer designed to provide lifetime income for most heirs.

Only a limited category of beneficiaries can stretch withdrawals longer:

- Surviving spouses;
- Minor children (and only until adulthood);
- Beneficiaries who are severely disabled or chronically ill; and
- Beneficiaries who are less than ten years younger than the account owner.

Everyone else must comply with the 10-year window.

Traditional Accounts and Roth Accounts Work Differently

Before we get into the mechanics of withdrawals, it helps to pause and separate two ideas that are often blended together: **traditional retirement accounts** and **Roth accounts**.

Traditional IRAs and 401(k)s are built around tax deferral. You generally get a tax benefit when you contribute, and you pay income tax when money comes out. Roth accounts flip that logic: you pay tax first, and qualified withdrawals later are tax-free.

That difference drives everything that follows.

IRAs, 401(k)s, and 403(b)s: Required Withdrawals

With traditional retirement plans, the government eventually wants its tax revenue. That's why required minimum distributions, often called RMDs, exist.

You are required to begin withdrawing money from traditional IRAs, 401(k)s, and 403(b)s by **April 1 of the year after you turn 73**. This date is known as your *required beginning date*. In plain English, it's the point when tax deferral ends and withdrawals must begin.

The amount you're required to withdraw each year is calculated using IRS life expectancy tables. The idea is to spread withdrawals over the rest of your expected lifetime. Each year, the fraction changes slightly as you get older.

If you die **before** reaching this required beginning date, your beneficiaries generally must start taking withdrawals the year after your death. They must also empty the account by the end of the tenth year. After taking the required distributions, they can decide how aggressively to withdraw the rest, slowly over time or all at once.

If you die **after** required distributions have already begun, the rules tighten slightly. Your beneficiaries must first take the distribution you would have been required to take in the year of your death. After that, they continue taking required distributions and still must fully empty the account within ten years.

Surviving spouses are treated differently. A spouse can roll an inherited IRA into their own IRA, effectively stepping into your shoes and resetting the rules as if the account had always been theirs.

> ***Example:*** *Suppose a 42-year-old inherits a traditional IRA from an older relative. Starting the year after the relative's death, withdrawals must begin. Over the next decade, the entire account must be emptied. How fast the money comes out during those ten years is a strategic decision, and one that often benefits from tax advice.*

Roth IRAs and Roth Workplace Plans

Roth accounts follow a different rhythm. Because Roth contributions are made with after-tax money, the government does not require you to take withdrawals during your lifetime. If you never need the money, it can continue growing tax-free for as long as you live.

That feature makes Roth accounts especially powerful in estate planning. When a Roth account is inherited, however, the beneficiary usually faces required withdrawals. Surviving spouses can roll the account into their own Roth IRA and continue the tax-free growth without required distributions. Other beneficiaries generally fall under the same 10-year rule that applies to traditional accounts.

The important distinction is this: **withdrawals from inherited Roth accounts are usually tax-free**, assuming the account has met the five-year rule. So while beneficiaries must withdraw the money on a schedule, they aren't handing part of it back to the IRS.

Example: Imagine someone contributes to a Roth IRA for many years but never touches it. Their spouse inherits it and rolls it into their own Roth IRA, letting it grow untouched for another decade or two. When a child later inherits the account, withdrawals must begin and be completed within ten years, but every dollar comes out tax-free.

Why These Rules Matter for Beneficiary Choices

At this point, the larger pattern should be coming into focus. Retirement accounts aren't just about *who* inherits. They're about *how* and *when* that inheritance is received, and what tax cost comes with it.

That's why beneficiary decisions deserve more thought than a quick form filled out years ago. Different beneficiaries face different rules. The same account can feel generous in one person's hands and burdensome in another's, depending on timing, tax brackets, and life circumstances.

You don't need to memorize the regulations to make good decisions. But you do need to know enough to ask the right questions and keep your paperwork aligned with your intentions.

And that brings us to the practical next step: identifying exactly **who you've already named**, and whether those choices still make sense today.

Naming Beneficiaries for Retirement Plans

Now that the withdrawal rules are on the table, the next step is deciding **who** should inherit each retirement account, and just as importantly, choosing beneficiaries in a way that doesn't accidentally force a faster payout than you expected.

On paper, naming a beneficiary sounds very flexible. You can name a spouse, children, other relatives, friends, a trust, or a nonprofit. And that freedom is real. The catch is that **not every type of beneficiary gets the same withdrawal options**, and with retirement accounts, the withdrawal timeline is where taxes and long-term value often live or die.

When a beneficiary can keep money inside the inherited account longer, the account has more time to grow with its tax advantages intact. People sometimes call this *"stretch"* planning. Currently, that full life-expectancy "stretch" is limited to a narrow group the IRS calls **eligible designated beneficiaries**, most notably: surviving spouses, certain minor children, disabled individuals, chronically ill individuals, and individuals who are not more than 10 years younger than the account owner.

Most other individual beneficiaries, such as adult children, siblings, and friends, are "designated beneficiaries" and generally fall under the ***10-year rule***, meaning the account must be emptied by the end of the tenth year after death. Whether annual withdrawals are required in years one through nine depends on the IRS rules in effect at the time and on whether the original owner died before or after their required beginning date (that is, whether they had already started RMDs). Because IRS guidance in this area has changed and may continue to evolve, beneficiaries should confirm the current rule before relying on a "no annual RMDs" assumption.

There's a third category: beneficiaries that are **not** "designated beneficiaries" at all, such as estates, many trusts, and organizations. When these are the beneficiaries, the payout rules can become faster and more rigid, depending on the facts. A common example is the **five-year rule**, which can apply in certain situations (especially when the owner dies before required distributions began).

A simple way to hold all of this in your head is this: retirement accounts don't just ask, *"Who do you love?"* They also ask, *"How quickly must this money come out, and who pays the taxes when it does?"*

> ***Example:*** *Picture an account owner who leaves an IRA partly to two relatives and partly to a nonprofit. The nonprofit will typically want to cash out quickly (it doesn't pay income tax on the withdrawal), while the relatives may benefit from spreading withdrawals over time to manage their tax brackets. That's not a problem, unless the paperwork and deadlines aren't handled correctly, in which case the "fast" beneficiary can accidentally make the "slow" beneficiaries' rules more complicated than necessary.*

> ***Note:*** *The most damaging beneficiary decision is not choosing the "wrong" person. It's* ***choosing no one****.*

If no beneficiary is named (or the named beneficiaries have died and nothing was updated), the retirement account often ends up payable to the owner's ***estate*** *by default. That's where trouble starts. When an account pays to the estate, probate may be required, and the withdrawal rules are usually less favorable, often forcing a quicker payout schedule than would have applied to an individual beneficiary.*

Spouse

If you're married, naming your spouse as primary beneficiary is usually the most natural choice emotionally, and it's often the most powerful choice financially too. That's because spouses receive options almost no one else gets.

Most notably, a surviving spouse can often treat the inherited IRA as their own through a **spousal rollover** (or, depending on the account type and circumstances, keep it in the deceased spouse's name temporarily and delay withdrawals until the schedule requires). The practical benefit is simple: it can allow continued tax deferral and more control over timing, especially if the surviving spouse doesn't need the money right away.

This is one of those places where the "estate planning" and the "retirement rules" truly intersect: the same dollars can be worth meaningfully more to a spouse than to an adult child, simply because the spouse can usually keep the tax shelter going longer.

> ***Note about spousal rights:*** *If you are married and want to name someone other than your spouse, especially with a workplace plan like a 401(k),*

be careful. Many employer plans are governed by federal rules that give spouses strong default rights, often requiring written consent if you name someone else. With IRAs, state property rules can also matter, particularly in community-property states.

This isn't a reason to panic, it's just a reason to treat someone other than a spouse as a decision that should be coordinated with the rest of your plan, not made casually on a form.

Children

After a spouse, most people want retirement assets to go to their children. And when children are adults, that's usually straightforward: you name them, they inherit, and they manage withdrawals under the 10-year rule.

The complications show up when children are still minors, or when they're legally adults but not yet ready to handle a large, taxable account responsibly.

Minors generally can't control inherited retirement assets directly. If you name a minor child as beneficiary and die while they're underage, someone will need legal authority to manage the account for them. Without planning, that can mean a court process to appoint a guardian, and once the child reaches the age of majority, they may suddenly gain full control, exactly when you might prefer continued structure.

This is where a coordinated estate plan earns its keep. Instead of naming a child outright, people often use one of two resources:

A custodianship under state law (often called UTMA). This can provide a built-in manager until a later age set by state law (commonly 21, sometimes 25).

A trust that you've already created for your children. This can keep management in responsible hands longer and control how distributions are used.

But here comes the trade-off that deserves a clear, calm explanation: trusts can create **higher income-tax pressure** if retirement distributions are retained inside the trust instead of being passed out to the individual beneficiaries. In 2026, a trust could hit the top 37% federal income tax bracket at **$16,000** of taxable income. This is an astonishingly low number compared to individual taxpayers.

So the idea isn't to "never name a trust." The idea is to "name a trust when supervision, protection, or family structure truly requires it, and make sure the trust is drafted to handle retirement distributions intelligently."

Even if the IRS rules allow a certain payout approach, **the plan's own rules can be more restrictive**. Some plans don't handle trust beneficiaries as smoothly as you'd hope. So when a trust is involved, it's worth confirming how the specific plan administrator will treat that designation.

Multiple Beneficiaries

It's also common to split a retirement account among multiple beneficiaries, say, several children plus a charity. That can work beautifully, but the plan needs to be handled with a bit of choreography.

A key concept *in certain retirement account situations* is the **beneficiary determination date** (often September 30 of the year after death). Essentially, it's a deadline used to determine who counts as the beneficiary for applying certain distribution rules, most commonly when there are multiple beneficiaries or when a trust is named as beneficiary. If you have a mix of beneficiary "types," you generally want the administration handled cleanly, so the individuals aren't accidentally stuck with rules intended for a non-individual beneficiary.

The practical fix is communication. Your executor or trustee should know these accounts exist, who is named, and which beneficiaries should be contacted quickly, especially any charity, so distributions and account separations happen on time.

Trusts

Trusts show up in retirement planning for two very different reasons. The first is straightforward: you want a trustee to manage money for minors, young adults, or someone who needs ongoing support or protection. In this context, the trust is functioning like adult supervision.

The second is more sensitive: you want to control what happens **after your spouse dies**, especially in a blended family, or you want a third party to manage assets because you don't want your spouse (or don't believe your spouse can) manage them alone.

Those can be legitimate goals, but naming a trust instead of naming a spouse directly is not a casual move. It can cost the family flexibility, and it can create tax compression inside the trust unless handled carefully.

So if a trust is being used primarily for "tax reasons," it's smart to pause and ask: *which tax, estate or income?* In modern planning, the income-tax consequences of inherited retirement assets often matter more.

Charities

Charities are a special case, and often a very smart one. Because qualified charities generally don't pay income tax on retirement account withdrawals, leaving retirement assets to charity can be one of the most tax-efficient gifts available. In simple terms: a dollar in a traditional IRA is often worth more to a charity than to an individual beneficiary because an individual must usually share that dollar with the IRS as withdrawals occur.

That's also why **donor-advised funds (DAFs)** can fit naturally here. A donor-advised fund is essentially a charitable account you establish at a sponsoring organization (often a community foundation or a financial institution's charitable arm). You contribute to the fund, receive the charitable deduction when you contribute (subject to the usual rules), and then recommend grants over time to charities you care about.

Naming a DAF as beneficiary of a retirement account can create a clean pipeline: retirement dollars flow into the fund, and the fund can then distribute to charities in line with the instructions you've left and the successor advisor you've named.

> ***Example:*** *Imagine Priya sets up a donor-advised fund and funds it modestly during life, using it to support a few local causes each year. She later names that donor-advised fund as beneficiary of part of her IRA. After her death, the IRA portion flows into the fund, and her adult niece, who she named as successor advisor, can recommend grants to the same causes going forward. The charitable impact continues, but the money is handled within a structure that's designed for it.*

Organizations (Not Charities)

It's important to pause here and clear up a common point of confusion. When people say they want to leave retirement assets to an "organization," they don't always mean a charity. Sometimes they're thinking about a private foundation, a club, an association, a business entity, or another organized group that matters to them. From an estate planning perspective, though, these organizations are treated very differently from qualified charities.

Essentially, **most organizations that are not charities do not receive any special tax treatment** when they inherit retirement accounts. Under IRS rules, they are usually *not* considered "designated beneficiaries." This has real consequences.

When a non-charitable organization is named as the beneficiary of an IRA or other retirement plan, the account generally must be paid out quickly, often within five years of the owner's death. There is no ability to stretch withdrawals over time, and the tax-deferred growth that makes retirement accounts so valuable is lost almost immediately.

Even more importantly, unlike charities, **non-charitable organizations may owe income tax on withdrawals**, depending on their structure. In other words, the same retirement dollar that would pass tax-free to a charity could be partially eaten up by taxes when left to an organization that doesn't qualify as tax-exempt.

Because of this, naming an organization that is not a qualified charity as a retirement plan beneficiary should never be done casually. It may still make sense in specific situations, but only after confirming exactly how that organization is classified for tax purposes and understanding how the required payout rules will apply.

If an organization matters deeply to you but is not a charity, it's especially important to get professional guidance before naming it as a retirement account beneficiary. A small amount of planning on the front end can prevent a large and unnecessary tax hit later.

Organize Your Retirement Plans

Now that you've seen how important retirement accounts and beneficiary designations are, it's worth pausing to do a bit of practical reorganization. This isn't glamorous estate planning, but it may be some of the most helpful work you do for the people you leave behind. A little organization now can spare your family confusion, delays, and unnecessary stress later. The first, and often biggest, step is simply consolidating what you already have.

Old 401(k)s, New Life

Many people change jobs several times over the course of their careers, and each job often leaves behind a 401(k). Some people roll those accounts over right away when they move on. Others don't. The accounts sit in the background, invested according to rules and fund choices set by a former employer.

Rolling an old 401(k) into an IRA puts you back in control. In other words, it means you choose where the money lives, how it's invested, and who manages it.

If you don't roll an account over, a few things can happen. Your former employer may keep the plan invested in a narrow menu of funds, sometimes heavily weighted toward company stock. Over time, plans change administrators; companies merge, shrink, or disappear; and occasionally, people discover, years later, that their retirement money has been moved without much notice.

> ***Example:*** *Eleanor worked for a midsize manufacturing company in her thirties and left after five years. She remembered having a 401(k) there, but life moved on. More than a decade later, while organizing her finances, she noticed that statements had stopped arriving. After several calls, she learned that her former employer had transferred its retirement plan to a new administrator years earlier. Tracking down the account took months. Eventually, Eleanor rolled the funds into an IRA she already owned, relieved to finally have everything in one place.*

Rolling over old accounts during your lifetime doesn't just benefit you; it makes things much easier for your survivors. If your retirement money is already in an IRA, your spouse or other beneficiaries will deal with one familiar institution instead of a long-forgotten employer or a plan administrator they've never heard of. The company managing your IRA has an incentive to help them because they want to keep the relationship.

In some cases, you may even choose to roll 401(k) funds into a Roth IRA, provided you meet the IRS income requirements. That decision has tax consequences and deserves careful thought, but the key point is that consolidation creates clarity and flexibility.

Fewer IRAs, Fewer Headaches

Once old 401(k)s are addressed, the next question is whether you have multiple IRAs scattered across different institutions. Many people do, often one from an early job, another from a later rollover, and maybe a third opened independently.

Consolidating IRAs into one or two accounts makes it easier to understand how your investments are performing, reduces duplicated fees, and cuts down on mail, emails, and login credentials. More importantly, it simplifies things for the people who will inherit these accounts. When survivors are grieving, it's surprisingly easy for a small account to be overlooked entirely.

Learning the Withdrawal Rules

Retirement accounts come with detailed withdrawal rules, and those rules apply differently to owners, spouses, and other beneficiaries. While this book explains the basics, it's also wise to know where to find reliable guidance.

The IRS, FINRA, and organizations like AARP publish up-to-date explanations about retirement plans and inherited accounts. Your own plan administrator is another important resource. While they must follow IRS rules, some plans impose additional restrictions, especially for beneficiaries.

Naming Beneficiaries Carefully

Once your accounts are organized, the next step is making sure the paperwork matches your intentions. Every retirement plan and insurance company has its own beneficiary forms, but they're all trying to accomplish the same thing: identifying who receives the money first, and who receives it if the first person can't. In short, you're naming a primary beneficiary and a backup.

Most companies allow you to change beneficiaries online or with a simple form. And while the forms vary, they usually ask for clear identifying information so there's no confusion later.

If you're married, it's always best to name your spouse by full name and other identifying details, rather than writing something vague like "my spouse." Life changes. Precision prevents disputes.

When children are involved, the wording matters even more. If your children are minors, the form should reflect how those assets will be managed until they're old enough to handle them responsibly, whether through a custodian under state law or a trust you've created.

Many forms also let you check a box labeled "per stirpes" or "right of representation." In simple terms, this means that if a beneficiary dies before you but leaves children of their own, those children step into their parent's place rather than losing the share entirely.

Divorce Changes Everything

If you've been divorced, beneficiary designations deserve extra attention. Sometimes a divorce agreement requires you to keep an ex-spouse as beneficiary for a period of time, especially when minor children are involved. In those cases, you must follow the agreement.

But many people simply forget to update their forms. That oversight can lead to painful surprises. Reviewing beneficiary designations after a divorce is one of the simplest ways to make sure your estate plan still reflects your life as it actually is.

Life Insurance

After retirement accounts, life insurance is often the next largest asset people leave behind. And like retirement plans, life insurance passes by beneficiary designation, not by your will or trust.

This makes reviewing life insurance beneficiaries just as important as reviewing retirement accounts. The form you filled out with the insurance company controls everything.

When you buy a policy, you name a primary beneficiary and usually a secondary one. The primary beneficiary receives the proceeds at your death. If that person has already died, the secondary beneficiary steps in.

> ***Example:*** *Martin bought a life insurance policy in his forties and named his partner, Elena, as the primary beneficiary. He named his longtime friend, Lucas, as the backup. Years later, Martin and Elena passed away in the same accident. Because Martin had named a secondary beneficiary, the insurance proceeds went directly to Lucas, without court involvement or delay.*

If you want to change beneficiaries on an existing policy, the process is usually straightforward. Ask the insurer for a change-of-beneficiary form or complete the update online, and keep a copy for your records.

Irrevocable Life Insurance Trust (ILIT)

For families with very large estates, life insurance can also serve a different purpose: providing cash to pay estate taxes. This is usually done through an irrevocable life insurance trust, often called an **ILIT.**

In simple terms, an ILIT owns the insurance policy, not you. You can pay the premiums, but you give up control. Because the policy isn't legally yours, the insurance proceeds aren't included in your taxable estate. After your death, the trustee can use those proceeds to help pay estate taxes or purchase assets from your estate, creating liquidity when it's needed most.

This is advanced planning, typically relevant only for estates well above the federal exemption. If this strategy seems worth exploring, professional guidance is essential, not because it's mysterious, but because the details matter.

Chapter | 10 | Assessment Test

1. **Why does the chapter say retirement accounts often shift from "retirement money" to "inheritance assets"?**

    a. Because withdrawals are no longer required
    b. Because many people don't need to spend all of them during life
    c. Because Congress redesigned them as inheritance tools
    d. Because they receive a step-up in basis at death

2. **Under current law, what rule applies to most non-spouse beneficiaries of inherited retirement accounts?**

    a. Lifetime "stretch" withdrawals
    b. Immediate full withdrawal
    c. Required withdrawals only after age 73
    d. Full withdrawal within 10 years

3. **Why are retirement accounts and life insurance treated together in this chapter?**

    a. They are taxed the same way
    b. They are always included in probate
    c. They pass according to beneficiary designations
    d. They are available only through employers

4. **Why can a $400,000 IRA be worth less to an heir than a $400,000 brokerage account?**

    a. IRAs cannot be inherited by children
    b. IRAs are subject to income tax when withdrawn
    c. Brokerage accounts are tax-deferred
    d. IRAs are excluded from the estate

5. **What is the most common problem people have with retirement accounts, according to the chapter?**

    a. Choosing the wrong investment funds
    b. Not contributing enough

c. Forgetting required minimum distributions
d. Outdated or mismatched beneficiary forms

6. What happens if a retirement account's beneficiary designation conflicts with a will or trust?

a. The will always controls
b. The trust overrides the designation
c. The beneficiary form usually controls
d. The court decides based on fairness

7. Why is naming a trust as beneficiary of a retirement account usually a "when-needed" decision?

a. Trusts cannot receive retirement assets
b. Trusts often face faster taxation at higher income-tax rates
c. Trusts eliminate beneficiary flexibility
d. Trusts invalidate SECURE Act protections

8. Why are retirement accounts often tax-efficient gifts for charities?

a. Charities receive a step-up in basis
b. Charities can stretch withdrawals indefinitely
c. Charities do not pay income tax on withdrawals
d. Charitable gifts bypass reporting requirements

9. What special advantage does a surviving spouse have when inheriting a retirement account?

a. Automatic tax-free withdrawals
b. The ability to roll the account into their own
c. Exemption from beneficiary rules
d. Guaranteed lifetime income

10. Why is failing to name any beneficiary on a retirement account especially risky?

a. The account is forfeited
b. The IRS imposes penalties
c. The account defaults to the estate and often faces worse payout rules
d. The account is frozen indefinitely

Answers

1. **B** – Many people don't spend all retirement funds during life, turning them into inherited assets.
2. **D** – Most non-spouse beneficiaries must empty the account within 10 years.
3. **C** – Both pass by beneficiary designation, not by will or trust.
4. **B** – IRA withdrawals are generally taxed as ordinary income.
5. **D** – Old or mismatched beneficiary forms are the most common problem.
6. **C** – Beneficiary designations usually override wills and trusts.
7. **B** – Trusts can trigger faster and higher income taxation if not carefully planned.
8. **C** – Charities do not pay income tax on inherited retirement withdrawals.
9. **B** – A spouse can often treat the inherited account as their own.
10. **C** – Accounts payable to the estate often face probate and unfavorable withdrawal rules.

Personal Notes

CHAPTER 11

Planning for Incapacity

> ***"The time to repair the roof is when the sun is shining."***
>
> ***— John F. Kennedy,***
> *35th President of the United States*

Estate planning has two "time horizons," and they call for different tools. One horizon is death. If you die, your will or living trust is what tells everyone how to wrap up your affairs and who receives your property. And if you never created either one, your state's default inheritance rules take over. In practice, the law picks your heirs for you.

The other horizon is incapacity. That's the situation people don't like to picture: you're alive, but you can't speak clearly, can't understand what's happening, or can't manage decisions because of an accident, a serious illness, or cognitive decline. In that moment, a will doesn't help much because wills generally don't authorize anyone to act for you during your lifetime.

So if you become incapacitated, your loved ones usually need **two separate documents:** one for medical decisions and one for money.

The first document is a **healthcare directive**. It's the paper that lets you choose a trusted person to speak with doctors if you can't. In practice, you're appointing a voice when yours isn't available. Most directives also give you space to spell out your preferences for end-of-life care, what procedures you would want to be performed or not performed, and what comfort should look like if recovery isn't realistic.

Depending on the state, this may be packaged as one combined form (often called an "advance" directive) or split into two: one that names your medical decision-maker and another (often called a living will) that expresses end-of-life instructions. These provide different packaging but fulfill the same purpose.

The second document is a **durable power of attorney for finances**. This names a person who can handle your financial life if you can't: paying bills, managing accounts, dealing with insurance paperwork, keeping the lights on, and preventing small problems from snowballing into big ones. "Durable" matters because it means the authority can continue even if you lose capacity.

And yes, these documents matter even if you're young, healthy, and don't think of yourself as someone who needs "estate planning." If you have no healthcare directive and no durable financial power of attorney, and for some reason you lose capacity, your family may have to ask a court to appoint a responsible adult to act for you. Depending on the state, that person may be called a *conservator* or *guardian.*

This path is typically slow, expensive, and public. It can require hearings, filings, and ongoing oversight. It also forces personal family matters into a legal process at the exact moment your loved ones are already overwhelmed.

> ***Example:*** *Imagine Ethan, who suffers a severe brain injury after a sudden fall. He can physically sign his name, but he can't understand what documents mean or why decisions are needed. His partner tries to get new powers of attorney signed, but the attorney explains the core problem: a power of attorney only works if the signer understands what they're signing. Without that, the family is pushed toward a court appointment so someone can legally manage medical and financial decisions.*

That entire ordeal is often avoidable if the documents are done earlier, when capacity is clear.

"But I Have a Living Trust; Isn't That Enough?"

No. A living trust is excellent for what it's designed to do: it allows a successor trustee to manage **assets titled in the trust** if you can't, and later to distribute those trust assets after your death.

But a trust doesn't automatically give anyone power over everything else. Many people still have important items outside the trust: an everyday checking account used for routine bills, retirement accounts, or other assets that don't sit inside the trust structure. And a trust doesn't authorize medical decisions at all. So even with a trust, a healthcare directive and a durable financial power of attorney are still the core incapacity tools.

Healthcare Directives

At the heart of a healthcare directive is a simple legal principle: you have the right to make decisions about your own body, even when you cannot speak for yourself.

United States law has long treated medical decision-making, especially end-of-life choices, as deeply personal, and courts have confirmed that when people express their wishes clearly, those wishes should be respected.

States implement that principle through forms that are usually easy to access and easy to complete. Hospitals and facilities that participate in federal health programs are generally required to provide information about these directives and to note them in a patient's records. In practice, that means the system expects these documents to exist, and knows what to do with them when they are completed.

You typically do not need a lawyer to complete a valid directive. If you're already working with a professional to coordinate an estate plan, it often makes sense to prepare the directive at the same time, simply so everything matches and nothing is overlooked.

Once you sign it, treat it like an emergency tool, not a keepsake. Keep the original, but share copies with your doctor, your healthcare system if you have one, and the people you've named. And a digital scan is worth its weight in gold because emergencies happen where filing cabinets don't.

A healthcare directive can be as simple or as detailed as you want, but most people cover the same core ground: who speaks for you, what you value if decisions get hard, and what comfort means to you.

It can also include preferences that feel "small" until you're the one living with them: where you would want to be cared for if home is no longer safe, whether you want visitors or quiet, whether music or faith practices matter to you, and how strongly you want pain relief prioritized. In simple terms, this isn't just paperwork. It's your chance to turn your values into instructions that a hospital can actually follow.

Your Right to Say "Yes" or "No"

Many directives include a section where you address treatment that can keep the body going through medical support, sometimes even when meaningful recovery isn't expected. This is often described as "life-sustaining treatment."

That phrase can sound cold. What it really means is care like ventilators, feeding tubes, dialysis, and other interventions that can maintain biological functions. When the topic turns to end-of-life choices, people respond in all kinds of human ways.

Some people want those measures used as long as there is any reasonable chance of recovery. Some people want limits if the treatment is only prolonging the dying process. Many people choose something in between, instructing: "Try for a period of time and reassess."

Some worry that declining aggressive measures today could mean missing a medical breakthrough tomorrow. Some have anxiety about organ donation. Some think about the financial strain of prolonged care. And some prefer to leave the decision to a spouse or adult children.

If "I'd rather not decide" is where you land, try imagining the scene you're creating for the people who love you: a crisis, a hospital team asking for direction, relatives trying to interpret what you "would have wanted," and no written guidance to settle disagreements. In the rare cases that become public or end up in court, the common thread is usually the same: the person left no clear instructions and no legally recognized decision-maker.

Instead, if you're thinking, *"I don't know enough to answer this,"* that's normal. You're allowed to learn as you go. You can read trusted resources, talk to your physician, and have a real conversation with the person you might name as your agent.

And you're not trapped by a form's checkboxes. If there's a value or boundary you feel strongly about, you can attach your own statement in plain language and ask that it be honored.

Comfort Care

One last thing matters here, because it's a frequent misunderstanding: choosing limits on life-sustaining treatment does **not** mean choosing suffering.

Care that prioritizes comfort, dignity, and quality of life is commonly called *palliative care*. In simple terms, it's a medical approach that focuses on relief, pain control, breathing comfort, anxiety management, and support for the patient and the family, rather than aggressive interventions aimed at cure at all costs. Palliative care can happen in a hospital, at home, in a skilled facility, or through hospice.

If you ever find yourself advocating for someone and the hospital culture seems geared toward endless tests and procedures, it can feel like you're shouting into the wind. This is where nurses and hospital social workers can be invaluable. They often know how to connect families to palliative teams and how to translate "We want comfort-focused care," into the right requests inside that system.

> ***Example:*** *Picture Monica, who completes her state's directive after watching a close friend endure a long ICU stay. Monica names her cousin as her medical agent and adds a short statement: "If doctors believe she is unlikely to regain the ability to recognize family or communicate in a meaningful way, she wants the focus to shift to comfort care rather than long-term artificial support." She signs the form properly, gives copies to her primary care clinic and her agent, and keeps a scanned copy in a folder that her agent can access.*

Physician Orders for Life-Sustaining Treatment (POLST)

A well-written healthcare directive is the foundation: it names the person who can speak for you, and it captures your values and end-of-life choices. It's tempting to think that one document should be enough.

But when someone is living with a serious, life-limiting illness, there's a practical problem: in an emergency, medical teams often don't have time to read a multi-page legal directive, or to interpret it the same way you meant it. That's where a **POLST** comes in.

A **POLST** (short for **Physician Orders for Life-Sustaining Treatment**) is not a "legal preference statement." It's a **medical order**, the kind of document clinicians are trained to follow quickly. It turns your end-of-life choices into **clear instructions that travel with you** from one care setting to another (home, ambulance, hospital, skilled nursing facility).

The POLST focuses on a few high-stakes decisions that tend to come up during crises, such as whether you want:

- **CPR attempted** if your heart stops;
- **High-intensity interventions** (for example, a ventilator to help you breathe); and
- **Artificial nutrition and hydration** through a tube.

A POLST is **not a replacement** for a healthcare directive. Think of the two as different tools for different moments.

Your healthcare directive, in practice, says: *"If I can't speak for myself, here's who speaks for me, and here's what matters to me."*

A **POLST**, by contrast, is usually appropriate only when there's a serious illness and a real risk that emergency decisions will be needed soon. A common rule of thumb is that a POLST is meant for people who may be in the last year of life, or who are living with advanced frailty or chronic illness, when emergency interventions may do more harm than good.

Because the POLST is binding on the clinicians who treat you later, it should be completed only after a **clear, specific conversation** with a medical professional (a physician, nurse practitioner, or physician assistant). What this means is, you don't want to check boxes unless you fully understand what those boxes will mean at 2:00 a.m. in an ER.

How a POLST Gets Created, and How to Make It Usable in Real Life

Unlike a directive, you don't typically fill out a POLST alone at your kitchen table. You complete it **with** your clinician, and **both of you sign it**. In many places, it's printed on brightly colored paper (often pink) so it stands out in a chart, and it becomes part of your medical record.

Then comes the piece that makes it work outside the clinic: **visibility**. If you're at home and paramedics are called, they can't follow a document they can't find.

So the practical habit is to keep a copy where first responders are trained to look, commonly the refrigerator door, or a clearly marked spot near the bed. Also, make sure it's in your doctor's file, and consider scanning or photographing it so your healthcare agent can pull it up quickly on a phone.

If you want to see whether your state has adopted POLST and how it works locally, the national POLST program keeps state-by-state information here: https://polst.org/programs-in-your-state.

DNR vs. POLST

People sometimes hear "POLST" and think it's the same thing as a DNR. They're related, but they're not the same.

A **DNR** (Do-Not-Resuscitate order) is narrower. In other words, it says one thing: *"If my heart stops, do not perform CPR."* You sign it with your doctor, and it's meant to guide emergency personnel.

A **POLST** usually includes a CPR choice **and** goes further, covering other life-sustaining treatments, not just resuscitation. That's why, in many situations, if you complete a POLST, you **don't also need a separate DNR;** the POLST already answers the CPR question.

Just like a POLST, a DNR should be kept **easy to find** at home, so emergency medical personnel can honor it.

If you're looking for a DNR form, the most reliable starting point is your doctor, or your state health department's website, because the formatting and rules can be state-specific.

Medical Aid In Dying (MAiD)

Some readers also ask about **medical aid in dying** (sometimes called MAiD). This is a separate topic from POLST/DNR. In simple terms, it refers to laws in certain states that allow a terminally ill person, under specific safeguards, to request a prescription they may choose to take to hasten death.

Medical aid in dying is available in a growing number of U.S. jurisdictions, including **California, Colorado, Delaware, Hawaii, Illinois, Maine, Montana, New Jersey, New York, New Mexico, Oregon, Vermont, Washington, and the District of Columbia**, with the details varying by state.

The rules can be strict and procedural. For example, some states require:

- Confirmation by qualified clinicians that the person is terminally ill within a specified time frame;
- That the person is an adult and mentally capable of making medical decisions; and
- That the person can self-administer the medication.

For state-by-state details and how the process is implemented, one of the better overviews is maintained by Compassion & Choices:

https://compassionandchoices.org/our-issues/medical-aid-in-dying/.

Healthcare Agent

A healthcare directive is powerful mainly because it lets you choose a person, your **healthcare agent** (sometimes called an *"attorney-in-fact for healthcare"),* to act if you can't. In practice, your agent is your voice when you don't have one.

As long as you can understand and communicate by speaking, writing, or even reliably signaling, your decisions stay in charge. The agent steps in only when you can't make or communicate informed choices. That might be because you're unconscious, too medically sedated, delirious, or unable to understand the risks and benefits of the options in front of you.

Most directives also let you shape the agent's authority: how much freedom they have, which doctors or facilities they can choose, and whether they can access your private medical information.

That last point matters because privacy laws (federal and state) limit who your clinicians can speak with. Many directives include language that authorizes providers to share information with your agent. If yours doesn't, you may need a separate HIPAA-style authorization. In simple terms, if your agent can't get information, they can't do the job, so it's worth confirming what your providers will require.

Unless you limit them, agents are typically authorized to make the kinds of decisions that come up in real life: consenting to or refusing treatment (including many mental health treatments, though some specialized treatments can have extra legal requirements), selecting or changing providers and facilities, approving tests or procedures, making choices about life-sustaining treatment (use, withholding, or withdrawal), and handling related end-of-life decisions, such as organ donation, autopsy authorization, and disposition arrangements where state law allows.

Choosing the Right Agent

Choosing an agent is less about who loves you most and more about who can carry out your wishes calmly under stress.

In many states, the basic eligibility rules are straightforward. Your agent must be an adult (typically 18+) and generally can't be your treating healthcare provider or the owner/operator of the care facility where you're receiving care. However, that person CAN be your agent, if they're also a close family member, such as a spouse, domestic partner, or close relative. (Some states also restrict employees of your provider or facility unless they're close family.) The goal is to reduce conflicts of interest.

Beyond the legal eligibility, the real questions are personal:

Can this person advocate for you with calm steadiness? Do they understand what you value, independence, comfort, longevity, avoiding burdensome procedures, faith considerations? Will they follow your stated wishes, even if other relatives disagree? And, practically, can they get to you if you're hospitalized, or will distance make that unrealistic?

It's wise to name **one primary agent and one backup**. Naming two people to act "together" sounds fair, but it can backfire, because if they disagree, your care gets stuck in the very conflict you were trying to prevent.

> ***Example:*** *Marisol, who lives alone and has two close cousins, initially wanted to name both as co-agents because she didn't want to hurt anyone's feelings. After talking it through, she realized the better plan was clarity: she named the cousin who lived nearby as primary agent because that person could actually be present, and named the other cousin as alternate, with a*

promise that the alternate would be kept informed. Everyone felt respected, and the plan became workable.

Once you've picked your agent and an alternate, the next step isn't paperwork; it's the ask.

This is a serious responsibility, and the right agent should be able to say, "Yes" freely. If someone is hesitant because of emotional burden, medical trauma, family dynamics, or time constraints, listen to that.

If they're willing, the most valuable thing you can do is talk through your wishes in plain language. No document, no matter how carefully drafted, captures every nuance.

It also helps to tell the people closest to you (a spouse, partner, adult children) who you chose and why, especially if you didn't choose the person everyone assumes would be in charge. That transparency now can prevent conflict later.

Keep Choices Organized

Many people find it helpful to keep a one-page "Who's in charge" worksheet with their estate planning documents. This could be your trustee, executor, financial agent, and healthcare agent (plus alternates). The point isn't the form, it's the clarity. In practice, it gives your family one obvious place to look when something happens.

Where People Find the Forms

Healthcare directive forms are widely available, often through hospitals, senior centers, doctors' offices, and reputable nonprofit organizations. In addition, federally funded facilities (those receiving Medicare or Medicaid) are generally required to provide information about advance directives and to note them in a patient's medical record.

If you want guidance and state-specific materials, well-known resources include Compassion & Choices and organizations focused on hospice and palliative care education. (And if you use a software tool to generate forms, treat it like any other legal document; make sure it matches your state's rules and is properly validated.)

Making It Legally Valid

Every state has its own signing requirements. Many require witnesses; some require or allow notarization; some limit who can serve as a witness. The instructions are typically printed right on the form. Essentially, this is the "don't skip the last step" moment, because an unsigned or improperly signed directive can create the same mess as having no directive at all.

After signing, make copies and distribute them intentionally to your agent, your alternate, your primary doctor, and any health system or hospital portal where you receive care. Keep the original somewhere safe, but also somewhere your agent can access if needed.

Revoke Your Directive

You can revoke and replace your directive at any time. Practically, the safest approach is two-part:

First, revoke the old document (many people simply destroy it, but a written revocation can create a cleaner record). Second, sign the new directive correctly and redistribute it.

In practice, the goal is to avoid "dueling paperwork", two different versions floating around, with different people holding different copies. When you update, you want the old one gone and the new one everywhere it needs to be.

Durable Power of Attorney for Finances

Once you've dealt with medical decisions, the next question is unavoidable: **Who handles the money while all of this is happening?**

Medical decisions and financial decisions move together. Hospital bills arrive. Insurance needs to be contacted. Caregivers need to be hired and paid. Rent or mortgage payments still come due. Accounts still need to be managed, even while you're focused on recovery, or unable to focus on anything at all.

That's where **a durable power of attorney for finances** fits into the picture. It is the financial counterpart to your healthcare directive. Just as your healthcare directive allows someone to step in and make medical decisions if you can't, a durable power of attorney allows someone to step in and manage money and property **while you are still alive**.

The word *durable* matters here for the same reason it mattered in your healthcare planning. It means the authority continues even if you become incapacitated. A basic power of attorney can stop working at exactly the wrong moment, when you're no longer able to act for yourself. A durable power of attorney is designed specifically for that vulnerable window

Most people create a general durable power of attorney that covers day-to-day life and the bigger financial tasks that can appear out of nowhere. But you can also make a power of attorney that's limited, only for one transaction, one account, or one time period (like while you're traveling or deployed). The structure is flexible; the purpose is practical: to keep your life functioning when you can't personally push the buttons.

Why It Matters

Here's the part people don't fully appreciate until it happens: without a power of attorney, your loved ones often can't do the simplest things, even if they're trying to help and even if everyone agrees they should be allowed to help.

From the perspective of a bank, insurance company, brokerage firm, or retirement plan administrator, that resistance isn't cruelty; it's risk management. If someone calls and says, *"I'm her brother and she's in the ICU; I need to move $1,500 to pay her rent,"* the institution can't just take that on faith. They don't know whether that person is a devoted helper or an opportunist. They also have legal duties to protect the account holder's privacy and prevent unauthorized transactions.

So without a valid durable power of attorney, people run into the same dead end over and over:

- You can't sign the person's checks;
- You can't access or even get clear information about accounts that aren't in your name;
- You can't negotiate with an insurer about coverage details;
- You can't manage or sell property that requires the owner's signature; and
- You can't make the kind of "adult life" decisions that become urgent during illness, like hiring caregivers, paying a facility deposit, or arranging a move out of an apartment.

The painful conclusion is that if you don't sign a durable power of attorney **while you're competent**, your family's alternative is often to ask a court to appoint someone to manage your affairs, usually called a ***conservator*** or ***guardian of the estate,*** depending on the state.

In simple terms, that court process is the legal system's version of: "Fine. If you don't choose who helps you, the court will choose." It's slower, more expensive, more restrictive, and public. It's also emotionally exhausting at exactly the wrong time.

Sharing Accounts Isn't Enough

Sometimes couples assume they're covered because they have a joint checking account. It's true that joint owners can often keep paying the household bills if one person is hospitalized. But joint accounts are only one small slice of real financial life.

Even married partners don't have unlimited authority over each other's separate property. Without a power of attorney, one spouse typically can't sell a car titled solely in the other spouse's name, refinance or sell real estate without the owner's signature, or handle certain tax and retirement matters that require the account holder's authorization. And even where the law gives spouses some rights, institutions often still want paperwork that clearly proves authority.

Also, the "we're fine" logic breaks the moment both partners are affected by the same event; car accidents don't politely injure only one person at a time. That's why backup agents matter. A durable power of attorney isn't just about your first-choice person; it's about making sure there's a clear second choice ready to step in.

And when illness becomes serious, the job is rarely just "pay the bills." Real life gets messy fast: someone may need to sell investments to fund care, cancel services, clean out a home, negotiate with landlords, settle insurance claims, manage disability paperwork, or coordinate the finances of a move to assisted living. Those tasks require authority, not just good intentions.

Even with a Trust, Something Is Missing

If you've created a living trust and you've actually funded it (meaning your major assets are titled in the trust), you've done something smart: you've made it easier for your **successor trustee** to step in and manage trust assets if you can't.

But a trust doesn't magically cover everything. In plain terms, your trustee can manage what the trust owns. Your trustee usually can't manage what the trust does *not* own.

That "outside the trust" category often includes:

- Small or forgotten bank accounts;
- Retirement accounts (which usually stay in your individual name, with beneficiary designations);
- Life insurance policies;
- Certain workplace benefits;
- Refunds, claims, and one-off payments that show up in your name; and
- Property you intended to transfer into the trust "later," but never transferred.

A durable power of attorney fills that gap. And it can do something else that's quietly powerful: it can authorize your agent to **transfer assets into your trust** if that becomes necessary.

In other words, that means if you're seriously ill and someone discovers your home or an account was never moved into the trust, your agent may be able to finish that "last-mile" funding work, assuming the power of attorney includes the right language and your state allows it in that situation. That can make an enormous difference for families trying to prevent a messy, last-minute probate problem.

What Your Agent Is Allowed to Do

A durable power of attorney can be *narrow* or *broad*. But if you're building it as part of a comprehensive estate plan, broad authority is usually the point. You're not creating this document for the easy days; you're creating it for the weeks when everything is on fire and someone needs the legal ability to act quickly.

Most durable power of attorney forms let you authorize your agent to handle the full menu of financial life: paying ordinary expenses, dealing with banks and brokerages, managing or selling property, handling taxes, managing investments, coordinating insurance, operating a small business, collecting benefits, paying for personal care, and supporting a spouse or dependents.

Sometimes the most sensitive power in the whole document is the power to **make gifts**. In simple terms, that means your agent may be able to give away your money or property. Done carefully, it can support longstanding family patterns (like annual gifts) or help with Medicaid planning in states where that's relevant. Done poorly, it can be abused. So if *gifting authority* is included, it should be thoughtful, with clear limits, clear intent, and the right person holding the power.

There are also hard limits. A financial agent cannot use a power of attorney to do things that are fundamentally personal to you, like making or revoking your will, marrying on your behalf, or adopting a child for you. And there are other tasks the law generally treats as non-delegable in certain contexts (for example, serving as a corporate director) because the role is supposed to be performed by the named individual.

Fiduciary Standards

The law doesn't treat an agent like a casual helper. Your agent is a **fiduciary**.

That means **they must put your interests first.** Not theirs. Not a sibling's. Not what they think is "fair." Yours.

That fiduciary duty usually includes some core behaviors that matter in real life:

- Your agent must act for your benefit, not for personal gain.
- Your agent must keep your money separate (no mixing your funds with theirs).
- Your agent must keep records because if questions ever arise, good records protect everyone.
- Your agent must avoid conflicts of interest, like buying your property for themselves, unless your document clearly authorizes that kind of transaction and state law permits it.

If an agent intentionally misuses the power, steals, self-deals, or hides transactions, they can be held responsible for the harm. But the law also recognizes that not every decision turns out well. If your agent makes a reasonable choice in good faith and an investment drops or a plan doesn't work as hoped, the agent typically isn't personally on the hook simply because the outcome was disappointing.

Choosing the Right Financial Agent

Choosing an agent for finances is not the same as choosing an executor or trustee, even if the names overlap.

Your trustee and executor are roles that matter primarily when you're gone. Your power-of-attorney agent matters while you're alive but vulnerable. That difference changes what "best person for the job" can mean.

Sometimes the best financial agent is the person who is nearby and organized, not the person who is the smartest investor. Sometimes it's the adult child who can handle day-to-day details calmly, even if another child will be the better choice for managing long-term inheritance issues later. Sometimes it's a sibling or close friend who has the time and temperament now, even if a professional fiduciary is named for the estate administration later.

It's also perfectly fine for your healthcare agent and financial agent to be different people. In fact, that can be ideal.

A healthcare agent may be chosen because they're steady in medical settings and can communicate well with doctors. A financial agent may be chosen because they're good at paperwork, negotiation, and staying on top of deadlines. The key is that the two agents must be able to communicate because health and money collide constantly: a care decision may require a deposit, a change in insurance, a facility contract, or a rapid reorganization of cash flow.

Couples often name each other as first choice for both roles, and that usually makes sense, especially because it reduces the risk of one spouse and a third-party agent fighting over control of a shared financial life. But the plan should never stop at "spouse as first choice." It needs a backup, for the simple reason that emergencies don't schedule themselves around convenience.

Single people often feel the weight of this decision more acutely. Many choose a trusted niece or nephew, a long-time friend, or where appropriate, professional fiduciaries. Not every professional fiduciary accepts the power-of-attorney role, but some do. If you're considering that path, the conversation needs to happen before you sign anything, so expectations and fees are clear and your plan is actually workable.

As for naming two people jointly, it sounds like a peacekeeping move, but it often creates a logjam. If both agents must agree on every action, your plan slows down when speed matters. If either can act alone, you risk conflicting instructions. For most families, one primary agent plus one alternate is the cleanest design.

And whatever choice you make, it's worth talking about it with your loved ones. If you expect objections, that's not a reason to hide the decision; it's a reason to explain it early, while you're healthy, so nobody is blindsided in a crisis.

Choosing When Authority Takes Effect

One of the most important design choices is **when your agent's authority becomes effective**.

You can make the power effective immediately when you sign it, or you can make it effective only upon incapacity. That second version is often called a **springing** power of attorney, because it "springs" into effect only when a triggering event occurs.

On paper, springing powers make sense. People like the idea of keeping the document dormant unless it's needed. The challenge is proving the trigger.

Most springing powers require a doctor (sometimes two, depending on the agreement or state practice) to sign a statement that you're unable to manage your affairs. That's often straightforward for a short-term crisis like major surgery. But it can become complicated in long, gray-area conditions, especially degenerative diseases, when capacity can fluctuate, when family members disagree about whether someone is still competent, or when you're in a remote location with limited access to timely medical evaluation.

And there's a problem that feels almost absurd until you live through it: to activate a springing power, your agent may need medical confirmation of incapacity, but medical privacy rules can make clinicians cautious about releasing information without consent. If the person is unable or unwilling to consent, the family can get stuck in a "prove incapacity to get authority, but need authority to get proof" loop.

The 'springing' power creates a Catch-22: to prove you are incapacitated, your agent needs medical records, but to get medical records, they often need the power of attorney. To avoid this, ensure your plan includes a standalone HIPAA Authorization specifically allowing your agent access to the records needed to trigger their authority.

Because of this, many estate planners pair a financial power of attorney with a written authorization that allows relevant medical information to be shared for this specific purpose. Another way around the mess is to make the power effective immediately, so no one has to argue about capacity at a time when the family needs help.

Still, immediate effectiveness is not automatically "better." It's simply a trade-off. In simple terms, an immediately effective power is like handing someone a spare key today. Most people only do that if they trust the person completely and have a reason they might need help, even while they're still generally capable (for example, older adults already relying on adult children for bill paying, or someone with an unpredictable medical condition). Younger, healthy people often prefer springing authority because it feels safer emotionally, and because, frankly, it reduces the fear of misuse.

There's no one right answer. But whichever approach you choose, the decision should be intentional, not accidental.

Making It Legally Valid

A durable power of attorney is only as useful as its acceptability.

Many states allow signing with witnesses, notarization, or both. But for finances, notarization is often the difference between a document that "exists" and a document that actually works in the world. Banks and brokerages commonly want notarized signatures. And if your agent ever needs to use the power of attorney in a real estate transaction, where documents may need to be recorded with the county, lack of notarization can become a deal-breaker.

So the practical rule is: sign it in front of a notary, and follow your state's execution instructions precisely. After that, make the document accessible. Your agent should have a copy, and they should know where the original is stored. Many people keep originals with their estate planning documents in a safe or safe deposit box, but think through access: if your agent can't get the document when they need it, your planning doesn't help. A scanned copy stored securely can be a lifesaver, even if the institution later asks to see the original for certain transactions. Especially if you chose to store your documents in a safe deposit box. A bank will want proof that your agent has the authority to access the safe deposit box. If all your documents are in the box and your agent does not have access to a copy of your durable power of attorney, they may need to get a court order to get access to the safe deposit box, which the court does not always grant.

Where to Get the Forms

Durable power of attorney forms often come from the same ecosystem as healthcare directive forms: senior centers, state agencies, legal aid resources, and sometimes financial institutions. Online, you'll find both free and paid versions. The important point isn't the price tag; it's whether the form matches your state's law and whether it's executed correctly.

Some people also use estate planning software that generates powers of attorney through a guided interview. That can be convenient, especially when it helps you cover the major powers most families need. But regardless of how you obtain the form, the same principle applies: the document must be properly signed and practical enough that institutions will honor it.

Institutional Forms

In theory, a valid power of attorney should be accepted by banks and financial institutions, and many states have laws that discourage unreasonable refusal.

In real life, institutions can be difficult. Some have internal review processes. Some delay. Some insist on their own forms for their own accounts. And in a crisis, delay is its own kind of harm.

That's why a very practical step, especially if you do most of your banking or investing with one institution, is to ask whether they have an **in-house power of attorney form** for accounts held there. Filling out the institution's form doesn't replace your general durable power of attorney; it just reduces friction.

In plain terms: you're removing excuses. You're making it easier for your agent to help you quickly.

If you do sign multiple power of attorney documents, the key is consistency. You don't want one bank form naming one agent and your general power naming someone else. That's how you end up with confusion when clarity is the whole purpose.

How to Revoke and Update It

You can revoke your durable power of attorney at any time, as long as you have the capacity to do so.

People sometimes think revocation is as simple as tearing up a copy. Destroying old copies is good housekeeping, but it isn't always enough because you can't be sure every copy is gone, and you can't be sure an institution won't later rely on an older version someone hands them.

The cleanest approach is usually two steps:

1. Create a written revocation (often called a notice of revocation) and sign it in front of a notary; and

2. Destroy old originals and copies to the extent you can, while also notifying the people and institutions who might rely on the old document.

If the power of attorney was ever recorded with a county for a real estate transaction, revocation needs to be handled with extra care. In that situation, it's wise to record the revocation too, so the public record doesn't keep pointing to an authority you no longer want in force.

Note: Don't leave an ex in charge. *If you divorce or end a domestic partnership, update your power of attorney as soon as it's appropriate. In many places, divorce changes certain inheritance rights automatically, but powers of attorney and healthcare directives don't always "self-destruct" the way people assume. Even when state law limits an ex-spouse's authority, you don't want ambiguity where you can have clarity.*

In basic terms, the goal is simple: the person who can access your money and make financial decisions for you should be someone you trust today, not someone you trusted years ago.

Using Your Documents Outside Your Home State

People travel. People retire in one state and spend winters in another. People end up hospitalized away from home.

So it's reasonable to ask: Will an out-of-state hospital or institution honor my documents?

In general, your documents shouldn't be treated as meaningless just because you crossed a state line. But unfamiliar forms can create friction. Bank staff and hospital administrators tend to trust what they recognize, and a form that looks "foreign" can cause delays, especially in urgent moments.

The practical answer is: It's better to have your documents than not have them. Keep them accessible when you travel; use paper copies if you prefer, but having a secure PDF on your phone can be an excellent backup. And if you spend substantial time in another state every year, it may be worth executing that state's versions too, so you're not depending on goodwill and improvisation in an emergency.

Chapter | 11 | Assessment Test

1. **Why doesn't a will usually help when a person becomes incapacitated?**
   - **a.** Because wills expire during life
   - **b.** Because wills apply only after death
   - **c.** Because courts invalidate wills upon incapacity
   - **d.** Because wills transfer medical authority

2. **What two documents are typically needed to cover incapacity planning?**
   - **a.** A will and a trust
   - **b.** A trust and beneficiary designations
   - **c.** A healthcare directive and a durable power of attorney for finances
   - **d.** A POLST and a DNR

3. **What often happens if a person becomes incapacitated without these documents?**
   - **a.** Assets are frozen permanently
   - **b.** Family members can act automatically
   - **c.** A court may need to appoint a guardian or conservator
   - **d.** The estate passes under intestacy laws

4. **Why is a living trust alone not enough for full incapacity planning?**
   - **a.** Trusts are invalid during incapacity
   - **b.** Trusts do not cover assets outside the trust or medical decisions
   - **c.** Trusts automatically end at incapacity
   - **d.** Trusts require court supervision

5. **What is the primary purpose of a healthcare directive?**
   - **a.** To manage financial accounts
   - **b.** To appoint an executor
   - **c.** To authorize inheritance distributions
   - **d.** To name someone to make medical decisions if you cannot

6. Which statement best describes palliative (comfort) care?

- **a.** Care that hastens death
- **b.** Care focused on cure at all costs
- **c.** Care focused on comfort, dignity, and symptom relief
- **d.** Care available only in hospice

7. What is the key difference between a POLST and a healthcare directive?

- **a.** A POLST replaces a directive
- **b.** A directive is a medical order
- **c.** A POLST is a medical order meant for immediate clinical use
- **d.** A POLST applies only after death

8. Why is a durable power of attorney for finances so important during incapacity?

- **a.** It avoids estate tax
- **b.** It allows someone to manage money and property while you're alive
- **c.** It replaces the need for a trustee
- **d.** It controls beneficiary designations

9. What fiduciary duty does a financial agent owe to the person who appointed them?

- **a.** To treat all family members equally
- **b.** To follow their own judgment
- **c.** To act in the principal's best interest and keep records
- **d.** To maximize investment returns

10. What is a common drawback of a "springing" power of attorney?

- **a.** It expires too quickly
- **b.** It cannot be notarized
- **c.** It may be difficult to prove incapacity when authority is needed
- **d.** It gives agents too much power

Answers

1. **B** – Wills generally operate only after death, not during life.
2. **C** – Medical and financial decisions require separate documents.
3. **C** – Courts may appoint a guardian or conservator if no documents exist.
4. **B** – Trusts don't cover medical decisions or assets outside the trust.
5. **D** – A healthcare directive names someone to speak for you medically.
6. **C** – Palliative care prioritizes comfort, dignity, and symptom management.
7. **C** – A POLST is a physician's order designed for rapid clinical decisions.
8. **B** – It allows continued management of finances during incapacity.
9. **C** – Agents must act loyally, keep records, and avoid self-dealing.
10. **C** – Proving incapacity can delay or block authority at critical moments.

Personal Notes

CHAPTER 12

Living With Your Estate Plan

> ***"Life is what happens when you're busy making other plans."***
>
> **— John Lennon,**
> *English singer, songwriter, and musician*

Even the most carefully built estate plan isn't something you finish and forget forever. Tax laws change. Rules get rewritten.

The point isn't the specific number. The point is uncertainty. Estate planning happens in a moving environment, not a fixed one. You plan with the best information available today, knowing full well that tomorrow may look different.

And historically, it always has. Over the past few decades, the estate tax threshold has been raised, lowered, expanded, "made permanent," and then changed again. For most people, though, these dramatic shifts don't end up driving their planning decisions. If your total estate is well below even the lower thresholds, taxes aren't the main issue. Clarity, control, and family harmony usually matter far more.

More often than not, what actually triggers an update isn't Congress, it's life. People revisit their estate plans when something meaningful changes. They buy or sell a home. Their finances grow or shrink. The people they once named as guardians, trustees, or executors move away, divorce, or no longer feel like the right fit. Children grow up and are suddenly old enough to take on responsibility. Marriages begin or end. Parents pass away. In one form or another, life keeps moving, and your plan needs to move with it.

Even without a big life event, every estate plan benefits from a periodic review. Assets change. Accounts get opened and closed. Beneficiaries drift out of date. A plan that was perfectly aligned five or ten years ago can become mismatched if no one ever looks at it again.

That said, now we need to understand what's already in your plan, how to store it properly, how to make sure the right people can use it when needed, and how to keep it current over time.

What a Well-Built Estate Plan Usually Includes

As we saw, estate plans are a small collection of tools, each doing a specific job:

- **Will:** Specifies who inherits your property. If you have minor children, it also names guardians for them.
- **Trust:** Holds your assets so they can pass to your loved ones without going through probate.
- **Healthcare Directive / Living Will:** Names an agent to make medical decisions if you are incapacitated and states your wishes for end-of-life care.
- **Durable Power of Attorney for Finances:** Authorizes an agent to manage your money and property if you are unable to do so.
- **Beneficiary Designation Form (Retirement Accounts and Life Insurance):** Names your primary and alternate beneficiaries. You keep copies; the original is held by the financial institution.
- **Property Deed:** Evidence of any transfers of real property, especially deeds used to move property into a living trust.
- **HIPAA Authorization:** Allows doctors and healthcare providers to share confidential medical information with people you choose.
- **Personal Inventory:** An up-to-date list of your assets, which can be extremely helpful to your trustee and executor.
- **Plans for Funeral, Cremation, or Other Final Arrangements:** Includes prepaid contracts or written instructions, kept with your important papers.
- **Letters to Guardians, Executors, or Trustees:** Personal letters explaining your choices and intentions, often meant to be read after your death.
- **Records of Outstanding Loans or Gifts:** Written documentation of loans or gifts that your will or trust may forgive or ask to be taken into account.

Storing and Sharing Your Documents

Once you've created these documents, the next question is surprisingly practical: where should they be stored? Many people assume a bank safe deposit box is the safest option. Sometimes it is, but it can also create problems. After your death, getting into that box may require court authorization unless someone else is already listed on the account. In some places, safe deposit boxes are scarce or unavailable altogether.

A simpler solution is often better. A fire-resistant home safe can hold your original documents and copies of important forms. The people who will need these documents must know where they are and how to get to them.

Your lawyer may keep copies, but the responsibility for safeguarding the originals is yours. After your death, your family or fiduciaries will need those originals to do their jobs properly.

Digital Copies

Today, much of what matters lives online. Documents are scanned. Accounts exist only in the cloud. Bills, records, and even entire businesses may be managed digitally.

Some people keep digital copies of their estate planning documents on a thumb drive. Others use cloud storage services. Both can work, but only if the people who need access actually have it.

Here's where things get tricky. Federal privacy laws restrict service providers from sharing the contents of emails, files, and online accounts without consent or a court order. That means your executor or trustee can't automatically access your digital records, even if they have full authority over your physical assets.

This mismatch has caused real headaches. Executors may need online records to run a business, locate assets, or even find the estate plan itself. In response, states have been updating their laws to give fiduciaries clearer authority over digital assets, provided you've granted that authority in your documents.

Many modern wills, trusts, and powers of attorney now explicitly allow executors, trustees, and agents to access digital accounts. Some tech companies also offer their own tools. You can name a legacy contact, set up an inactive account manager, or specify what happens to your data after death.

The safest approach, for now, is redundancy. Use the tools providers offer. Make sure your estate planning documents authorize access. And, if you want someone to have access, make sure they have the necessary passwords or instructions.

This area of law is evolving fast, but the goal is simple: don't let your digital life become a locked room no one can enter.

Who Should Have Copies

Not everyone is comfortable sharing their entire will or trust during their lifetime, and that's fine. At a minimum, though, the people involved need to know where the documents are and how to find them.

Healthcare agents and financial agents should always have copies of the documents that give them authority. In an emergency, time matters. Doctors should have your healthcare directive in your medical file. If you've completed a POLST or a DNR, it should be visible in your home, where emergency responders will see it immediately.

While you're alive, you'll sometimes need to prove that your trust exists and that you're the trustee. Fortunately, you don't have to hand over the entire trust document. Most states allow you to use a short summary, often called a certification of trust, which confirms the trust's existence and names the trustees, without revealing private details about beneficiaries or assets. It's a small but important tool that keeps your information private while allowing everyday transactions to move forward.

Updating Your Plan Over Time

An estate plan is never frozen in time. Even when it's carefully thought out and well drafted, it reflects a snapshot of your life at a particular moment. And life, of course, doesn't stay still. For most people, that means revisiting their plan every few years, often every three to five years, or sooner if something significant changes for them or for the people they've named as guardians, trustees, executors, or beneficiaries.

No matter how confident you feel about the decisions you've made, the chances that you'll never need to review or revise your estate plan during your lifetime are very close to zero.

Changes in Relationships

Some of the most important triggers for revisiting an estate plan involve changes in marital status. **Marriage and divorce** don't just affect your personal life; they change your legal rights and obligations in ways that ripple through your entire plan.

If you're getting married for the first time, it's worth stepping back and thinking about how you want to treat property going forward. This is often when people consider a prenuptial agreement, essentially a written understanding of what property stays separate and what becomes shared. These conversations can feel uncomfortable, especially if money has never been an easy topic. But having them early can save confusion and conflict later, and many couples end up grateful they talked things through while everyone was calm and optimistic.

Divorce or remarriage also demands careful attention. During a divorce, many people want to update powers of attorney and healthcare directives right away, since those documents control decisions while you're alive. You may also want a new will. A living trust can be rewritten during the process, but it usually can't be fully funded until the divorce is final. Beneficiary designations are often locked during divorce proceedings unless your spouse agrees, so once the divorce is complete, updating those forms should be a top priority, always keeping in mind any promises or requirements set out in the divorce settlement itself.

The death of a spouse brings a different kind of urgency. It's an emotional loss first and foremost, but it's also a moment when your estate plan almost certainly needs attention. If you already have a plan, you'll want guidance on what steps come next and how your documents should change. If you don't, this is the moment to create one.

Children

Children are often the biggest drivers of estate plan revisions, simply because so much evolves over time. Children are born. They grow up. Sometimes they struggle. Sometimes they surprise you, in good ways or hard ones.

Parents often revise trusts to respond to a child's needs. Some families decide to keep assets in trust for a child dealing with addiction or mental health challenges, rather than distributing money outright at a certain age. Others start with protective trusts, only to realize years later that their child has grown into someone perfectly capable of managing an inheritance directly. As parents learn who their children really are, their plans change to match that reality.

Adding a new child, whether by birth or adoption, almost always calls for an update. Even if your documents technically include after-born children, most people want to name the child explicitly. That might mean amending a trust, updating a will, or creating new documents altogether, depending on what else you want to change.

Having more children can also affect **guardianship choices**. Someone who felt confident agreeing to care for one child may hesitate at the thought of raising two or three. It's important not to assume; checking in and adjusting your plan accordingly is part of responsible planning.

As children get older, your choices may shift again. Teenagers have different needs than toddlers. Family relationships evolve. Guardians age. A choice that made perfect sense when your kids were small may no longer be the best fit years later.

And sometimes, heartbreak forces change. If a child dies, you may want to rethink how assets are handled for surviving children or whether grandchildren should be included differently.

Grandchildren often prompt another round of reflection. You might want to make gifts to them, or you might decide that timing and structure matter more than generosity alone. It's important to understand one key limitation here: beneficiary designation forms are simple but rigid. You can change them easily while you're alive, but you cannot attach conditions. A retirement account won't wait to see whether someone finishes school, gets sober, or finds stable work. For those kinds of goals, a trust, not a beneficiary form, is the right tool.

People, Pets, and Financial Changes

Even pets can require updates. If you've set aside money for an animal's care and that pet dies, your documents should change. Some plans are drafted broadly to allow for future pets, while others are very specific, sometimes intentionally so, especially for animals likely to outlive their owners. The key is making sure the plan still reflects reality.

Changes to guardians, trustees, or executors are also common. People move. Relationships change. **Marriages and friendships happen and end.** When the people you've chosen are no longer the right fit, geographically, emotionally, or practically, it's time to revise.

Financial changes are another frequent trigger. Inheritances, job losses, new businesses, real estate purchases, or unexpected windfalls can all affect whether your plan still makes sense. Good or bad, a major shift in finances is a signal to take another look.

Moving to a new state deserves special attention. Estate planning laws vary widely, especially when it comes to marital property. Moving between community-property and common-law states can have serious consequences if your plan isn't adjusted correctly. This is one situation where professional help is often essential.

How Changes Should Be Made

When it's time to update your plan, it's important to do it properly. Crossing out names, scribbling notes in the margin, and initialing changes might feel efficient, but courts hate uncertainty and will not enforce a change made like this. If a document is ever challenged, a judge needs to know who made a change, when, and with what intent. Informal edits make that impossible.

The safe approach is formal replacement. Create new documents, clearly revoke the old ones, and make sure everyone who had a copy of the old version knows to destroy it.

Updating a Will

Updating a will is usually straightforward. Many people simply create a new one, which automatically revokes prior wills. While codicils, short amendments, are legally valid, they often create more confusion than clarity. A clean, updated document is easier to understand and harder to misplace.

Updating a Living Trust

Trusts offer flexibility, but how you update them matters. Small changes, like switching a successor trustee or adjusting a specific gift, can often be handled with an amendment. Larger or more numerous changes are usually better handled through a restatement.

A restatement keeps the trust's original name and date but replaces the entire text with an updated version that reflects current wishes and law. Assets stay where they are, and beneficiaries see one coherent document instead of a patchwork of amendments. This approach is especially helpful when simplifying old tax structures, adjusting how long children's inheritances stay in trust, or adding new beneficiaries.

Sometimes revoking a trust entirely makes sense, such as after a divorce involving a joint trust. But revocation is more work than restatement, because assets must be moved out and into a new structure.

If you created your trust yourself, the program or book you used likely includes amendment forms. If a lawyer drafted it, going back to that lawyer is often the most cost-effective option. New attorneys are cautious about amending documents they didn't write and may prefer restatement instead.

Whenever a trust is updated, the related will usually needs updating too, since the two documents reference each other.

Updating Powers of Attorney, Healthcare Directives, and Beneficiaries

Keeping powers of attorney and healthcare directives current usually means confirming that you still trust the people you've named, and that the documents are valid where you live. If you replace them, revoke the old versions clearly and destroy copies.

Beneficiary designations for retirement accounts, insurance policies, and payable-on-death accounts are updated separately, using the institution's forms. Always keep copies with your estate planning documents so your family knows what you intended.

Chapter | 12 | Assessment Test

1. **Why does the chapter emphasize that estate planning happens in a "moving environment"?**
   - **a.** Because estate plans automatically update
   - **b.** Because laws, finances, and family circumstances change over time
   - **c.** Because courts frequently reinterpret documents
   - **d.** Because estate plans expire after a set number of years

2. **For most people, what most often triggers the need to update an estate plan?**
   - **a.** Changes in federal estate tax thresholds
   - **b.** Advice from financial institutions
   - **c.** Periodic court reviews
   - **d.** Major life events such as marriage, divorce, or moving

3. **Which document primarily controls who inherits property at death?**
   - **a.** Durable power of attorney
   - **b.** Healthcare directive
   - **c.** Will
   - **d.** HIPAA authorization

4. **Why can storing original estate planning documents in a safe deposit box create problems?**
   - **a.** Banks destroy documents after death
   - **b.** Safe deposit boxes are not fireproof
   - **c.** Courts do not recognize documents stored in banks
   - **d.** Access may be restricted after death without court approval

5. **What is a major challenge related to digital assets in estate administration?**
   - **a.** Digital assets are excluded from estates
   - **b.** Executors automatically receive passwords
   - **c.** Privacy laws can limit access without proper authorization
   - **d.** Digital assets must be probated separately

6. **What is a certification of trust primarily used for?**

a. Updating trust terms
b. Proving a trust's existence without revealing private details
c. Naming beneficiaries
d. Funding the trust

7. **How often does the chapter suggest most people review their estate plan, even without major life changes?**

a. Every year
b. Every six months
c. Every three to five years
d. Only at retirement

8. **Why are informal handwritten changes to estate planning documents discouraged?**

a. They are always illegal
b. They increase tax liability
c. They can create uncertainty and invite disputes
d. They automatically invalidate the entire plan

9. **What is usually the safest way to make significant changes to a living trust?**

a. Adding handwritten notes
b. Filing a codicil
c. Ignoring outdated provisions
d. Using a formal amendment or restatement

10. **Why is it important to keep beneficiary designation forms updated and consistent with the rest of the plan?**

a. They are difficult to change later
b. They control asset distribution and override wills and trusts
c. They expire after a set time
d. They reduce estate taxes automatically

Answers

1. **B** – Estate planning must adapt to legal, financial, and family changes.
2. **D** – Life events are the most common reason plans need revision.
3. **C** – A will directs who inherits property at death.
4. **D** – Safe deposit boxes may be inaccessible without court authority.
5. **C** – Privacy laws can block access unless authority is clearly granted.
6. **B** – A certification of trust confirms the trust exists without exposing details.
7. **C** – Regular reviews every three to five years help keep plans aligned.
8. **C** – Informal edits create ambiguity and legal risk.
9. **D** – Amendments or restatements provide clarity and legal certainty.
10. **B** – Beneficiary forms often override other estate planning documents.

CHAPTER 13

After a Death

> ***"What we do for ourselves dies with us. What we do for others and the world remains and is immortal."***
>
> ***— Albert Pike,***
> *American author, poet, and lawyer*

Planning an estate is a bit like packing for a trip. Before you start filling your suitcase, you want at least a rough idea of where you're going. You wouldn't pack flip-flops and linen shirts if your destination was Iceland in January. Estate planning works in a similar way, except the journey itself is mysterious, and the people who will actually experience it are the ones you leave behind.

I can't tell you what happens after death in any philosophical or spiritual sense. But I *can* help you understand what happens in practical terms: how the plan you've carefully put together actually gets carried out, step by step, in the real world.

If part of you is thinking, *"Why does this matter to me? I won't be here,"* that's a fair thought. The answer is simple and very human: the more organized you are now, the less confusion, stress, and extra work your loved ones will face later. What you do today doesn't make things easier for *you*, it makes things easier for the people who are grieving and trying to do the right thing at the same time.

What Comes Next

When someone dies, a surprising number of details need attention, often right away. What happens next depends heavily on how that person planned, or didn't plan. Dying without any estate plan, dying with just a will, or dying with assets properly held in a living trust all lead to very different legal paths.

There are entire books devoted to probate and trust administration, and they're incredibly useful if you're the one doing the work. This chapter isn't meant to turn you into an executor or trustee. Instead, it gives you a clear, practical overview, so you can see *why* the planning you've done matters so much later.

No matter how simple or complex a plan is, the people left in charge almost always face the same five core tasks:

- **Determining who has legal authority** to act;
- **Finding and securing assets;**
- **Notifying heirs and beneficiaries**;
- **Paying debts and taxes**; and
- **Distributing what's left**.

Every document you create, every list you keep, and every conversation you have in advance makes each of these steps smoother for the people who will eventually handle them.

Proving Death and Proving Authority

After someone dies, one question comes up immediately: *Who is legally allowed to act?* Someone has to pay bills, secure property, deal with banks, file tax returns, and eventually distribute assets. That authority doesn't arise automatically.

If someone was already helping under a durable power of attorney or a health-care directive, that authority **ends at death**. In simple terms, those documents are "while you're alive" tools. The most common mistake families make is assuming a power of attorney allows them to pay for a funeral or settle a debt after death. The second a person dies, the power of attorney becomes a scrap of paper. Authority must then be 're-proven' through the will (executor) or trust (successor trustee).

Once death occurs, only two roles matter:

- An **executor** (also called a personal representative), if there's a will and probate is required; and
- A **successor trustee**, if assets are held in a living trust.

Without a will or trust, no one can act quickly. Everything slows down until a court steps in.

Banks and financial institutions won't just take someone's word for it. Before they release information or allow access, they'll ask for proof of two things: that the person has died, and that the person standing in front of them has legal authority to act.

Proof of death comes from a certified death certificate. Proof of authority usually comes in one of two forms:

- **Letters testamentary**, issued by a probate court, naming the executor; or
- A **certification of trust**, showing who the successor trustee is and what powers they have.

On paper, this can sound complicated. In practice, it's usually very methodical. Every bank, brokerage firm, and insurance company deals with estates all the time. They'll tell the executor or trustee exactly what they need to see before they'll act. Each step builds on the one before it. And every step becomes easier if the right documents are easy to find.

Death Certificates

A death certificate is the starting point for almost everything. Without it, accounts can't be transferred, insurance proceeds can't be paid, and property can't move.

Funeral homes usually handle filing the paperwork with the county and will ask how many certified copies you want. It's smart to order several, perhaps 10, depending on how many assets are involved. They're inexpensive, and it's far easier to order enough at the beginning than to scramble later.

Some institutions will accept copies. Others, especially when real estate is involved, require originals. Having extras saves time and frustration.

Finding the Documents

Having a well-drafted estate plan doesn't help much if no one can find it.

It has happened many times that adult children search garages, closets, storage units, and old file cabinets for weeks, unsure whether their parent even had a will or trust. Sometimes the lawyer is gone. Sometimes the documents are decades old. Sometimes the electricity gets shut off before anyone even figures out who's in charge.

So once your plan is finished, the next step is simple but critical: put it somewhere accessible. That might be a fire-resistant box, a home safe, a desk drawer, or secure cloud storage. There's no single right answer. What matters is that the *right people know where to look and how to get in.*

Some people share copies with a trusted family member or friend. Others keep digital backups. Many do both. Any of these approaches can work, as long as you keep them updated when changes are made.

Without access to your will or trust, your plan can't be carried out. Guardians can't be identified. Authority can't be proven. Everything stalls.

> ***Note:*** *At this point, it's worth remembering the inevitable question: What happens if someone dies without a will or a trust?*
>
> *Things still get done, but slowly. A court must appoint an administrator, and state law dictates who inherits. Even in states with simplified probate or small-estate procedures, there are still forms, waiting periods, and formalities.*

For families, this often feels impersonal and frustrating. Decisions are made by statute, not by the person who died. And no one can move forward until the court gives permission.

This contrast is intentional. It highlights why even a modest estate plan is better than none, and why organization matters just as much as the documents themselves.

Avoiding a Treasure Hunt

The weeks after a death are disorienting even under the best circumstances. Grief alone takes energy. Adding financial confusion on top of that makes everything heavier.

Executors and trustees need a complete picture of assets and liabilities. Without it, they become detectives, opening mail, tracking automatic payments, searching old tax returns, and trying to reconstruct a financial life from fragments. This work takes time, delays distributions, and often costs money.

Over the years, one lesson becomes very clear: **simplicity is a gift** to your family. Consolidated accounts, clear records, and even a basic list of assets and debts can dramatically reduce stress. It doesn't need to be perfect. It just needs to exist.

A practical habit helps here. Reviewing accounts once a year, often at tax time, or at major life milestones creates a living snapshot your loved ones will rely on later.

Making a List

You don't need a perfect spreadsheet to help your family. You just need something that gives them a reliable starting point.

One approach is to tie the habit to something you already experience: tax season. When you're gathering documents for your return, you're already looking at bank statements, investment statements, mortgage interest forms, and retirement tax forms. That's an ideal moment to update a basic list of accounts and major debts and to note where the original estate plan documents live.

If tax season is chaotic, another surprisingly workable trigger is milestone birthdays. People remember them, and you don't need to do it often for it to matter.

Without such a list, your executor must piece everything together manually. That work delays distributions and increases costs.

Safe Deposit Boxes

Safe deposit boxes seem like a natural place to store "important papers," but they can create a classic catch-22 after a death. If no one else is listed on the box, the bank may restrict access until the right legal authority is shown. And sometimes the very document needed to prove authority, the will, is inside the locked box.

Rules vary by state and by institution. Some states allow limited access to a box after death for the narrow purpose of locating estate documents. Other places require a court order. Some banks have their own internal policies that are stricter than people expect.

If you use a safe deposit box, the best prevention is to plan for access while you're alive. That might mean adding a trusted person as a co-lessee (if appropriate for your situation), clearly documenting where the key is, or, if your bank allows it, titling the box in the name of your revocable living trust so your successor trustee can step in more smoothly.

And if you're the family member trying to get in after someone dies, the most practical advice is also the simplest: ask the bank what they require, and if the answer isn't clear, ask the probate court in the county where the person died what the local rule is.

Inventory

Eventually, all of this detective work leads to one result: a final inventory of everything you owned at death. Only then can assets be valued, appraisals ordered, and distributions made.

Until every asset is identified and valued, nothing moves forward.

And that brings us full circle. When you organize your plan, your papers, and your lists now, you're not just planning for death, you're protecting the people you love from confusion, delay, and unnecessary hardship later.

Digital Accounts

Now that we've talked about *finding the papers* and proving who's in charge, there's another category of "property" your family can't settle with a key, a filing cabinet, or a banker's phone number: your **digital accounts**.

If you want your loved ones to have access to your online accounts, email, cloud storage, photos, social media, subscriptions, and anything else tied to your identity, you need to leave them **credentials**. In practical terms, credentials are the login pieces: **your usernames, passwords, and any sign-in method that confirms it's really you** (for example, a code texted to your phone). Without those, your family can't simply "prove they're the executor" and access your inbox the way they can access your checking account.

And here's why: under federal privacy rules (and the contracts to which we all click "I agree"), many online service providers are **not allowed** to hand over the *contents* of stored electronic communications without the account holder's consent. That makes digital assets fundamentally different from most other assets. Your executor may automatically have authority over your property, but that doesn't automatically unlock your email messages, your saved files, your direct messages, or your private photo archives.

Digital access law has improved in recent years, but it's still uneven and highly dependent on **state law plus the provider's rules**.

Many states now have statutes, often based on a widely adopted "uniform" framework, that allow a legal representative (executor or trustee) to access digital accounts *if* you've clearly authorized that access. In practical terms, you usually create that authorization in one of three ways:

1. **You use the provider's own planning tool.**
   This is when you flip a setting that tells the company, "If I die, disclose my account (or parts of it) to this person."
2. **Your will or trust gives explicit authority.**
   This is language that says your executor or trustee may access, manage, copy, and close your digital accounts, and may request disclosure from the provider.
3. **The provider's terms of service allow it.**
   Some companies' contracts are more cooperative than others. Some will share limited information with proper documentation; others refuse unless you've used their tool.

But the opposite is also true, and this is the part families discover the hard way: if you **don't** provide passwords, **don't** use a provider's tool, and the provider's terms **forbid access**, your loved ones may have only one route left: **a court order**.

That means delay, legal fees, and uncertainty. It also means your family is asking a judge for permission to do something that would have been easy if you'd left a simple list.

Tools That Actually Help

Some major service providers have recognized this problem and built in ways to plan ahead:

- **Google's Inactive Account Manager** lets you decide when an account is considered inactive and who can receive access to specific data. You control the timing and the scope.
- **Apple's Legacy Contact** feature allows you to designate a trusted person who can access your Apple account after death using a special access key.
- **Meta's memorialized accounts** let you choose whether your profile remains as a place for remembrance, appoint someone to manage it, or have it deleted entirely.

Other providers may simply delete accounts upon request, sometimes after reviewing a death certificate. The landscape is still changing, but one thing is certain: if you don't plan for digital access, you are leaving your loved ones to navigate a confusing and often frustrating system.

Notifications

Once the person in charge has legal authority and can access the core information, another nonnegotiable step kicks in: **notice**.

When you're building your estate plan, it's easy to focus only on the distribution and who gets what. But after death, the law cares about process, and part of that process is making sure the right people are informed.

If your estate goes through **probate**, your heirs and beneficiaries generally must receive **formal legal notice** of the probate hearing and of their right to object to the appointment of the executor. They can also see your will because the will becomes part of the probate court file. In other words, probate is a public and structured process, and notice is how the system gives interested people a chance to speak up.

If the estate is handled through **trust administration**, beneficiaries (and in some states, certain heirs) must also be notified of your death. States differ on the details, but in many places, beneficiaries are entitled to receive either:

- A copy of the **entire trust**; or
- The sections that describe **their rights and distributions**.

You can't administer a trust in the background without telling the people whose legal rights are affected by it.

That's why one of the most practical things you can do is leave your loved ones a clean, updated list with the **names, mailing addresses, email addresses, and relationships** of:

- Your trust beneficiaries; and
- The heirs who would inherit under state law if you had no plan (even if you *don't* want them inheriting).

Because if that information isn't available, someone will have to go looking.

When People Are Hard to Find

Here's what that search looks like in real life. Imagine an older person who never married, doesn't have children, and has outlived most close relatives. They leave everything to a longtime friend who lives abroad. But state notice rules still require the trustee to identify and notify certain family members, perhaps a sibling, perhaps nieces and nephews. If the trustee doesn't have addresses, the trustee may have to hire a professional locator to find them.

That costs money, and it slows everything down, not because anyone is being difficult, but because the trustee has legal obligations that must be satisfied before distributions can safely be made.

Essentially: **missing addresses can freeze an estate**.

Debts, Taxes, and Distributions

Now we get to the part people dislike talking about, but the law treats as sacred: **creditors get paid before beneficiaries**.

It's often hard to identify everything a person owns. But it can be even harder to identify everything they owe, especially if they died unexpectedly, were disorganized, or didn't discuss finances openly. Yet no matter how clear your will or trust is, the person in charge generally should not distribute assets until debts and taxes have been handled.

Probate usually requires two things:

1. **Known creditors must be paid** (or properly disputed); and
2. **Unknown creditors must be given a chance to come forward.** This is often done by publishing a legal notice in a local newspaper for a prescribed period.

Then comes the **claims period**, a defined period of time in which creditors may file formal claims against the estate. The executor must address each claim by either paying it, negotiating it, or rejecting it. If the executor rejects a claim, the executor typically has to follow the court's procedure to explain why.

And here's the practical consequence: **probate generally cannot close until creditor issues are resolved**. Even a perfectly cooperative family can't always speed that up, because part of the timeline is baked into the process.

If you want to make this part easier, your most helpful work is boring, but powerful. You should list:

- Mortgages and home equity loans;
- Credit cards;
- Bills;
- Car loans and personal loans;
- Medical debts or ongoing payment plans; and
- Business liabilities, if any; and
- Keep copies of promissory notes for money you loaned to others (so the trustee/executor knows whether to collect or forgive).

And timing matters. In many states, creditors may have **up to a year** to assert claims. Tax authorities may have longer windows for tax issues (often discussed in "years," not weeks). The point isn't to memorize deadlines; it's to understand why the person in charge cannot responsibly "just distribute everything next month."

Automatic Bills

Monthly bills also deserve a spot on your list, especially when they're paid automatically out of a bank account or charged to a credit card.

When someone dies, accounts can freeze, balances can drop, and automatic payments can start failing. The result is not just annoyance, it can mean:

- Utilities get shut off;
- Insurance policies lapse;
- Late fees accumulate; and
- Property is placed at risk (for example, a home without insurance).

Sometimes a family member pays bills personally during the gap between death and appointment of an executor. And in many cases, that person later seeks reimbursement from the estate as a creditor. That's a common and sensible workaround, but it's far easier when everyone knows what's being paid and why. In practice, **automatic payments don't grieve**; they just keep pulling money until the account runs dry.

Trust Creditor Rules

Successor trustees also have a legal duty to pay valid debts before distributing trust property. Some states allow trustees to use creditor-notice procedures similar to probate. But even where the law is flexible, the risk is the same: distribute too soon, and a late bill can create a mess.

That's why many trustees are advised to **hold back a reserve**, often for a meaningful period of time (commonly around a year in many situations, though it varies), so there's cash available if a legitimate claim arrives late. The trustee holding a reserve is a way to ensure the trustee has the funds to pay for any unexpected expenses.

Think about it like this: if a trustee distributes everything and then an unexpected tax bill arrives, the trustee has only two bad options:

- Pay it personally; or
- Go back to beneficiaries and ask them to return money they may have already spent.

Neither is fun. Both are avoidable when a trustee holds back a reserve.

A very normal approach looks like this: distribute a large share once the trustee has paid the obvious bills and has a strong sense of the estate's shape, then keep a portion aside for late claims or final expenses, and distribute the remainder when the risk window has passed.

Taxes Don't End at Death

After death, a final income tax return typically has to be filed. And if prior returns weren't filed, those issues must often be cleaned up before the estate can close.

This is why it's so helpful to leave:

- Copies of annual tax returns;
- The name and contact information of the person who prepares your taxes;
- Any login information needed to retrieve tax documents (if you use online portals).

If you use an accountant, having that same accountant prepare the final return is often smoother because they already know the patterns, income sources, deductions, carryovers, and what records exist.

It is not uncommon for people in poor health to fall behind on taxes. When that happens, the executor or trustee may have to deal with multiple years of filings and payments before distributions can safely occur. In short: **unfiled taxes can hold an estate hostage**.

How Property Is Finally Distributed

Only after all the earlier steps are complete—authority, inventory, appraisals, notice, debts, taxes—does the last step finally arrive: distributing what remains.

If your plan uses a **will**, distribution happens through probate in an orderly sequence. The court typically requires:

- An inventory of assets;
- Proper valuation;
- Proof that heirs and beneficiaries were notified;
- Proof that known creditors were paid and proper notice to potential creditors was given; and
- Ultimately, a court order authorizing distribution.

Once the executor has the order, the executor distributes assets, collects receipts from beneficiaries, and files those receipts with the court.

If your plan uses a **living trust**, the successor trustee supervises the same logical sequence, but privately notifies the right people, identifies and values trust assets, pays debts and taxes, prepares a trust accounting, makes distributions, collects receipts, files any required tax returns, and formally closes things out, sometimes after a reserve period ends.

In simple terms, trust administration is not "no work." It's "no court supervision," which often makes it faster and more private, but it still requires methodical steps.

The Bottom Line

The more information you provide now, the easier this becomes later. When your executor or trustee has your:

- Documents;

- Account lists;
- Debt lists;
- Beneficiary/heir contact list;
- Digital access plan; and
- Tax records,

then estate settlement becomes what it's supposed to be, a structured process that can be completed without unnecessary drama, delay, or expense. And that's the practical promise of estate planning: **relief**.

Chapter | 13 | Assessment Test

1. **What is the main reason estate planning focuses on what happens *after* death, even though you won't experience it yourself?**
    - **a.** Because courts require advance preparation
    - **b.** Because it reduces taxes for the deceased
    - **c.** Because it reduces stress and confusion for loved ones
    - **d.** Because it speeds up funeral arrangements

2. **Which roles have legal authority to act *after* a person's death?**
    - **a.** Healthcare agents and financial agents
    - **b.** Executors and successor trustees
    - **c.** Guardians and conservators
    - **d.** Beneficiaries and heirs

3. **What two things do banks and financial institutions typically require before allowing access to accounts?**
    - **a.** A will and a list of beneficiaries
    - **b.** A court order and tax returns
    - **c.** Proof of death and proof of authority
    - **d.** Identification and a power of attorney

4. **Why are durable powers of attorney no longer useful once a person has died?**
    - **a.** They expire automatically at death
    - **b.** They are invalid if probate is required
    - **c.** They apply only to medical decisions
    - **d.** They must be approved by a court

5. **Why is ordering multiple certified death certificates recommended?**
    - **a.** They expire after use
    - **b.** Some institutions require originals rather than copies
    - **c.** Courts require one per asset
    - **d.** They are difficult to obtain later

6. **What is the biggest practical problem when estate planning documents cannot be found?**

   a. Taxes increase
   b. Beneficiaries lose inheritance rights
   c. Legal authority cannot be proven and everything stalls
   d. Probate becomes mandatory

7. **Why is creating and updating an asset and debt list such a powerful step?**

   a. It eliminates creditor claims
   b. It avoids the need for probate
   c. It reduces the executor's legal responsibility
   d. It prevents loved ones from having to reconstruct finances from scratch

8. **Why can digital accounts be harder to access than physical assets after death?**

   a. They are excluded from estates
   b. Providers delete accounts immediately
   c. Privacy laws and provider rules restrict disclosure without consent
   d. Courts lack jurisdiction over digital property

9. **Why must executors and trustees usually delay distributions to beneficiaries?**

   a. Beneficiaries must approve first
   b. Assets must increase in value
   c. Debts, taxes, and creditor claims must be resolved first
   d. Probate courts impose waiting periods arbitrarily

10. **What is the central message of the chapter's conclusion?**

   a. Estate settlement is simple if assets are modest
   b. Trust administration requires no work
   c. Planning eliminates all conflict
   d. Organization now creates relief later

Answers

1. **C** – Good planning reduces stress and confusion for the people left behind.
2. **B** – Only executors and successor trustees have authority after death.
3. **C** – Institutions require proof of death and proof of legal authority.
4. **A** – Powers of attorney are "while alive" tools and end at death.
5. **B** – Many institutions require original certified certificates.
6. **C** – Without documents, no one can prove authority or move forward.
7. **D** – Clear lists spare loved ones from detective work and delays.
8. **C** – Privacy laws and provider contracts often block access.
9. **C** – Creditors and tax obligations must be handled before distribution.
10. **D** – Preparation and organization now translate into relief later.

CONCLUSION

Estate planning has a reputation for being complicated, technical, and a bit grim. By now, you know that reputation isn't quite deserved. What makes estate planning hard isn't the documents themselves; it's the thinking that comes before them. Deciding who should act, who should receive what, and how those decisions should unfold over time requires clarity more than clever drafting. That's the hard work you've done here.

If you've worked through this book carefully, you now understand how the major pieces of an estate plan relate to one another. You've seen how wills, trusts, guardianship nominations, incapacity documents, and fiduciary roles are not isolated forms but parts of a single system designed to function under stress, after a death, during illness, or in moments when quick decisions matter. That perspective alone puts you far ahead of most people who sign documents without ever seeing the full picture.

For many readers, this will be enough to move forward with confidence. You may decide to draft documents yourself, using reputable forms and the guidance you've gained here. Others will take what they've learned into a lawyer's office, not as passive clients, but as informed clients who know what questions to ask and what decisions they've already made. Either path is valid. Understanding the terrain makes every route safer.

Along the way, you've also seen where professional help truly matters. Complex family structures, property in multiple states, closely held businesses, special needs planning, or exposure to estate or inheritance taxes are not places to improvise. Getting help in these situations isn't a retreat from independence; it's an extension of it. You're choosing expertise where the stakes justify it.

If you do work with professionals, approach those conversations deliberately. Be clear about what you want help with and what you've already decided. Pay attention to how you're treated. A good advisor will respect the work you've done, explain options plainly, and help translate your intent into documents that actually work. If someone seems dismissive or unwilling to engage at that level, keep looking. This is personal work, and the relationship matters.

Before you set this book aside, take a moment to tie up the practical ends. Make sure documents are signed correctly. Confirm that assets are titled the way your plan assumes they are. Let the people you've named know where originals are kept and how to find them when needed. These final steps are not dramatic, but they're what turns planning into protection.

Most importantly, remember that an estate plan isn't a one-time event. Lives change. Families grow. Relationships evolve. Laws shift. The real success of a plan isn't that it was perfectly drafted once, but that it gets revisited when it should. Use what you've learned here as a framework you can return to, not a checklist you never open again.

You've done something meaningful by engaging with this process. You've reduced uncertainty for the people you care about. You've replaced guesswork with direction. And once the plan is in place, you're free to let it fade into the background, doing its work while you focus on living the life it was meant to protect.

Glossary

401(k) / 403(b) — *Employer-sponsored retirement accounts funded with pre-tax contributions; grow tax-deferred until withdrawal.*

529 Plan — *Tax-advantaged investment account for qualified education expenses.*

A/B Trust — *A married couple's trust that splits at the first death into a revocable Survivor's Trust (A) and an irrevocable Bypass Trust (B).*

ABLE Account — *Tax-advantaged savings account for individuals with disabilities that preserves Medicaid and SSI eligibility.*

Administrator — *Court-appointed person who manages an estate when there is no will.*

Advance Healthcare Directive — *Legal document naming a healthcare agent and stating end-of-life treatment preferences.*

Annual Gift Tax Exclusion — *Amount you can give per person per year without filing a gift tax return (2026: $19,000).*

Annuity — *Insurance contract providing regular payments in exchange for a lump sum or series of contributions.*

Beneficiary — *Person, trust, or entity designated to receive assets from a will, trust, account, or policy.*

Beneficiary Designation — *Form filed with a financial institution naming who receives the account at death; overrides a will or trust.*

Beneficiary IRA (Inherited IRA) — *Retirement account inherited after the original owner's death, subject to its own withdrawal rules.*

Blended Family — *Family where one or both partners bring children from a prior relationship.*

Bond (Fiduciary) — *Insurance guarantee protecting beneficiaries against misconduct by an executor, trustee, or guardian.*

Buy-Sell Agreement — *Contract among business co-owners governing what happens to a departing or deceased owner's share.*

Bypass Trust (Credit-Shelter Trust / B Trust) — *Irrevocable trust funded at the first spouse's death to use their estate tax exemption.*

Capital Gains Tax — *Tax on profit from selling an asset for more than its cost basis.*

Certification of Trust — *Summary proving a trust exists and identifying trustee powers, without revealing private details.*

Certified Death Certificate — *Official document proving death; required before banks, insurers, or courts release assets.*

Charitable Deduction — *Tax reduction for qualifying gifts to recognized charities.*

Children's Trust — *Trust holding assets for minors or young adults until a specified age.*

Clayton Election — *Flexible trust option letting a surviving spouse choose, after the first death, how assets are allocated between trusts.*

Codicil — *Formal amendment to an existing will; generally discouraged in favor of writing a new will.*

Community Property — *Property acquired during marriage in a community-property state, owned equally by both spouses.*

Conservator — *Court-appointed person who manages financial affairs for someone incapacitated or a minor.*

Contingent Beneficiary — *Backup beneficiary who inherits if the primary beneficiary cannot.*

Cost Basis — *Original purchase price of an asset, used to calculate capital gains when sold.*

Creditor Claims Period — *Legal window after death during which creditors may file claims against the estate.*

Custodial Account (UTMA/UGMA) — *Account managed by an adult for a minor until the child reaches the age set by state law.*

Death Benefit — *Amount paid by a life insurance policy to the beneficiary; generally income-tax-free.*

Decedent — *A person who has died, in legal context.*

Designated Beneficiary — *Individual named on a retirement account subject to the SECURE Act's 10-year withdrawal rule.*

Digital Assets — *Online accounts, files, cryptocurrency, and social media profiles that may need management after death.*

Disinheritance (Pretermitted Heir) — *Intentional or accidental exclusion of a potential heir from a will or trust.*

DNR (Do-Not-Resuscitate) — *Medical order directing that CPR not be performed if the heart stops.*

Donor-Advised Fund (DAF) — *Charitable account where the donor gets a tax deduction at contribution and recommends grants over time.*

Durable Power of Attorney for Finances — *Document authorizing someone to manage your finances; remains valid if you become incapacitated.*

Ed/Med Exception — *IRS rule allowing unlimited tax-free payments for tuition or medical bills paid directly to the provider.*

Elective Share — *Minimum portion of a spouse's estate the surviving spouse can claim in common-law states, regardless of the will.*

Eligible Designated Beneficiary — *Narrow category (surviving spouse, minor child, disabled, chronically ill, close in age) who may stretch retirement withdrawals beyond 10 years.*

Enhanced Life Estate Deed (Lady Bird Deed) — *Deed transferring property at death without probate while the owner keeps control during life.*

Estate Plan — *Collection of legal documents governing who manages your affairs and who inherits your property.*

Estate Tax (Federal) — *Tax on assets at death exceeding the federal exemption (2026: $15M per person, 40% rate).*

Executor (Personal Representative) — *Person named in a will to manage the estate through probate, pay debts, and distribute assets.*

Federal Estate Tax Exemption — *Amount each person can leave tax-free at death (2026: $15M individual / $30M couple).*

Fiduciary — *Person legally obligated to act in another's best interest (trustee, executor, agent).*

Final Income Tax Return — *Last personal tax return for a deceased person, covering January 1 through date of death.*

Five-Year Rule — *Rule requiring full withdrawal of an inherited retirement account within five years in certain situations.*

Form 706 — *Federal estate tax return; also used to elect portability of a deceased spouse's unused exemption.*

Funded Trust — *A trust to which assets have actually been transferred; an unfunded trust controls nothing.*

Gift Tax — *Federal tax on lifetime transfers; shares the same exemption and 40% rate as the estate tax.*

Guardian / Guardianship — *Person appointed to care for a minor's personal needs (of the person) or finances (of the estate).*

Healthcare Agent — *Person named in a directive to make medical decisions when you cannot.*

HEMS Standard — *Trust distribution standard: health, education, maintenance, and support.*

HIPAA Authorization — *Form allowing healthcare providers to share your medical information with specified people.*

Homeowner Exclusion — *Tax rule excluding up to $250K/$500K of capital gain on sale of a primary residence.*

ILIT (Irrevocable Life Insurance Trust) — *Trust that owns a life insurance policy to keep proceeds out of the taxable estate.*

Incidents of Ownership — *Control rights over a life insurance policy that can pull proceeds into the taxable estate.*

Incapacity — *Inability to make or communicate informed decisions due to illness, injury, or cognitive decline.*

Intestate / Intestacy — *Dying without a valid will; state law determines who inherits.*

Irrevocable Trust — *Trust that generally cannot be changed once created; removes assets from the grantor's taxable estate.*

Joint Tenancy with Right of Survivorship (JTWROS) — *Co-ownership where the survivor automatically inherits the deceased owner's share.*

Kiddie Tax — *Rule taxing a child's unearned income above a threshold at the parent's rate (2026: $2,700).*

Letter of Intent — *Nonbinding personal letter to a guardian, trustee, or executor offering guidance and context.*

Letters Testamentary — *Court-issued document authorizing the executor to act on behalf of the estate.*

Life Insurance — *Contract paying a death benefit to named beneficiaries; passes by designation, not by will.*

Lifetime Gift and Estate Tax Exemption — *Total transferable during life and at death before federal tax applies (2026: $15M).*

Living Trust (Revocable Trust) — *Trust created during your lifetime that holds assets, avoids probate, and provides for incapacity management.*

Living Will — *Document expressing end-of-life medical treatment wishes; often part of a healthcare directive.*

Marital Deduction (Unlimited) — *Tax rule allowing unlimited transfers between U.S. citizen spouses free of estate or gift tax.*

Medical Aid in Dying (MAiD) — *State laws allowing a terminally ill adult to request life-ending medication under strict safeguards.*

Medicaid — *Government health insurance for low-income individuals; eligibility affected by how assets are held.*

Notarization — *Having a document signed before a notary public who verifies identity; required for many estate documents.*

Palliative Care — *Care focused on pain relief and quality of life for seriously ill patients, regardless of prognosis.*

Payable-on-Death (POD) — *Bank account designation transferring funds directly to a named person at death, bypassing probate.*

Pension (Defined-Benefit Plan) — *Employer-funded plan paying guaranteed monthly income based on salary and years of service.*

Per Capita — *Distribution method where each living beneficiary in the same generation gets an equal share.*

Per Stirpes — *Distribution method where a deceased beneficiary's share passes to their children.*

Pet Trust — *Trust that sets aside funds and names a caretaker for a pet after the owner's death.*

POLST — *Physician-signed medical order covering CPR, ventilation, and nutrition for seriously ill patients; stronger than a living will.*

Portability (DSUE) — *Rule letting a surviving spouse use the deceased spouse's unused estate tax exemption; requires Form 706.*

Pot Trust — *Trust pooling assets for all children, letting the trustee distribute based on individual need.*

Pour-Over Will — *Backup will that directs unfunded assets into a living trust at death.*

Prenuptial / Postnuptial Agreement — *Written agreement between spouses defining property rights; prenuptial before marriage, postnuptial after.*

Probate — *Court-supervised process of validating a will, paying debts, and distributing assets.*

Required Minimum Distributions (RMDs) — *Mandatory annual withdrawals from traditional retirement accounts starting at age 73 (75 in 2033).*

Reserve (Trustee Holdback) – *Funds a trustee retains temporarily after initial distributions to cover late debts or taxes.*

Residuary Estate – *Everything remaining after specific gifts, debts, taxes, and expenses are paid.*

Revocation – *Formal cancellation of a will, trust, power of attorney, or directive.*

Right of Survivorship – *Ownership feature where the surviving co-owner automatically inherits the deceased owner's share.*

Roth Conversion – *Paying tax now to move funds from a traditional account to a Roth for tax-free growth and withdrawals.*

Roth IRA / Roth 401(k) – *Retirement accounts funded with after-tax dollars; qualified withdrawals are tax-free.*

SECURE Act / SECURE Act 2.0 – *Federal laws requiring most non-spouse beneficiaries to empty inherited retirement accounts within 10 years.*

Self-Proving Affidavit – *Sworn statement attached to a will confirming proper execution; avoids locating witnesses at probate.*

Separate Property – *Property owned individually by one spouse, typically acquired before marriage or by gift/inheritance.*

Settlor (Grantor / Trustor) – *The person who creates and funds a trust.*

Small Estate Affidavit – *Simplified document to transfer assets from a small estate without full probate.*

Special Needs Trust – *Trust for a person with disabilities that preserves government benefit eligibility.*

Spousal Rollover – *Surviving spouse's ability to treat an inherited retirement account as their own.*

Springing Power of Attorney – *Power of attorney that activates only upon a triggering event, usually incapacity.*

State Estate Tax – *Estate tax imposed by certain states, often with exemptions far lower than the federal threshold.*

State Inheritance Tax – *Tax paid by heirs on inherited property; imposed by a small number of states.*

Step-Up in Basis – *Revaluation of an inherited asset to market value at death, eliminating unrealized capital gains for heirs.*

Successor Trustee – *Person or entity who takes over trust management when the original trustee dies, resigns, or becomes incapacitated.*

Taxable Estate *— Total value of everything owned at death, before exemptions and deductions.*

10-Year Rule *— SECURE Act rule requiring most non-spouse beneficiaries to fully withdraw an inherited retirement account within 10 years.*

Tenancy by the Entirety *— Joint ownership for married couples providing survivorship rights and creditor protection.*

Tenancy in Common *— Co-ownership where each owner's share is separate and does not pass automatically to the other.*

Testamentary Trust *— Trust created within a will; takes effect only after death and goes through probate.*

Title *— Legal ownership of property; how title is held determines how it transfers at death.*

Traditional IRA *— Retirement account funded with pre-tax contributions; grows tax-deferred, withdrawals taxed as income.*

Transfer-on-Death (TOD) *— Designation on an investment account or deed transferring assets directly at death, bypassing probate.*

Trust *— Legal arrangement where a trustee holds and manages assets for beneficiaries according to terms set by the creator.*

Trust Administration *— Process of managing and distributing trust assets after the creator's death, typically without court supervision.*

Trust Amendment vs. Restatement *— An amendment changes specific provisions; a restatement replaces all terms while keeping the original trust intact.*

Trustee *— Person or entity responsible for managing trust assets for the benefit of the beneficiaries.*

Uniform Prudent Investor Act *— Law requiring trustees to manage investments with the care and skill of a prudent investor.*

Will *— Legal document specifying who inherits your property, naming an executor, and designating guardians for minor children.*

Bonus Worksheets & Resources

This book includes a set of downloadable bonus worksheets designed to help you organize your estate plan and put what you've learned into practice.

As part of the bonus section, you'll find:

- **Estate Plan Property Worksheet** — to inventory your assets, understand how they're titled, and decide how each one should be handled in your plan.
- **Will Planning Worksheet** — to organize your decisions about beneficiaries, executors, guardians, and specific bequests before drafting your will.
- **Trust Planning Worksheet** — to map out your trust structure, including trustees, successor trustees, beneficiaries, and the property you intend to place inside.
- **Guardianship Planning Worksheet** — to evaluate and compare potential guardians for your minor children, so you can make a confident, well-thought-out decision.
- **Fiduciary Roles Worksheet** — to keep track of every key person in your estate plan, from executors and trustees to healthcare agents and financial powers of attorney, all in one place.

Estate-planning needs vary from person to person, and the rules can differ by state. These worksheets are designed as practical planning tools to help you think clearly, stay organized, and prepare effectively, whether you're building your plan on your own or getting ready to meet with a professional.

For convenience, the worksheets are available in two formats:

- **Printable PDFs**, if you prefer to fill them out by hand
- **RTF files**, which you can open and edit on your computer

Use these materials at your own pace, revisit them as your understanding grows, and treat them as tools to support clearer thinking and better preparation. To download them, scan the QR code or click on the link if you are on Kindle.

https://financeknightspublications.aweb.page/exclusive-bonuses-unlock

About Us

FINANCE KNIGHTS
PUBLICATIONS

Finance Knights Publications is an independent publishing company focused on business, law, and finance education.

We started in 2023 with a simple idea: understanding the fundamentals of complex topics like LLCs, accounting, estate planning, and investing shouldn't require expensive courses or a law degree. So we create step-by-step guides that give our readers a solid foundation to make informed decisions.

Every book is developed alongside CPAs, attorneys, and industry specialists, not as a marketing claim, but because accuracy matters when someone's building a business or protecting their assets.

Since launch, thousands of entrepreneurs and small business owners have used our books to navigate decisions that once felt overwhelming.

My name is Carmelo Nacci, founder of Finance Knights Publications. After *17 years in the Armed Forces*, I shifted my focus to building an independent publishing business centered on business, finance, and personal planning. The same discipline that guided my military career now guides how I create books.

At *Finance Knights Publications*, I work alongside my partner and a team of dedicated collaborators, each title begins with in-depth research: statutes, regulations, trusted treatises, and real-world practice. To ensure accuracy and reliability, the manuscript is reviewed internally and then independently certified by multiple licensed professionals before publication. Only after this multi-layered verification do we go to print.

This book reflects that process. It is designed to be clear, usable, and responsible, offering step-by-step structure without unnecessary jargon and highlighting when professional advice is wise.

Thank you for your trust. I hope these pages make your planning easier, and your next steps unmistakably clear.

Before You Go

If you've made it this far, thank you for reading. We truly appreciate your time and trust.

You've just gone through the entire book, which makes your perspective one of the most valuable out there. If you have a moment, sharing a few honest words on Amazon could help someone who's still deciding whether this book is right for them.

You can scan the QR code or use the link provided (if you're on Kindle):

https://www.amazon.com/review/create-review/?ie=UTF8&channel=glance-detail&asin=B0GS6717MK

If you noticed any issues, such as typos, printing problems, or a defective copy, or have suggestions for improvement, feel free to contact us at:

info@financeknightspublications.com

If your feedback leads to a correction, we'll make sure you receive an updated, corrected copy.

Thank you again for reading.

Finance Knights Publications

Made in United States
Cleveland, OH
06 November 2026

47653964R00140